MIDNIGHT IN MEXICO

THE PENGUIN PRESS   NEW YORK   2013

MIDNIGHT
IN MEXICO

A REPORTER'S JOURNEY
THROUGH A COUNTRY'S DESCENT
INTO DARKNESS

Alfredo Corchado

THE PENGUIN PRESS
Published by the Penguin Group
Penguin Group (USA) Inc., 375 Hudson Street,
New York, New York 10014, USA

USA · Canada · UK · Ireland · Australia
New Zealand · India · South Africa · China

Penguin Books Ltd, Registered Offices:
80 Strand, London WC2R 0RL, England
For more information about the Penguin Group visit penguin.com

Copyright © Alfredo Corchado, 2013
All rights reserved. No part of this book may be reproduced, scanned, or distributed in any
printed or electronic form without permission. Please do not participate in or encourage piracy
of copyrighted materials in violation of the author's rights. Purchase only authorized editions.

Library of Congress Cataloging-in-Publication Data

Corchado, Alfredo.
Midnight in Mexico : a reporter's journey through a country's
descent into darkness / Alfredo Corchado.
pages   cm
Includes index.
ISBN 978-1-59420-439-5
1. Corchado, Alfredo.   2. Drug traffic—Mexico.   3. Organized crime—Mexico.
4. Investigative reporting—Mexico.   I. Title.
HV5840.M4C67 2013
364.10972—dc23
2012046885

Printed in the United States of America
1   3   5   7   9   10   8   6   4   2

BOOK DESIGN BY MARYSARAH QUINN AND AMANDA DEWEY

Penguin is committed to publishing works of quality and integrity.
In that spirit, we are proud to offer this book to our readers;
however, the story, the experiences, and the words
are the author's alone.

ALWAYS LEARNING   PEARSON

To Herlinda and Juan Pablo, my parents,
for teaching me the art of believing against all odds

MIDNIGHT IN MEXICO

INTRODUCTION

Before I had written the first words of this book, John D. Feeley, a veteran American diplomat with deep, proud Irish and Italian roots and a big heart for Mexico, asked me what my book would be about. I rattled off a list of themes I hoped to cover, from immigration into the United States, to the ongoing violence and corruption in a country I once thought I knew, to the role of the United States in shaping Mexico's destiny.

Feeley grinned. You're making *mole*, he said, referring to the traditional sauce made from any number of ingredients, from almonds to chocolate to *pipián* chili, all blended to create a uniquely Mexican flavor. I told John I had no idea how to make *mole,* but I would pour every bit of my soul into these pages.

"Great," he said. "Stories heal you and others."

Midnight in Mexico is my attempt to investigate the complex questions facing my country. These challenges marked me first as a boy and then as a reporter. This isn't meant to be a comprehensive history of arguably the most transformative time in Mexico since the revolution of 1910. But in my half century on Mexican and U.S. soil, I have had a front-row seat to great change. This book offers a glance at some of the moments when the Mexican people stood between hope and fear.

During my career as a journalist, I have been blessed. I reported on Mexico as much as I could while I was based in the States. But in 1994 I came to live and work in Mexico City permanently. Since then, four presidents—Carlos Salinas de Gortari, Ernesto Zedillo, Vicente Fox and Felipe Calderón—have governed the country. I knew all of them, some better than others. Three milestones marked the period and defined my work: the 1994 North American Free Trade Agreement, the 2000 election that ushered in the first changeover in power in seven decades, and the ongoing battle against the cartels and the culture of violence they spawned. Hope and fear. Fear and hope.

By the time this book is published, nearly one hundred thousand people will have disappeared or been killed since President Calderón launched a war on the cartels. When it began in 2006, the new president promised that an increasingly violent Mexico would at last become a nation of laws. The situation was dire. Less than 20 percent of those detained on drug trafficking charges in Mexico were convicted. Cops were underpaid and undertrained and forced to rely on bribes as a way to put food on the table. Inequality marred the country's future and left too many living on too little. Mexico's low rates of tax collection left limited funding for infrastructure or social programs. The education system was run by a corrupt union. Millions of young men and women were ripe for recruitment by drug traffickers.

*M*idnight in Mexico draws on my reporting from 1986 to the present, beginning with the now extinct *El Paso Herald-Post;* I continue to blame the *Herald-Post* for infecting me with the incurable disease of journalism. I also relied on reporting I did out of Mexico—often on my vacation time—for the *Wall Street Journal*. Most of the work represents the eighteen years I have been honored to report for readers of the *Dallas Morning News*. In 1994, the newspaper hired me for what it said was a foreign correspondent job. To this day it still feels like a dream come true. But the term "foreign correspondent" is a bit misleading. Mexico has never been foreign to me. Mexico has always been personal—a story not necessarily of two countries but of one people.

I am a son of Mexico. I come from a typically large Mexican family—I'm the eldest of nine. Tradition in my Durango town of San Luis de Cordero dictated that our ancestors bury the umbilical cord of every newborn to remind us—especially those destined to leave—of a place of first sunsets and sunrises: No matter how far I traveled, I'd never forget. More than half the town's population of two thousand worked in the United States at some point—among them, my father, a bracero, part of a generation of temporary guest workers whose sweat slowly transformed the face of the United States.

I arrived in the United States in 1966, kicking and screaming, pledging to my parents—Juan Pablo and Herlinda—that one day I'd return to Mexico and prove them wrong about the promise of the United States. I'd echoed the words of my Tío Delfino, who refused to go north. He reminded us that Mexico wasn't cursed by history but by betrayal. My parents proved my distrust of the United States wrong by giving us the possibility of reinvention in a new land.

In California's San Joaquin Valley, my father drove tractors and my mother stooped over a short hoe weeding fields of sugar beets and lettuce. My brothers and I joined her picking every imaginable crop to help keep America fed. We grew up cramped in a trailer house surrounded by fields of melons. Later my parents took our dreams to El Paso, a city along the U.S.-Mexico border, across from Ciudad Juárez.

The excitement of that place was a catalyst for an aspiring journalist, the profession that paved my way home. From my parents' small restaurant, Freddy's Café, three blocks from the international bridge, I plotted my return to Mexico. As a student at El Paso Community College, followed by the University of Texas at El Paso and later as a reporter for the

Herald-Post, I crisscrossed the border and shook with excitement at what, throughout the 1980s, felt like a people's revolution taking place just feet from U.S. soil. I was inspired by men and women hell-bent on reclaiming a nation beset by one-party rule, a powerful oligarchy and entrenched monopolies.

Even when I went north to further my career, Mexico remained close. In Philadelphia, where I worked in the *Wall Street Journal*'s regional bureau, I'd spend long winter nights alongside my new friends Ken Trujillo, David Suro and Primitivo Rodriguez. At the time, we believed we were the only four Mexicans in Center City, where we talked about the same big ideas of what Mexico could be as we nursed tequila. We were nostalgic about our *paisanos* back home, their resilience, the daily greetings of *"Buenos días," "Buen provecho," "Buenas tardes,"* the haunting smell of corn on a cob and the sounds of Javier Solís.

Just as Mexico's hopes fell with the latest peso devaluation, mine rose with my job at the *News* in 1994. I was finally home. *Mamá* was proud that her son, a high school dropout, had finally made something of himself, but she would have preferred I had done something else—and, certainly, somewhere else. She had dreaded the day when we'd drive to the El Paso International Airport, where I would catch a flight to my new home, Mexico City. As we said good-bye, she watched me with her lips pressed together and eyes that said, "I've lost one. I will not lose another."

The homecoming was bittersweet. I loved the strength I saw in the streets, the cry for democratic change, the young and old, the men and women marching through the streets of Ciudad Juárez, of Guanajuato, San Luis Potosí, Monterrey and, of course, Mexico City. But I've lost count of the number of times I walked back from El Zócalo or the Angel of Independence, feeling hopeful about Mexico's future, only to watch the country gradually plunge further into darkness.

I arrived as the Party—the Partido Revolucionario Institucional, or PRI, as the regime was known—was in a nosedive, as was the peso. The party had been created in response to the instability and political assassinations that followed the Mexican Revolution. It worked so well that the PRI had ruled Mexico since 1929, taming any unrest by crushing or co-opting rivals.

Twelve years after the peso devaluation of 1982, however, the regime could no longer mask gaping problems in the economy, impunity in the justice system or pervasive social inequality. I watched the clock tick past midnight on New Year's 1994 with my then best friend, Angela. Uneasiness hung in the air. Mexico City seemed to stand still, eerily quiet, as did the rest of the nation.

I was convinced that my coverage would serve as a bridge between two countries. The United States had long pushed Mexico to clean up its house, tackle corruption, strengthen wobbly judicial institutions and stem the cartel tide. Few listened. I certainly didn't. It wasn't my reporting beat. We had one of the best reporters covering drug trafficking and all the ills that came with it. But the newspaper industry was unraveling. A staff of twelve led by Tracey Eaton, our narco beat reporter, was dwindling. Suddenly, I was thrust into a darker story of Mexico as I took up the cartel beat.

Like many in Mexican society, I had convinced myself that the country was on the right track, but we now watched hopelessly as a small, powerful group of men with big guns, protected by corrupt government officials, held a nation hostage. The conditions—poverty, impunity, corruption—were so deeply rooted that any region facing the threat of traffickers was swallowed by violence.

All I could do was hold on to the best of my ability. This book is an account of the stories I found and the country I tried to speak the truth about.

Driving from my home in La Condesa to the PRI headquarters was painful on July 1, 2012, election day. The sky was gray, threatening more rain. I felt sad again for Mexico. The PRI was back, and Enrique

Peña Nieto, a former governor of the state of Mexico, would be the new president. His boyish face and pompadour gave no hint of the past. His focus was on the future, he insisted.

Days later, I interviewed him. He was curious about whether I considered myself Mexican or American and how immigrants abroad could help Mexico transform. It depends where I am at the moment, I told him. I arrived in the United States when some five million Mexicans called the U.S.A. home, I said. Today, that number is an estimated thirty-five million—more than 10 percent of the U.S. population—and soon to be fifty million.

Did your family vote for me? the president-elect asked. Some did, some didn't, I responded. Some did support you, I added, but more because of your wife. He laughed; his wife is Angélica Rivera, a beloved actress known as *La Gaviota* for her role in a widely popular soap opera. Peña Nieto vowed he wouldn't disappoint my state of Durango, or Mexico. He promised to bring down violence, continue to strengthen judicial institutions, improve the economy, reform labor, privatize parts of the oil industry and work to improve equality.

I stared at him, nodded my head and realized it really didn't matter anymore whether this was the new and improved PRI. Mexico had changed. It was not just a new generation but a new country. That change, however, would be tested like never before.

I hope that in these pages I will answer one of the questions that I get from friends on both sides of the border, from my father, brothers and sisters, but mostly from my mother: Why in the world would I pick the title *Midnight in Mexico* when all I ever want to do is talk about Mexico's potential?

You may marvel at how a veteran correspondent, trained to be skeptical, would have so much hope for his embattled country. I have been amazed at my own naïveté. Sure, I get angry at times, vowing to leave and never set foot in Mexico again. But the more secrets I discover, the more complicated the story has become, and the more curious I've grown.

The truth is, I really have always been—I still am—in love with Mexico. Even with wisdom gained, flaws uncovered, I haven't stopped believing. This book, *Midnight in Mexico,* is about searching for a flickering light during the darkest night and believing in the promise of a new day.

PART I

When summer rains fall on Mexico, all is forgiven. The raindrops cleanse the metropolitan Mexico City sky, sweeping away the smog that traps twenty million people in its suffocating embrace, bringing everything into sharp focus over the southern edge of the city. Two hulking volcanoes stand guard: According to ancient legend, they are Popocatépetl, "Smoking Mountain," lying next to his lover, Iztaccíhuatl, "Woman in White." Washing away the smog, the rain reveals them on rare occasions, the same way it swept the desert sky of Durango decades ago.

The cleansing is una limpia, *the ancient rite, healing a scarred, misunderstood land always on the cusp of greatness, a country writhing to free itself from the curse of history and geography, for better or for worse tucked in the indifferent shadow of my adopted homeland, the United States. The moment of forgiveness is fleeting. The hole in heaven closes.*

ONE

2007

I walked onto the balcony of my sixth-floor apartment in my neighborhood of La Condesa and fixated on the thin sheets of rain falling on a late summer afternoon. In the center of a roundabout on the street below, theater students rehearsed their lines. A young valet parking cars for tips, dressed in a gray hooded pullover and tan jeans, struggled to light his cigarette. In the center, the actors moved gracefully around a pale blue fountain that, usually dry, was now filling with rainwater. Somewhere in the distance the sound of the steam whistle of *el camotero,* the man selling roasted sugared sweet potatoes, pierced the wet air.

Inside my apartment the Eagles sang through the speakers, welcoming me to the Hotel California. My girlfriend of more than a decade, Angela, and a friend were chatting over Malbec and tequila before we were to head out for dinner with some journalist colleagues. A tall vase of calla lilies sitting on a table between them reminded me of Diego Rivera's timeless frescoes of indigenous women gathering flowers into their arms.

My cell phone vibrated in my jeans pocket.

I hesitated. It was bound to be work. But I didn't want to miss a tip. I set my tequila down and flipped the phone open.

It was July 2007. The last time I felt safe in Mexico.

I recognized the low-pitched voice on the other end: a longtime trusted source, a U.S. investigator with informants inside some of the most brutal drug cartels in Mexico. I grabbed a pen and notepad and slipped into my bedroom. I closed the door. The skyline was still visible through the windows. It was dusk.

I spoke his secret code name and joked, "Hey———, *¿Qué onda?* What's up?"

He got to the point: "Where are you?"

"In Mexico."

"Where exactly?"

"In my apartment. Why?"

"They plan to kill an American journalist within twenty-four hours," he said. "Three names came up. I think it's you. I'd get out."

"What? Who are they?"

"I can't tell you more because I don't know more. But this may be serious—Zetas business."

The Zetas, a Mexican paramilitary group on the payroll of a powerful drug cartel, had gained unprecedented control of key drug routes to the United States by terrorizing Mexico's bloodstained northeastern region. They tortured enemies, cut them into pieces, dropped bodies in barrels of acid and captured the horrors on video to be sent to TV stations or posted on YouTube. The killings spread at a rapid pace. They were terrorists without a political agenda. Now they were apparently after me.

"Who are the other two reporters?" I asked in disbelief.

"Could be anyone, but I'd put my money on you. Just hide out."

"What? *¿Dónde? ¿Por qué?*" I was speaking in Spanglish, my natural language, furiously scribbling down his every word.

"Let's talk tomorrow. Don't know enough yet."

"Wait, wait—tomorrow may be too late."

"Bro," he scolded me. "Stop pissing them off. Lay off."

He hung up. As usual, his calls were too brief; he was always afraid his phone could be tapped. My own cell phone almost dropped from my hand. The floor-to-ceiling windows that gave me a beautiful view of the Mexico City skyline now left me feeling exposed. I looked out at the new fifty-five-story Torre Mayor building beaming in the distance. Down below, six narrow streets converged at the roundabout Popocatépetl. Two stray dogs joined the actors near the fountain and splashed in the falling rain. I had a fleeting urge to jump into the nearest closet or hide in the bathtub. But my feet wouldn't move.

Had I been betrayed?

As a journalist in Mexico, I'd been threatened on three previous occasions: A source once had to hide me in the back compartment of his SUV after I received a menacing phone call; a mysterious man once walked up to me at a bar and said the Zetas would chop my head off if I kept asking questions; and Angela and I once had reason to fear that either a top government official or the military, or both, were after us because of a story we'd reported on about the first video that surfaced showing criminals spilling confessions and then being executed. Each instance had left me terrified.

But there was something about that finite deadline—twenty-four hours—that felt more real, more imminent. The clock had begun ticking already.

I scanned my recent work, a stack of notepads with "Ciudad Juárez," "La Línea," "Nuevo Laredo" and "Zetas" scrawled in my chicken-scratch, looking for the story that could have pissed them off—whoever *they* were. Some of my stories had glimpsed the spreading influence of the Zetas in cities across the Southwest of the United States. There were stories about the massacre of young women in Juárez, of an informant gone rogue, of Americans missing in the border towns of Laredo and Nuevo Laredo.

It could be any one of them, really, or all of them.

One thing lingered in my mind. The tip for my latest story had come from the same U.S. investigator.

My report had outlined a peace pact between Mexican government officials and drug cartels. A few days earlier the investigator and I had been at a bar along the border. We had developed a rapport over the past two years. I'd fly to meet him somewhere in Mexico or the United States so he could give me information to break stories. He was handsome, with a sharp nose and a full head of hair combed back, and he always dressed casually in slacks and loafers. He had a penetrating look, framed by deep circles under his eyes. No matter the occasion, he wore his poker face.

We cut into juicy pepper steaks sprinkled with *chiles toreados* while an eager waiter poured more and more tequila. Suspecting the waiter was a cartel mole, or *halcón,* the investigator stopped talking every time the server approached, and he kept his back to the wall, eyeing everyone and everything. He finally loosened up, thanks to the tequila.

"The violence is about to stop," he said, observing me intently.

I looked up from my plate.

"Yeah, right," I said, and teased him. "No more tequila for you."

He paused and his fingers began tapping on the table. The waiter turned away.

"Go ahead," I said.

Since 2000, the dynamic of drug trafficking had changed. Mexico's two strongest cartels—the Sinaloa organization and the Gulf organization—had gone to war. There were some personal feuds, but the fight was still about business. Sinaloa wanted a bigger piece of the profitable cocaine trade, whose route led from Colombia up through the Gulf coast states to the southern Texas border. To fight the encroaching

Sinaloans, the Gulf cartel dispatched its newly formed paramilitary arm, the Zetas. Heavily equipped and well trained for urban warfare, the Zetas were established to protect territory, known as *plazas,* personnel and drug trafficking operations.

Zetas were often Mexican military personnel who had been trained by the U.S. military to fight the cartels. Neither government knew how many army deserters—lured by the bigger paychecks offered by drug kingpins—eventually became Zetas. But the number didn't really matter, because the knowledge from the American training had already been passed down. It was said the Zetas knew forty-three ways to kill a person in three minutes or less.

By 2007, the Zetas were showing signs of increased independence from the Gulf cartel. They expanded their operation, leaning on Texas gangs that served as paid mercenaries and operated out of San Antonio, Houston and Dallas, key trans-shipment points for all kinds of goods, legal and otherwise. Their victims were even appearing on the U.S. side of the border. The headlines were bad for business, and the cartels had agreed to a secret meeting.

The U.S. investigator lowered his tone. He had deep intelligence about the meetings, the initial one held at the home of drug trafficker Arturo Beltrán Leyva outside Mexico City, in Cuernavaca. Rival cartel leaders and corrupt government officials had met to end the spiking violence and get back to the business of moving drugs and making money. The plan was to divide drug distribution routes evenly and realign themselves, as they had done decades before. The men talked, drank and agreed to meet again. Tension between kingpins Édgar Valdez Villarreal, known as La Barbie, and Miguel Ángel Treviño Morales was deep. Treviño Morales suspected La Barbie of having ordered his brother killed. They cursed and challenged each other to a gunfight. Their bosses, particularly the host, got between them and sternly warned them that they were there to talk business and not settle personal scores.

The U.S. government had a snitch inside, collecting information on who was there.

The Mexican drug czar, high-level military leaders, intelligence officials and federal cops all knew about the pact, the investigator said. The leading officials hadn't been there personally, but they had representatives to protect their interests and back one cartel or another. Each interest had to be on the take for shipments to move north smoothly. At the meetings there were so many representatives mingling with cartel leaders, my source explained, that it was difficult to tell who was good and who was bad. In other words, who were members of the government and who belonged to organized crime?

The old-timers in the cartels wanted things to return to the way they were before Mexico underwent its so-called democratic process. For decades since the revolution, the authoritarian regime, Partido Revolucionario Institucional, or PRI, ran the country. During its heyday PRI members forced the cartels to share the profits, particularly with themselves.

When there was only one political party, one authority, negotiating was easy. But political power had become increasingly decentralized since the changing of the guard in 2000, when the conservative Partido Acción Nacional, or PAN, finally took the presidency. State and local politicians were no longer simply taking orders from the top of a single-party hierarchy. Many politicians took advantage of their newfound authority and independence.

Political decentralization also created a power vacuum. The cartels were ready to prey on the delicate fledgling institutions that were now exposed in the new democracy. Criminal files disappeared, investigators were killed and witnesses vanished, with near total impunity for those responsible. Almost overnight, the so-called rule of law fell to Mexico's modern-day conquerors: the drug cartels.

After his election in 2006, Mexican president Felipe Calderón talked about building a country of laws, recapturing territory that had been lost to criminal groups. He sent out the military to rein in the cartels, but failed to fully measure the consequences or the capacity of existing institutions.

Some regions were facing a slow-burning conflict among factions with shifting loyalties, in cities and villages—many close to the border—with tangled histories and changing dynamics. Every local commander, every official and every community had to work out an accommodation with the cartels and their members. Corruption alone didn't explain the violence. Having your head between a vice didn't give you many choices. The government was either helpless or co-opted. More than 430,000 state and local police officers, and a federal police force growing fast to more than 35,000, some more corrupt than others, could not counter the narco billions. But the increased press coverage of the violence threatened a delicate balance.

As we sipped tequila, I didn't hide my surprise about a peace pact. Even for Mexico, this was brazen. The investigator seemed both appalled and annoyed at my reaction.

The government had long, historic ties to the cartels, especially Sinaloa, he said, and it knew the cartels well, particularly the Zetas. After all, the Zetas had belonged to the army before they deserted. Officials had records of them, knew their families, histories, addresses and even nicknames. Someone inside had to be covering for the Zetas in exchange for tens of thousands of dollars a month. How else could they move drugs and migrants and kidnap victims with such ease?

"This shit has never worked without the government in on the take," the investigator said defensively. "The two coexist, side by side. They have to. Trust me—the killings will stop any day now. You watch—

"And start again, like that," he added, snapping his fingers.

The investigator finished his dinner, wiped his mouth, stood up and threw his napkin on the table.

"Be careful out there," he said. "And remember my advice."

I nodded. Of course I remembered. U.S. citizenship wasn't enough to protect me. Don't get too comfortable. To the cartels, I looked as Mexican, and as disposable, as anyone.

The investigator preferred to leave the dark bar on his own. I watched him cross the street and walk into a park across from the bar; dressed in black slacks, loafers and a guayabera, he cautiously and constantly looked behind him. I caught his gaze through the window and quickly looked away.

I asked the waiter for the bill. He handed it to me with a wry smile. On the border everyone had become suspect. I paid and quickly retreated to my hotel room on the U.S. side of the border, so close to Mexico I could hear the sirens there.

After I broke the peace pact story, the Mexican media picked it up. The information compromised both the government and the cartels and jeopardized millions of dollars in future kickbacks. In a country where the rich and powerful are rarely, if ever, scrutinized, the story would have upset more than a few people, people with the *huevos*—and the impunity—to kill an American journalist.

I took a deep breath as I gazed through the curtains. Angela and our friend Cecilia, a writer, were chatting in the living room and making their way to the balcony where it now seemed like hours since I'd stood. I was forty-seven years old, unmarried, no kids. I had lived for my work, which now might put a bullet in my head.

Were there hit men downstairs in the lobby? Were they already making their way up the stairs? Should I make a break for the airport? The previous scares had instantly sent me packing for the United States. But I was tired of running without knowing why or from whom. There was nowhere to hide—certainly not in this apartment.

Goddamn it. The investigator had played a role in one of my most important stories. He was the best source I had, and now the most dangerous one too.

He kept three—sometimes up to five—cell phones, each dedicated exclusively to key contacts from the different criminal organizations. Whenever he couldn't answer one of my questions, he'd go to the speed dial on one of the phones and call someone from deep inside the cartel who could answer it, providing crucial details as I whispered follow-up questions or wrote them down on my notepad. Calls didn't last more than thirty, forty-five seconds.

I hardly knew him. I had trusted him, shared details of my life. He knew where my family lived. He knew our history, how we'd come from Mexico to work as farmworkers in the United States. He knew where I'd grown up, about my struggle to belong on one side of the border or the other. He had even met Angela.

Some of his sources—all traitors to the cartels—had been killed over the past year. One afternoon he had called me to pass on information that two police officers had been gunned down by Zetas in a Mexican border town. He knew I was there working on a story.

"You still on the Mexican side?" he asked.

"Yeah. Why?"

"Can you get to this location downtown and call me when you get there?"

"Sure," I said, and literally ran down the street, the sound of sirens growing louder as I got closer.

I called him back. Two cops down, I told him, one a female with a bullet to the head, blood spilling. Her brains on the car floor.

"Thanks," he said gravely and hung up.

Later that evening he told me the female officer had been a contact of his. Her husband, motivated by fear of what Mexico was becoming, ratted out the Zetas until they discovered his betrayal and had him killed in front of her. The wife sought out the U.S. investigator, vowing revenge, and told him she would finish the job and hand over the Zetas' top leader. She was also angry about the women they raped. She was one of them. The Zetas, with the help of the local police force, found her first.

To the cartels, I was just another one of his people. I'd be just another dead Mexican. Some estimates have it that fewer than 5 percent of all homicide investigations in Mexico are ever solved. Mexico's conviction rate is worse than that of Honduras. If you are on a hit list, you are as good as dead. Especially journalists—or rather, Mexican journalists. So far the foreign correspondent community in Mexico had stayed relatively safe.

I remembered what the U.S. investigator had told me a couple of years before.

"Look, I won't bullshit you," he said one night at a seafood restaurant in Washington's Georgetown district after I asked him what the likelihood was that an American journalist would ever be the target of a hit by Mexican cartels.

"First, the good news: Drug traffickers don't want to mess with an American correspondent. The attention threatens their business."

"That's great," I said. "So what's the bad news?"

"You don't look American, bro."

I dug my cell phone out of my pocket and nervously pounded his number. The call went to voice mail. I pressed redial. Again, no answer. Redial again. Voice mail. Goddamn it! I threw my phone on the bed and let my notepad fall to the hardwood floor amid a mess of books and magazines, unable to even muster the energy to hurl it against the wall. I felt helpless.

Thoughts of my mother, my father, my family, Angela, haunted me.

¡Puta madre!

I walked back to the living room and cranked up the volume on my iPod. Angela, wearing a salmon-colored shawl wrapped around her bare shoulders, was still deep in conversation with Cecilia. Angela commuted back and forth every few weeks and was in town now because she and I were planning to head to Baja California to do some reporting about Americans working illegally in the beach communities there. We expected it to be an easy assignment about retirees and young people lured there by the promise of a new life. Angela and I had been living our relationship long-distance for years, so whenever possible we planned to report stories together for the newspaper and she for television.

A threat against me was a threat against her too. The cartels knew her and they knew no limits; family and lovers were fair game. She was my best friend, the woman I had wanted to marry. Even though she never said yes, I urged her to keep the engagement ring, just in case. Everyone thought she was my wife because we had been together for so long. I loved her deeply.

Neither Angela nor Cecilia noticed me leaning against the doorjamb. "Lyin' Eyes" was now blaring. I slipped back into my bedroom.

They plan to kill an American journalist within twenty-four hours.

Ya sabes, my mother and father would say. You know the risks.

I began pacing. I tried to distract myself by thinking of something normal. What was I going to do with the eight bottles of Siembra Azul tequila a friend had shipped me that day as a celebratory gift for an award I had received for my work? The tequila, from the highlands of Jalisco, had been carefully cultivated with the help of classical music from Vivaldi and Mozart, to inspire passion in the yeast. I really wanted a drink.

Angela would ask the tough questions I didn't know how to answer. What would I do? Where would I go?

So instead I dialed my editor back in Dallas. Tim Connolly's calm temperament and flat North Dakota accent always put me at ease. He had been by my side through the other threats. Little ruffled him.

"Hey, Alfredo," he said. "I was about to call you."

Tim had just heard from the editors at the *San Antonio Express-News* about the threat. I pictured Tim's pensive eyes and red-gray beard.

Slowly, measuring his words, he said, "Maybe you should get out. Maybe you should follow your source's advice."

I told him I'd get back to him. I needed to talk to Angela, speak to sources, poke around, find out what was really going on and whether the information was "raw," or unconfirmed. What had happened to the peace pact that the cartels had allegedly agreed on?

If I needed to get on the next flight, Tim repeated, I shouldn't hesitate.

I hung up and wandered into the living room again. This time I lowered the music and joined Angela and Cecilia standing by the balcony, where the air was cool and inviting. The rain had given way to open patches of clear evening sky.

Sweeping aside her blond bangs, Angela looked over at me and smiled.

"Finally going to join us?" she teased.

Her green eyes read the worry on my face and her smile disappeared.

"You okay?" Angela asked, her face turning serious. "You've been on the phone this whole time? What's going on?"

Angela and I had met in El Paso at my family's restaurant, Freddy's Café, in the summer of 1988. I noticed a stunning blonde sitting alone at a table I had reserved for friends. I was about to move her to a different table when a friend of mine walked in, kissed her on the cheek and sat down next to her. There was nothing to do but take her order and hope she would notice me.

I'd introduced myself, told her I was back home in El Paso for a story I was doing for the *Wall Street Journal,* where I worked in the

Philadelphia bureau. At twenty-eight years old, I thought I was hot shit. But whenever I was home, my mother would put me right to work seating customers, taking orders and picking up dirty plates.

Angela just kept on eating.

"Did you like the huevos rancheros?" I asked. "Or should I berate the cook, my mother? Just tell me how I can be of service, *güerita*." Blondie.

She barely looked at me. Later, when the conversation heated up around the table about El Paso's changing political landscape, I leaned in close and, trying to be flattering, asked, "So, you're a real blonde?" She shot me a look of disgust. This was El Paso—at least 80 percent of the city's population was of Mexican descent, meaning largely brown skinned and dark haired. Her blond hair stood out. "What are you?" I continued.

"I'm a human being. What are you?" she replied.

That was nearly that except I had felt something powerful pass between us, though I could not name it yet. She'd been born in Mexico City, the daughter of an American mother and a Ukrainian father. She had grown up between Mexico and the United States, but her Spanish was flawless, crisp, more sophisticated and lyrical than mine.

She kept coming to my parents' cafe and I kept trying to engage her in conversation.

Hey, what's going on?" Angela repeated. "What happened?"

I didn't say anything. I looked into my snifter with its splash of tequila. I wished there was more.

"You look pale," she continued. "What's wrong?"

"I think we should cancel dinner." A group of journalist friends were joining us to celebrate an award I had won for stories that I now began to regret ever writing.

Angela looked puzzled and crossed her arms.

"There is a hit on an American journalist within twenty-four hours and my source thinks it's me," I said.

Angela stared at me. Cecilia's brows furrowed deeply. They set their glasses down.

"Oh, my God," Angela said. "Why?"

She had a pretty good idea. Again, I'd gotten too close to the story.

Cecilia murmured, "Wow, shit, Alfredo. What are you gonna do?"

I shook my head. We all took a drink.

The last vestiges of a red sun briefly peeked through the clouds, then moved behind distant skyscrapers.

On my iPod, Marco Antonio Solís crooned, "Si No Te Hubieras Ido": *The rhythm of life suddenly doesn't seem right anymore.*

The rain would begin again any minute.

We stood in silence and felt the humid wind whip through the trees below. The electrical wires fluttered gently. A stronger breeze blew, stirring the branches even more, making the leaves hiss. A blanket of clouds circled Mexico City. A storm was forming in this valley of twenty million souls.

We moved away from the windows.

Angela broke the silence. She suggested I call our friend and colleague Dudley Althaus to tell him about the threat and cancel dinner. A correspondent for the *Houston Chronicle,* Dudley was usually relaxed, the voice of reason and experience. He was from Ohio and he had the look of a quintessentially big, burly gringo. He was anything but an overbearing American. He had been in Mexico so long we joked that his first byline had appeared when Mexico City was still Tenochtitlán, the Aztec capital before the Spaniards set foot in Yucatán in 1517. Like Angela and me, Dudley had covered plenty of tough stories on the drug cartels.

One thing had become abundantly clear in my years of writing on Mexico: There was no solace in reporting about organized crime—just grief, heartache, threats and death. All too often it's the reporters who lose when reporting about cartels and their endless fights to control distribution routes into the world's single biggest drug market. The characters may change, but the business goes on no matter what we write. The reporter watches and records this shadowy world where everyone is a ghost, where life means nothing. And then he, or she, is silenced.

I dialed him.

"Don't think it's a good idea to get together," I said.

Dudley resisted. He organized a weekly gathering of correspondents at a local bar. Fridays were cantina night. Tonight, Thursday, was a special night—correspondents from the Associated Press and the *Washington Post,* a photographer for the *Dallas Morning News* and the New York–based American correspondent for Mexico's *La Jornada* were all supposed to be there to celebrate. He felt we needed to keep our dinner as planned, alert U.S. authorities and show solidarity. If we didn't band together—like our Mexican colleagues, who were prone to infighting—we could be setting a dangerous precedent. Dudley thought we should also share the news with the minister counselor for public affairs at the U.S. embassy, Jim Dickmeyer, who would also be joining us. He had the ear of the U.S. ambassador, Tony Garza. If we could get to Garza, he could get information out about the threat and perhaps even brief the Mexican president, or at least get his attention. This wasn't just about me, Dudley said.

The dinner was on.

The challenge is to get to dinner safely, I thought as I hung up the phone.

Erich Schlegel, a friend and photographer, had just joined us as we all grabbed our umbrellas and nervously rode the elevator down six flights and stepped outside and into a cab I had called minutes before. I had insisted on going on my own, but the three adamantly opposed the idea. Safety in numbers, Angela said firmly.

Outside, rain fell lightly. The air was chilly. Winters in Mexico City felt like spring, while summers—often cold, gloomy, dark—felt like winter. As we drove, the streets seemed unusually empty. My eyes were alert to every shadow. The city, the country, felt turbulent to me, frantic. Neon lights illuminated the seafood restaurant, but Calle Atlixco was otherwise dark. The reflection of headlights traveled from one puddle to the other, tires splashing water on stray cats.

TWO

Around the table, we debated the merits of the threat and what steps to take. Some took notes while others just listened, stunned. Threats didn't happen to Americans. Our Mexican colleagues—friends like Ramón Cantú Deándar in Nuevo Laredo—were the ones on the firing line.

In 2007 alone, more than two thousand Mexicans, among them cops, politicians and journalists, were killed. Of the journalists, all but one was Mexican—so far, at least. No one in power seemed to care enough to do anything about it, or even thought anything could be done about it. Postmortem, the dead were often labeled as shady characters linked to organized crime. In Mexico, they kill you twice: First, with a bullet, an ax to your head or a bath full of acid. Then they spread rumors about you.

Angela was quiet and hardly touched her food. I nervously munched on guacamole and scallops and drank more tequila, and I left the table to take calls from the editor of the *Laredo Morning Times* as well as the border reporter from the *San Antonio Express-News,* who'd been ordered to leave Laredo and return to San Antonio immediately. His editors doubted that even the U.S. side was safe, especially Laredo, which shared the border with Nuevo Laredo, Mexico, the Zetas' base of operation. We exchanged notes. But I told him I wasn't ready to leave. Not just yet. I needed more information.

I found a quiet corner and made calls. I needed to speak to Ramón, the publisher and editor of *El Mañana,* the family-owned newspaper in Nuevo Laredo. *El Mañana* faced constant threats and attacks by the two warring cartels that fought for territory as well as control of the news. Already there had been fatal consequences for not heeding their demands.

The *El Mañana* offices had been hit by grenades and riddled with bullets. The night-side reporter was paralyzed after being shot. Three years earlier, city editor Roberto Mora had been stabbed twenty-eight times. The Zetas kidnapped Ramón's brother, Heriberto, shortly afterward. The release of his brother carried a price: self-censorship. Ramón's paper became a mouthpiece pressured into covering the cartel's interests.

Because of the relationship, he had gained rare access to the Zetas. But he was not proud of the contacts. The cartels and the Zetas had "invited" him more than once to remote areas or dark parts of town where in the front cab of a bulletproof truck or SUV he met with Mexico's most wanted criminals. Such invitations could not be refused. Lives were at stake.

He picked up on the first ring. I could imagine his unruly hair, a cross between Fher, the singer for Maná, and Jim Morrison of the Doors. Ramón had been raised in Mexico but was born in the United States. Like me he was unable to separate the two nationalities, although if you pressed, or pissed him off enough, he'd say, *"¡Mexicano hasta las cachas, compadre!"* Mexican to the core.

He hadn't heard anything about the threat but offered to check it out.

"No te preocupes, cabrón," he said, using one of the many terms of endearment he had for me. "I'll ask around."

I also called law enforcement sources, including a Mexican intelligence official I knew and trusted, to compare notes. We had known each other for some time now. Days before, I had walked into his office to check the information from the U.S. investigator regarding the peace pact story. As I entered, he motioned for me to close the door behind me. As always, we had just a few minutes. He was busy and didn't like to be seen with me. Mexico's intelligence system was undergoing a restructuring at the time. Many in the agency had been fired. Mistrust among the agents was particularly high. When we met it was always brief. At his suggestion, I'd lie to his secretary and tell her I needed a meeting to discuss some minor issue.

When I began to frame the question about the peace pact based on the information I had from the U.S. investigator, the Mexican official held up his hand. He sat there for a moment in his large leather chair drumming his fingers on top of his messy desk, eyes darting, looking for the remote control to his TV. He found it, aimed it at the television and landed on a music channel, Telehit, which features bubblegum Latin pop. He raised the volume.

"Yes," he said. "I can confirm the account. There have been ongoing attempts to reach a peace pact. But it's too soon to know whether this one is any different, whether it'll work. And yes, I'm afraid, some members of the government are involved. They have to be. Otherwise the system doesn't work—nothing works."

"Who in the government?"

"That's under investigation. Not ready to talk yet," he responded. "That's all I can give you."

"The fighting in the north and at the border is for control of the key *plazas*"—critical border crossing points to the lucrative routes north—"and the government now controls those *plazas*?" I asked. "Is that why the killings have suddenly stopped? Just like that?"

"To a certain extent," he said. "That's all I can give you now."

He looked at me impatiently. I shook his hand and walked away quickly, avoiding eye contact with the agents and informants crammed on a torn-up love seat in the hallway, waiting to see the Mexican intelligence agent. I touched my back pocket to make sure my notepad was tucked deep inside. I felt clumsy.

Now I was on the phone with him. Yes, he said, he had heard about the threat from inside contacts but, like the U.S. investigator, he didn't know more. "Who told you?" I asked. He wouldn't say. I wanted to know whether this was blowback—had he heard about the threat from the U.S. investigator? I wanted to ask, although I knew such a question would break protocol. I couldn't get anything out of him as he quickly hung up. I called the U.S. investigator and was relieved when he finally answered. He was still at his office, leaving a meeting.

"I'm going nuts here," I said. "Just tell me—should I leave? How serious is this? Just answer me!"

"Working on it," he said. He hung up.

"Hey, goddamn it!" I screamed into the phone.

I thought I was alone. I had been trying to remain calm, in front of friends, in front of Angela, but David Brooks, the correspondent for *La Jornada*, had been watching me as I stood outside the restaurant. He lit a cigarette. Like Angela, David had gone to school in Mexico and his Spanish was impeccable. Every time he visited from his current home base in New York City, he was dumbfounded by what was happening to his homeland. His politics leaned left, something he was not shy about. He wasn't sold on Mexico's embrace of American-style democracy or the fight against organized crime. He was constantly questioning whether or not democracy would change Mexico for the better. We were all being duped by high-priced New York City and Austin consultants hired by the Mexican government, he'd tell me.

Our homeland remained a place of extremes. In the seven years since the election of the first opposition government, led by the PAN, signs of a growing Mexican middle class had multiplied, at least in terms of access to TVs, cars, homes, cell phones. But Mexico remained a country of contradictions, where forty million people lived in poverty, 15 percent of them on less than one dollar a day. The gap of inequality remained wide, even after NAFTA was signed in 1994. Despite cleaner elections and having the second-largest economy in Latin America, Mexico faced her future with one of the most corrupt government bureaucracies on earth. Annually, the country lost an estimated $50 billion to tax evaders, criminals and corruption.

A lifetime of humiliations, betrayals and defeats is embedded in the Mexican psyche. Many of Mexico's founding fathers rose just as the Spanish empire was falling apart—men like Miguel Hidalgo y Costilla, José María Morelos and Ignacio Allende. All died for their cause. But one lived long enough to define an entire century. General Antonio López de Santa Anna spent the better part of the 1800s in the military, as president or in exile. He served as president for eleven nonconsecutive terms between 1833 and 1876, during which years he lost the territory comprising Texas, California, Arizona, Nevada and New Mexico. Yet it would be hard to argue that Mexico has seen much better since, with the exception of a few courageous leaders. The political and religious men who have governed the country have swallowed the rivers, eaten the forests, destroyed the coastline and robbed the country of its oil, crying nationalism if anyone got in their way. Mexico has been mocked by its history every step of the way.

For much of my life I have believed that Mexico was on the verge of transformation, of creating a civil society, believing rule of law could heal a self-imposed curse. We are always almost there.

"*Está cabrón, ¿no?*" I shrugged and looked at David, avoiding his eyes. "Pretty fucked up, huh?"

"Where's the long-awaited political change?" he responded, a tinge of sarcasm in his voice. "What happened to the American-style democracy?"

"Maybe this is it," I said, reminding him we—Mexicans raised in the United States—were supposed to help usher in that democracy.

David puffed away his last drag, paused and said, *"Entonces estamos de la chingada."* Then we're fucked.

The smoke lingered in the rain.

We returned and took our seats at the table. Dickmeyer asked how raw the information was. A threat with a twenty-four-hour deadline was dead serious if confirmed by multiple intelligence sources. But no one seemed to have confirmation yet. "Raw" could mean worthless as a rumor.

"Source is checking on that now," I answered. "I was hoping you'd tell me."

"I'm just a spokesman," he said.

He calmly announced he would brief the ambassador the next morning, if that was all right with us.

We nodded in agreement.

We drank too much.

"If they're gonna kill you, we all need to be liquored up," said Dudley, half joking. Then he paused, looked me in the eye and said, "A threat on you is a threat against all of us."

Angela and I got home and headed straight to our room. Not wanting to disturb Cecilia, we strategized in hushed tones. Baja California sounded good to me, better than hiding out in some hotel in Dallas or, worse, heading for El Paso—with a bull's-eye on my forehead in the city where my family lived and where a transnational gang wouldn't necessarily stop. Angela wanted to cancel the Baja trip and immediately leave for the United States with me.

I wanted to go with her to Baja. I didn't want us to be alone and apart from each other. And the thought of working on a non-narco story at a beach popular with Hollywood stars sounded safe. What I really wanted was to buy time to work the phones from Mexican soil, closer to the answers, if there were any.

I wasn't ready to leave, I insisted.

"When will you be?" she asked.

"Not yet," I responded.

Sleep on it, she said. "Remember what Dudley said. Let's not be hasty," she reasoned.

While Angela slipped into bed, I called my editor, Tim, and told him about the plan. I'd write about golf courses, beach resorts—anything but drug trafficking.

"But you'll still be in Mexico," he said, sounding skeptical.

I reminded Tim of past threats and how the newspaper had responded: by installing bulletproof windows in our office, welding iron bars onto the windows in my apartment, flying in a security consultant who we believed was former CIA and hiring Mexican security consultants, who went as far as to provide a red panic button that supposedly connected us to them instantly. I never pressed it, fearful I would rile up the wrong people. For weeks the security detail had shadowed Angela and me, until Angela felt less safe with them than without them. I told Tim what I believed: If a cartel hit man wants to kill you, he will. It would be just a matter of time. And if the cartel can't kill you, it'll send you a message by killing a relative, a loved one. I had relatives on both sides of the border, I explained to Tim. No place was safe. I needed more time on the ground to find the truth.

Tim didn't sound very convinced, but he trusted my judgment.

I hung up and began to shove clothes and notebooks into my green duffel bag. I looked over at Angela, passed out in a deep sleep. She looked so peaceful. She had lost her mother to cancer months earlier. Now she feared she'd lose me too. I finally crawled into bed. I tried to coax sleep by fixing my eye on every object in my room, one at a time, as if trying to memorize what my room looked like.

The bookshelf against the wall was loaded with music: the great singer-songwriter Juan Gabriel from Ciudad Juárez, love songs by Luis

Miguel, Marco Antonio Solís, Shakira and, of course, Miguel Bosé, whose Spanish lisp and outlandish way of dressing I used to imitate. I went through a regrettable phase as a teenager in which I wore red ballet tights and a short T-shirt in honor of Bosé. I was fifteen. The Doors, the Eagles, Coldplay, R.E.M., David Gray, Bruce Springsteen, U2; a giant Christmas collection that friends loved to poke fun at; Miles Davis and John Coltrane; *ranchera* music from Alejandro Fernández and Pepe Aguilar and their fathers, and Los Relámpagos del Norte. Music, my first love, always grounded me in the moment.

The light of the palisade glass of the Torre Mayor spilled into my bedroom. I fixated on Mexico's tallest building. I got up and e-mailed the U.S. investigator, hoping he was awake.

I wandered into the bathroom, exhausted. My whole body ached. Maybe it was age, I thought, or tense muscles from so much stress. I leaned on the countertop, inspecting my bloodshot eyes in the large mirror. In front of me I saw a man aging fast. Hair thinning, turning gray; circles under sad, dark eyes; sunken pockmarked cheeks.

My mother, Herlinda, wanted me safe in the United States with her and my father, Juan Pablo, and my five brothers and two sisters. She had sacrificed all she knew to get us out, because she saw Mexico as stuck between hope and despair, divided between the rich and those who lived with nothing but their stubborn faith. I had neither riches nor faith. Just brown skin, an accent and ideas bleached by American ways, and a deep, deep love for Mexico, *mi tierra,* that I couldn't even explain anymore.

Mexico, forty years after we'd left, remained unpredictable, untamed and raw. But I had been lured back thirteen years earlier by nostalgia and the promise of what Mexico could be.

Mamá, look, this bedroom alone is bigger than the entire trailer where we lived as migrants in California and twice the size of our living room in the adobe house in Durango. *Mamá, ¡ya mero, ya casi!* Almost!

I had chosen journalism as a profession after a guidance counselor managed to convince me that reporting was a better career plan than working the fields or becoming a hairdresser, the job I had settled on after watching Warren Beatty chase girls in the film *Shampoo.* I had worked for the *Ogden Standard-Examiner* in Utah, the *El Paso Herald-Post,* the *Wall Street Journal* in Philadelphia and now the *Dallas Morning News,* which had paved a road back to Mexico.

In a photo on a bookshelf, my mother and brothers stared back at me in sepia tones. Four young boys in button-down checkered shirts making awkward faces, with our mother in the middle, stern and unsmiling, the sadness still in her eyes, looking uncomfortable in a borrowed black dress. Lupita, her beloved daughter, my baby sister, is missing in the photograph. I couldn't look at that photo without also seeing that dark, gaping absence. It was the last photo we took before crossing the border to start a new life. I repaid my parents' sacrifice by writing exactly the kinds of stories I had promised them I wouldn't touch.

My American cell phone started vibrating. It was the U.S. investigator.

The information about the threat, he said, was "definitely raw." The source would need a day, maybe two or three, to get more information and run it by other contacts, confidential informants, to verify the threat further. Keep your guard up, stay vigilant until I know more, he said and hung up.

My whispering on the phone woke Angela. I apologized but explained that the information about a possible hit was unconfirmed. This could all be a huge mistake, I said. Angela wasn't convinced.

"Does it really matter whether the information is raw or verified?" she asked quietly. "Do you really want to find out? Do you want confirmation? Come to bed. You need rest."

"I'm going with you to Baja," I said.

"Okay," she responded, and closed her eyes. "We'll go together." She went back to sleep.

I stretched out in bed beside Angela and slipped my arms around her body, warm with sleep. I felt a surge of desire to protect her, to make her feel safe. Next to Angela, I felt secure. I *needed* her. The thought gripped my throat. I squeezed her close. I lay there, hoping the mercy of sleep would come and claim me in my bed, in my apartment in La Condesa, in the city that I loved and in the country that I now felt had betrayed me.

It was midnight in Mexico.

THREE

Hours later, we were running.

Samuel, our driver, was weaving in and out of traffic on our way to the airport, where we'd catch a flight to Baja California. In Mexico a lot of people with money have a driver. In my case, earning dollars meant having the money for a driver and a housekeeper. Samuel was also part assistant, part bodyguard. He was a Mexico City native who kept me out of trouble with his knowledge of the city. I was especially grateful this morning for his habit of driving like a madman. The car radio blared news that the U.S. embassy had issued a warning to any criminal organization threatening the life of an American foreign correspondent. I wasn't sure if publicity was good or bad. One thing was clear: Everyone knew now.

Angela and I found our seats on the plane. As she settled into her seat and I shoved my backpack into the overhead compartment, my phone vibrated. I froze. The caller ID read "Unknown." I didn't answer. A minute later it rang again. This time I saw "MiguelM," for Miguel Monterrubio, a spokesman for President Felipe Calderón, on the screen. We were not close friends, but I considered him more than a source. Miguel and I had met in Washington when I served as D.C. correspondent for the *News* and he and his family had just moved there from abroad. Lean and balding, Miguel was always in a hurry, with a cell phone pegged to each ear. Months earlier he had returned from Washington and we'd shared coffee in Polanco, near Los Pinos, the presidential residence and office, where he worked as the president's point person for foreign correspondents. He had lectured me against reporting too much on the drug violence, insisting I was missing out on Mexico's grandeur. Mexico was changing, and changing fast. We walked for blocks around the coffee place, as I patiently heard him out, without saying much. I liked hearing the hope in his voice. Don't get jaded, he said.

"*Güey*, dude, why don't you answer your phone?" he asked.

"I didn't hear it, *güey*," I lied. I was scared of who could be on the line.

Miguel had briefed the president's top communications director about the threat. He told me the president had expressed his concern and pledged to punish anyone making threats against journalists. I thought of Ramón and the countless other Mexican journalists more vulnerable than me. I wondered whether it was nothing more than empty promises.

Miguel said President Calderón had asked him to get to the bottom of it. I wondered why Calderón cared about a threat against an American journalist. Perhaps it was because Ambassador Garza was making a big deal out of the violence spreading across the country. Perhaps he believed that a threat on an American was only steps away from a threat against Mexican government officials, his inner circle, maybe even his family, himself.

"What do you know?" I asked Miguel.

"Nothing, other than what I read. Maybe it was your last article. I really don't know."

The piece about the peace pact had incensed the president so much that Miguel had called me immediately to deny the president was in any way involved. I never said "the president," I reminded him, and offered to write a clarification, but he rejected it, saying he just wanted to be clear: The president doesn't believe in peace pacts.

That was just days ago. Now he was on the phone expressing the president's concern.

"I don't know if it was the peace pact story," he said. "But I would start there."

"What can the government do?" I asked Miguel.

"What are you planning on doing?"

"I'll be in touch," I said. "I promise."

The flight attendants asked us to shut off our phones.

"Where are you going?" he asked, hearing the intercom.

I didn't trust anyone, especially over the telephone, especially a bureaucrat, friend or not.

"Can't tell you, but you can always reach me."

"I understand. We'll be in touch."

As I was about to turn the phone off, Miguel called back with one urgent request:

"No more calls. Text me."

"Why?" I asked.

And then his voice disappeared.

As I recounted the conversation to Angela, I searched for her hand and held it tight. She suddenly pulled away.

Angela always said Mexico was her refuge, a place of happy childhood memories in a sea of uncertainty. Her mother, a native of Chicago, had escaped to Mexico when her first marriage ended in divorce. That's where she'd met Angela's father. The pregnancy would put an end to the romance—her father did not want the child. Angela's mother refused to end the pregnancy. Her father left Mexico, right before Angela was born at the American-British hospital in Mexico City a week before Christmas.

Sometimes her mother had enough money; other times it wasn't so clear whether she would be able to keep a roof over their heads. Times were especially tough when they moved to south Texas to live near Angela's grandmother, who'd settled there after marrying a Texan with a ranch in the lush, humid Rio Grande Valley right on the Texas-Tamaulipas border, a region now taken over by drug traffickers. At one point the financial uncertainty forced Angela to drop out of school. When she returned to high school she quickly made up for lost time. She made good grades, graduated near the top of her class and was voted "Most Beautiful."

At the University of Texas at Austin, Angela began searching for her father. She had never needed him, but his absence made her curious. She put an ad in the English-language newspaper in Mexico City seeking information. She learned he was living in San Diego with his family. She eventually sought him out, although she never expected much from the relationship. Initially he was defensive, refusing to acknowledge her even though his sons bore a remarkable resemblance to their newfound half sister. Years later, her father came to accept her as his daughter. She was with her brothers as he struggled to take his last breath. By then Angela had learned not to count on anyone but herself.

She told me I was the first person she could lean on and now, as we sat on the runway, she feared that was slipping away. She pressed her lips together. Even when sad she was lovely. She whispered that she wanted me to come back to El Paso—to safety. I didn't know how to respond.

"I'm not convinced I'm the target," I protested. I couldn't bear the thought of leaving. "It could be someone else."

I reminded her that the threat didn't make sense. The peace pact by the cartels was in place. The killings were diminishing. Murdering an American reporter would be bad for business.

"Stop fooling yourself," she said. "You know I love Mexico, but things are getting crazy. Next time there won't be a warning."

She waited for a response.

"It's time for you to leave Mexico," she insisted again. "You're too damn obsessed, and this story is getting too dangerous."

The blue fabric on the airplane seat in front of me looked worn.

"Hey, did you hear anything I just said?" she asked.

I didn't know what to say.

"You need to think beyond yourself and start thinking of your family, your mother, your father—me," she said. "Come home, at least for a while."

I saw my reflection in the airplane's tiny window.

As the plane took off, I watched the city below. I normally close my eyes when planes take off. That morning I wanted to remember everything. The city was anticipating that afternoon's summer rain. I knew she was right. She squeezed my hand.

Accompanied by a cameraman and photographer, Angela and I worked on our stories. We were hundreds of miles away from Mexico City, in San José del Cabo. We traveled between beaches and drank hard. Emotions raw. With each day that passed, I settled into the slow rhythm of Mexico's wild and rugged seaside towns. That Mexico of pueblos and pristine beaches, *mercados* and palm trees, captivated me completely, as ever. My immediate fears subsided, but I still looked over my shoulder, wanting to know why the threat had come and who was behind it.

I texted Miguel incessantly.

Patience, he replied.

The more we drove around Baja California, the more I longed for the endless fields of the San Joaquin Valley where I grew up. I wanted to drive the eight hundred or so miles to the border and keep driving on Highway 1 to Carmel, turn right to the Salinas Valley, past the Missions

Trail, and cross Highway 101 to Pacheco Pass, Route 152 and then home, beyond the San Luis Obispo dam, over the yellow hills where my brothers and I spent Easter afternoons hunting for painted eggs in the grass. I yearned to visit the valley where my parents and I had labored, drenched in sweat. I once despised those fields. Now I missed the smell of garlic, the sweet taste of oranges, and tomatoes dusted in salt and pepper.

That night I stood on the balcony of our hotel room in Todos Santos, an isolated rocky beach town with art galleries, cafés, a bar and the Hotel California where the Eagles supposedly found their inspiration. The tar-black ocean looked inviting at night. The stars seemed so close. I leaned against the door and nursed tequila in a cognac glass and stared out at the darkness, comforted by the sound of ocean waves. The bright July moon etched a sparkling silver path across the water. The lights of Todos Santos dappled the waves. Across the street was a mission, its bells silent.

Angela called me to bed, but I wanted to stay outside a little longer. It was getting late. The tequila was taking its effect. I dug my phone out of my pocket—one more attempt. I scrolled down to "Durango"—and dialed. I didn't worry about calling so late, as this was our usual hour.

Paisana's voice came on the line. *"¿Eres tú, paisano?"*

I met Paisa at my parents' restaurant in the 1980s, shortly after we all moved from California to El Paso to be closer to Mexico. My mother's home-cooked meals quickly became a hit, while my father sold her burritos from a food truck. I loved working at Freddy's, waiting tables, always finding new ways to attract customers. Freddy's consisted of six tables and a kitchen crammed into a tiny storefront just four blocks from the border on South El Paso Street, and it was always packed. People came from both sides of the border to sample my mother's *caldo de res* and her famous enchiladas.

On Sundays, friends from El Paso Community College, UTEP and I organized Freddy's Breakfast Forum, where we'd sit with political leaders and debate the future of El Paso, a fast-growing city with the permanent problem of brain drain. Big-name politicians would drop by on Sundays, with cameras clicking, to shop for votes. Hillary Clinton campaigned there for her husband in the fall of 1992. That morning I served her *menudo* and watched her take a big spoonful. When she realized she was eating cow stomach sprinkled with white hominy, she didn't take another bite, but she smiled a lot.

During the week our favorite customers were named Chano, Perica, Pilín, Neto, Memo, Botas, Chapulín, and Chiquilín. Their nicknames referred to parrots, grasshoppers, boots and other objects. No one ever gave a real name. No one asked. We weren't curious. The men and women roamed South El Paso Street, hustling on a street that seemed like an extension of Juárez, crammed with vendors of cheap goods, T-shirts, lipstick and other trinkets. They would trust us with packages for a few hours. On the border, it was best to keep our mouths shut about what we saw and heard.

One of our most loyal clients was a tall, attractive woman with long black hair. Many knew her as La Chola. I nicknamed her Paisana, or "countrywoman," because she came from my native Durango. She'd begun her career as a smuggler in El Paso and Juárez. She came from a middle-class family but had traded stability for the excitement of the border, where she found it easy to make a fast buck.

Paisana was one of several *fayuqueras,* small-time smugglers who catered to demands on both sides of the border. I knew Paisana moved goods banned by the U.S. government, whether Argentine wines, mangos, avocados, guavas, cigarettes, Cuban cigars, illegal drugs—anything American clients wanted. On her trips back to Mexico, in the days before NAFTA, she transported electronics, including TVs and stereos.

One day she brought in several bottles of Malbec in sacks. She stood them up on the light green plastic cushions of our white metal chairs. As I balanced a heavy bowl of my mother's *caldo de res* and a plate of red enchiladas stuffed with cheese and topped with cream, I tripped and busted one of Paisana's bottles. Wine spilled. Amid the shards were thumb-sized balloons stuffed with something white.

I hadn't seen anything like Paisana's white balloons before. I had a hunch but discretion was a must at my parents' café.

"Oops, sorry," I said. "What is this stuff? Sugar, salt, flour?"

"I don't really know, but Americans love it," she responded edgily.

To make up for my clumsiness, I didn't charge her for her meal. My kid sister, Monica, who followed me around wiping down tables and delighting customers with her little-girl smile, looked shocked. Monica was a tip machine and collected the money left on tables; we called her "Ching Ching" for the sound of the cash register. Paisana just smiled as she walked out, carefully clutching her other bottles.

Years later Paisana was arrested for trafficking drugs and spent a year in jail before agreeing to work as an informant for a U.S. law enforcement agency in exchange for her early release and a promised green card. She commuted between the United States and Mexico and infiltrated two major cartels.

I met her again when a senior U.S. agent connected us. I didn't recognize her until much later; she had gained more than a few pounds and was going by a different name. But one day she told me a story about moving Argentine Malbec over the border in El Paso and something clicked. I asked her if she ever ate at Freddy's; she said she couldn't remember but she ate a lot—and her laugh reminded me of that laugh all those years ago.

"I'm sure if you met me then you wouldn't have been able to forget me," she said. "I was that hot. Had a really hot body."

After that, we never talked about the past. But I started calling her Paisana again, and she became a trusted source.

. . .

Now I needed a favor. I told her about the threat. I was not sure if the threat was against me or the sources that fed me information.

"It better not be me," she said. "Remember, protect me. Or I'll see you in *el infierno*—the fires of hell."

"Don't worry, Paisana," I said. "I'm sure it's not you. I need your help."

She asked questions I couldn't, or wouldn't, answer, like the identity of my sources. "You know the rules," I reminded her.

"Yes, but I need all the information if you want me to help," she argued.

"Can't," I replied. "This is all I can give you."

She offered to find out whether the threat was real and why it had been issued. She said she'd find a way to mediate between the cartel and me if necessary. Finally, she told me to take this threat seriously.

"These guys will stop at nothing," she said in her deep, scratchy smoker's voice. *"No tienen madre.* They're motherfuckers."

She knew the cartel men well. Some had been her lovers; she was careful not to ever name them by anything other than their nicknames. Information, she'd warn, can get you killed. Corruption was systemic. Didn't Moctezuma bribe Cortés too?

"You gringos are crazy," she'd say, bursting out in a guffaw, exposing her gap teeth and running her hands through her long hair.

"Yes, we are," I'd respond.

"And hypocritical too," she'd add.

"No doubt."

Through the years, over cups of coffee with Paisana—she didn't drink alcohol because it makes you do and say stupid things, she'd tell me—I learned the story of the cartels.

Mexico's first great drug traffickers came mostly from the same town, or near it: Badiraguato, a tiny enclave in the fertile hills of Sinaloa's Sierra Madre, where tomatoes, soybeans, sesame seeds, wheat, cotton, marijuana and opium poppies grew in abundance. Pedro Avilés, Mexico's first kingpin, a gentleman who many say quietly promoted deals with government officials and avoided flashy headlines, was born there in the 1930s. Miguel Ángel Félix Gallardo, the "godfather"—*el padrino*—of Mexico's modern cartels, was born in 1946 outside the capital, Culiacán, not far from Badiraguato, as was Amado Carrillo Fuentes, the "lord of the skies," who would rule Juárez's underworld. The Beltrán Leyvas were also born nearby. Joaquín Guzmán Loera—nephew of Pedro Avilés and the man destined to lead what would become the powerful Sinaloa cartel—was born in 1957 in La Tuna, a tiny town outside Badiraguato. His top associate, Ignacio Coronel Villarreal, was born around the same time just across the Sinaloa border in tiny Canelas, Durango.

Sinaloa lies along the Pacific coast, a narrow strip of beach, tropical coastline and fertile highlands. It's touched by four states: Sonora to the north, Nayarit to the south, and Chihuahua and Durango to the east. It's not far from my hometown. Three states form an area commonly known as the Golden Triangle, once famed for its poppies, now notorious for its marijuana. Badiraguato lies at the tip of the triangle, about an hour's drive from the state capital of Culiacán and about a day's drive to the U.S. border, with easy access to California and the rest of the U.S. market. Badiraguato is tucked into the Sierra Madre and boasts a near perfect climate for growing poppies, the first lucrative narcotic crop.

People in the region say the cultivation of opium came with the Chinese settlers who arrived in the nineteenth century to build railroads. At first, distribution proceeded in an ad hoc fashion. The first U.S. drug policy did not regulate opiates until 1914; Mexico enforced antidrug laws from the 1890s on. Mexicans had long been nervous about marijuana, associating it with madness and violence. Commercial production of opium gained momentum in the 1940s, when the U.S. military needed morphine for its soldiers during World War II. The business was so important that Mexico, under pressure from the United States, sent soldiers to the hills to protect poppy plants—even though growing opium was illegal in Mexico. Mexican politicians looked the other way as smugglers lined their pockets with cash.

The first shipments of Mexican pot also began in the 1940s, but demand exploded in the 1960s and 1970s. Drugs brought in bigger profits than tomatoes and offered a lucrative black market free of the hassle of international trade laws. American demand for marijuana proved as easy to satisfy as the demand for fruits and vegetables.

The cartels grew ever stronger. Over the decades, locals faced two viable options for earning a living: Work in the United States, legally or not, or stay put and work for the cartels, growing or moving drugs. Migrant workers in the United States strove to earn a couple thousand dollars a month holding down two or more jobs while Mexican cops made a few hundred dollars a month. Smugglers were kings. El Chapo, as head of the Sinaloa cartel, later made the *Forbes* list of the world's billionaires. El Chapo and others were able to reach such heights in part because they were able to exploit a family-oriented business model. Like the mafia, the Mexican cartel men married one another's sisters; brothers-in-law baptized one another's children; cousins watched one another's backs. Family members controlled the entire drug production and distribution chain. Law enforcement proved no match for such ties, and so joined in without much hesitation. Money and power were concentrated in an underworld economy controlled by the cartels.

The flow of Mexican drugs into the United States seemed unstoppable, and American efforts to stop it were entirely futile. In 1969, President Richard Nixon unleashed a massive twenty-one-day policing effort on the U.S.-Mexico border called Operation Intercept. He conferred with President Gustavo Díaz Ordaz and timed the crackdown to the autumn marijuana harvest, when smuggling went into high gear. Díaz Ordaz knew it would hurt Mexican border communities, but Nixon could do what he wanted in his own territory. The operation didn't stop the flow of marijuana, but it did severely disrupt licit trade. Traffic on international bridges, both personal and commercial, snaked for miles, causing legitimate merchants on both sides of the border to lose business—as much as 80 percent of retail sales in U.S. border cities alone.

The next major drug war operation targeted the source. Mexican president Luis Echeverría Álvarez, who previously, as interior secretary for Díaz Ordaz, had been on the payroll of the CIA, closely cooperated with Americans on Operation Condor. Ten thousand Mexican soldiers mounted the attack on drug growers and traffickers in the Golden Triangle, with financing from the United States and help from Drug Enforcement Administration agents. Violence raged for days in the mountains. An unknown number of people were killed; hundreds were arrested, tortured and jailed. Not a single top boss was captured. The locals became permanently suspicious of the Mexican federal government, which they felt had turned against them without warning. The bosses who escaped capture moved out of the sierra and set up a new home base in Guadalajara, where they worked with the military—which had one of the largest barracks there—to avoid another such disruption to their business.

Drugs kept flowing north. Guadalajara was near the Pacific Ocean, which meant transportation and easy access to docking ships; it had roads to and from arable land in Sinaloa and routes leading north to U.S. cities on the West Coast and in the Midwest and Northeast. It was just a forty-five-minute plane ride from Culiacán in Sinaloa, but Guadalajara was culturally on the other side of the world: conservative, Catholic, preoccupied with family names and old money. It was jarring for *los tapatíos*, the original Guadalajara folk, to see ostentatious homes springing up alongside those of the conservative oligarchy. The children of drug traffickers went to the same pricey private schools as the children of moneyed families; their teenagers frequented the same dance halls and played soccer for the same teams; their wives shopped in the same posh malls and danced in the same nightclubs—many of them owned by the smugglers themselves. The narcos were the new money in town, and they would grow smarter, stronger and wealthier.

Officers at the military base there could offer the necessary protection for cartel leaders and their merchandise en route north, in return for large sums of cash. Everyone from the poorly paid military all the way up to the federal government in Mexico City became eager partners of cartel leaders. The infrastructure they needed was largely in place. During the Cristeros' bloody fight against the government in the 1920s, Catholic rebels had created an underground network in the area to smuggle guns, secret documents and persecuted priests to safety. These tunnels would be exploited by the smugglers, who used them to move dope to roads leading north.

By the time the organization had moved to Guadalajara in the late 1970s, the boys from Sinaloa were bringing in millions annually under "El Padrino," who was connected to many of the local political families. He had spent time first as a federal policeman and later as bodyguard to the governor of Sinaloa. A trusted member of the inner circle of the top political families, he attended their *quinceañeras,* weddings and baptisms. From this network, he developed a massive organization that included production of marijuana in the Golden Triangle, its shipment north and its distribution in the United States. Others from Badiraguato became his lieutenants. Like most of the bosses who came before him, Félix Gallardo had little formal education—elementary school, some junior high school at best. But he was a shrewd businessman with quick instincts.

One of the most important and lucrative shifts in the trade was cocaine. By the 1980s Americans had developed a taste for cocaine, and

Colombia had become a willing supplier. Pablo Escobar's Medellín cartel began trafficking tons of cocaine annually in superconcentrated bricks flown over the Caribbean, boated into Florida or moved overland or by air through Mexico to the U.S. border. Félix Gallardo wanted in on the take. While Mexico didn't produce coca, it could provide Colombian cartels with an alternative to the risky Caribbean route, where American ships and planes were increasingly intercepting shipments as part of the continuing "war on drugs." It was an offer too good for the Colombians to refuse.

Throughout the 1980s and early 1990s, U.S. operations along the Florida straits put territorial control of drug supply routes firmly into the hands of Mexican drug trafficking organizations. The Mexican cartels were the U.S. government's beneficiaries, becoming the land bridge between the top drug-consuming market in the world and the Andean cocaine supply. In time, Mexico would become more of a victim to the United States, as American demand for drugs would increase while Mexico's weak institutions would further crumble under the stress of the growing cartel power.

Mexico's powerful neighbor to the north facilitated the corruption in some agencies. The CIA infiltrated the Mexican army and the Dirección Federal de Seguridad (DFS), a Mexican intelligence agency in collusion with drug traffickers. Throughout its history, DFS had been viewed as influenced by the CIA. The DFS was responsible for the death of Manuel Buendía, one of the first journalists to write about the connections between the Mexican and U.S. governments and the cartels. The CIA role in the DFS's illegal activities remains hotly disputed.

Like many drug traffickers, Félix Gallardo enjoyed the protection of the DFS. He and other drug kingpins carried their own DFS badge and worked closely with the DFS chief, Miguel Nazar Haro. El Padrino had federal officials—including customs, port authorities and soldiers on orders of their superiors—on his payroll. Colombian snow would move swiftly and without incident through Mexico after traveling through the first human pipeline between Colombia and Mexico.

El Padrino used the young Guzmán Loera, whom everyone called "El Chapo," or "Shorty," as his logistics coordinator. His men dug dozens of tunnels along the U.S.-Mexico border as early as the 1980s, often using migrants, some unwittingly, to cross packages for the northern market. Planes from Colombia landed in makeshift airstrips in Zacatecas, Chihuahua and Sinaloa; ships docked quietly at the ports in Acapulco, Puerto Vallarta and Lázaro Cárdenas. All the while, corrupt Mexican authorities would let the merchandise pass in exchange for a cut of the proceeds.

During this period of prosperity and relative peace, the cartels formed alliances. Félix Gallardo controlled Mexico's central corridor, the north and all of the western coast, from the Pacific ports in the south up to the northern border with California, Arizona, New Mexico and west Texas. But the Gulf of Mexico and the eastern coast belonged to Juan Nepomuceno Guerra, who'd begun his career as a bootlegger smuggling whiskey into the United States in the 1930s. His nephew Juan García Ábrego would later join him. Like Félix Gallardo, Guerra had cultivated a deep network of friends and relatives on both sides of the border. He counted among his key contacts powerful members of the PRI. Tall and burly in a white Stetson, Guerra was feared and revered on both sides of the border.

Guerra wasn't a producer—marijuana didn't flourish in the hot, humid Gulf region—but he was a powerful distributor who controlled the exit and entry of contraband in his region. Guerra and Ábrego controlled the port and airport of Cancún, the port of Veracruz and the highways running up Mexico's Gulf coast through Tamaulipas to the Texas border. Anything that passed through had his approval. El Padrino contracted Guerra to move Sinaloa marijuana over the border to markets east, including New Orleans, Miami, Philadelphia and New York.

Guerra and Ábrego charged him a 15 percent commission on shipments. The two factions didn't make war; there was enough demand for Mexican pot and Colombian snow to go around.

El Padrino began to worry that a DEA operation could bring down his fortune, so he franchised his empire—and its risk—by distributing the most valued smuggling routes, or *plazas,* to trusted lieutenants, many of them from his home state of Sinaloa. He would continue to oversee his empire from the base of his operation in Guadalajara.

He divided the country into four main distribution routes and parceled them out to the families of his favorite lieutenants: the Tijuana corridor, bordering California, went to the Arrellano Félix family; Juárez, across from El Paso, went to the family of Ernesto Fonseca Carrillo, the Carrillo-Fuentes clan; the Sonora region, adjacent to Arizona, went to the Quintero family; the Pacific region would be shared by the Guzmáns and Zambadas. This newly partitioned organization would later become known as the Federation, the precursor to the Sinaloa cartel. He left the Gulf region untouched under Guerra's control.

What had been essentially a family business became a global conglomerate. Today, the Sinaloa cartel can buy a kilo of Colombian or Peruvian cocaine for around $2,000. The kilo finds its way to the El Dorado of cocaine markets, the United States, by overwhelming weak, corrupt authorities and judicial institutions and leaving behind a path of death and destruction. In Mexico, that kilo fetches more than $10,000; when it crosses into the United States, its value triples to about $30,000 depending on the city. Once broken up for retail distribution, that same kilo sells for upward of $100,000. The drug trade creates at least half a million jobs.

The United States continued to fight the powerful flow of drugs from the south, but it was rarely able to punish the cartels without wounding legitimate Mexican businesses. The DEA tried to disrupt the cartels, including by embedding agents in their ranks. Few got in deeper than

Enrique "Kiki" Camarena, born in Mexico and raised in California. He infiltrated the heart of the Federation: Félix Gallardo's Guadalajara cartel. In 1985, with intelligence Camarena had gathered, U.S. agents pressured Mexican authorities to bring down a Chihuahua marijuana plantation with an estimated value of $2.5 billion. Camarena went missing for four weeks. When his badly tortured body turned up, the consequences were severe. The U.S.-Mexico relationship would never be quite the same again. The political repercussions started immediately.

Mexican president Miguel de la Madrid, under pressure from the U.S. government, declared illegal drugs a national security issue. To further appease his northern neighbors, he disbanded the DFS. President Ronald Reagan signed National Security Decision Directive 221, which linked narco trafficking to "insurgent groups" and "terrorist cells" abroad. He declared the narcotics trade a "threat to United States national security," opening the door to a greater U.S. interventionist role in Mexico and Latin America. The drug trade militarized the war on drugs, converting what had once been a matter for domestic law enforcement into an issue of foreign policy.

During the first Bush administration, with NAFTA negotiations under way, the United States pushed for Félix Gallardo's arrest. Carlos Salinas de Gortari was now president of Mexico, and he needed to keep the Americans happy to make NAFTA a reality. In 1989, Félix Gallardo was finally jailed. Business promptly resumed, with the kingpins he had picked earlier taking over the same operation amid periodic bloody feuds.

"The more the United States tries to bully Mexico, the more ballsy these men become," Paisana had told me. "What do they have to lose when they come from practically nothing? They're cold-blooded motherfuckers. Hardheaded and nationalistic too, resentful sons of bitches who will kill for everything they've earned by killing others."

The investigation into Camarena's murder reinforced how broken the system was, with allegations of corruption all the way to the top of the

De la Madrid administration. Even so, U.S. consumption kept growing and Mexican cartels kept meeting demand. The collusion among cartels and the Mexican government continued.

The PRI had every reason to quietly partner with the cartels. The leaders were pragmatists, after all, not ideologues. As long as the demand existed in the north, there would be market pressure to supply. So why not negotiate with the cartels, keep the flow of commerce smooth and pocket a cut of the profits? The PRI regime was viewed as a paternal figure for Mexican society and the same held true in its dealings with criminal organizations. While the cartels would resort to violence to resolve internal disputes, few of these battles ever got too out of hand, lest the PRI step in to exercise its authority.

But as the PRI grew older, weaker, more divided and bankrupt, its authority on such matters began to erode. By the late 1980s, fledgling calls for democratic reform began to take hold just as the cocaine business was reaching its height. Without a strong central authority to hold them in check, the cartels started running wild.

FOUR

Nearly a week after Angela and I had arrived in Baja California, the text message I'd been anxiously awaiting finally arrived: Miguel wanted to talk to me in person. Angela and I caught a flight the following morning back to Mexico City. Samuel dropped off Angela at my apartment and sped me to a restaurant not far from Los Pinos.

Miguel asked to meet at Lago, an upscale restaurant overlooking Chapultepec Lake. He walked in late, wearing his round glasses and impeccable suit and tie. He smiled as he greeted me and tried joking in his usual way about how his favorite team, the Pittsburgh Steelers, would destroy my team, the Dallas Cowboys. I was in no mood.

"Skip the bullshit, Miguel," I said as I took out my notepad and pressed him.

"We're off the record," Miguel said.

"That's fine," I said, writing in my notepad. "This is for me."

The threat, Miguel announced unsurprisingly, likely came as a result of the story I'd written on the peace pact. The information in the story, as I suspected, had jeopardized millions of dollars in future kickbacks—as much as $500 million annually.

Corrupt authorities and cartels weren't angry about the charges of corruption and illegitimacy. It was about money.

Miguel told me to back off.

Was it the cartel or the government?

He wouldn't tell me more—or he didn't know.

If I knew about the peace pact, what else did I know? Miguel asked me. Names? What else? That's what you need to worry about, because that's what these guys are going after: names, snitches.

I thought about the worth of that information. What the cartels paid, what the U.S. government paid, the price of moles. Leaks were worth millions, if not billions, of dollars. The business of pushing drugs remains murky, earning anywhere from less than $10 billion to more than $40 billion, which if accurate would be nearly twice the size of the estimated $22 billion in remittances sent from emigrants abroad. A chunk of that money went to pay for the information and protection that would provide competitive advantage.

They wanted to know what I knew.

"That's what they're after," he said. "What else do you know?"

Now I wished we could talk football. He didn't press me. He didn't necessarily want to know, he added. The less he knew, the better.

I shouldn't be surprised, he told me.

From our table at Lago, I watched ducks splashing in the placid lake water. Miguel reached for another duck taco and advised me to lay off for a while and watch my back.

"They won't hesitate to put *un pinche balazo a tu cabeza, cabrón,*" he said. A fucking bullet to your head.

I wrote that down in my notepad.

"They might hesitate to put a bullet into a gringo," he said. "You? You're open game." He laughed at the contradiction. I didn't.

Lunch was over. He put his hand on my shoulder: Don't trust anyone. And text is better because it is more difficult to trace.

"The more we dig, the more dirt we find," he said. "*Todos tienen su precio*. Everyone has his price. Including you. Remember that."

Yes, I've come to terms with that, I said.

"*No seas pendejo*," he added. Don't be stupid.

Best to Angela, he said.

I tried my hardest to grin, knowing the most difficult part of the afternoon was just beginning. Angela.

Samuel pulled up to the curb in my beat-up blue Volkswagen Jetta as Miguel's car pulled away. I wondered what Miguel thought about our little walk now, the one in Polanco when I'd told him how covering narcos hadn't become an obsession, but a necessity. He'd insisted then that the problem was more of an invention of the media. Now Miguel was advising me on how to stay alive while I reported the story previous governments had tried for so long to keep quiet.

No seas pendejo, I thought. I should remember that every now and then. As we drove, the sun began to appear behind a blanket of clouds. I asked Samuel what his price was, how much money would it take for him to sell me to a narco. He thought I was joking and then he got offended.

"*Yo tomaría un balazo por ti, Alfredo—no manches*," he said. I'd take a bullet for you—don't kid around.

Mexicans often use such hyperbole. Most of the time it's heartfelt, but I had learned not to take things too literally. Politeness and niceties can feel like all that's left in a country where the system has long been so unfair, where everyone fends for himself.

The sun was deceptively bright now. I felt like shit for having put Samuel on the spot. I reached for the stereo volume and cranked up R.E.M.'s "Losing My Religion," one of his favorite songs. I didn't say another word. We steered along the scenic road that winds through Chapultepec Park, the "Hill of the Grasshoppers" in Náhuatl, the ancient Aztec language. It's a sprawling forest of pines, pathways and lakes, the

largest city park in Latin America. Moctezuma had once put an imperial resort on the hill. In the 1780s, a viceroy started building a summer palace but never finished it. It wasn't until 1867, during the French occupation, that Emperor Maximilian and his wife, Carlota, turned the buildings into a castle to resemble their home in Trieste, on the Adriatic. From the ramparts of this castle legend has it that a group of young Mexican cadets chose to leap to their deaths rather than surrender to the conquering troops of General Winfield Scott at the end of the U.S. war against Mexico in 1847.

I stared out the window at the families strolling around, the children riding bikes, the stands selling freshly fried potato chips, a teenage girl putting on her roller skates. A man selling colorful balloons walked around, his two short legs jutting out from below the bunch.

I looked at Samuel again. I liked seeing his crooked smile and his slicked-back black hair parted in half. I'd met Samuel through Angela, who had hired him as a driver years before. She trusted him. He was young. He had trained to be a boxer. He was loyal. He would tell me when he thought someone might be following us. He watched my back. He had dreamed of becoming a mechanical engineer but, like millions in Mexico, instead became a *trabajador de mil usos,* a jack-of-all-trades, because money ran out and he was never able to finish his degree. For a time Samuel left Mexico City, leaving behind his family, including an abusive father who once slapped him so hard he broke his front teeth, giving him a crooked smile that only appeared on rare occasions.

"Why did he do that?" I once asked him.

"I don't really know," he said. "It's a chapter in my life that I have worked to erase. So far I've done a good job."

Samuel was determined to make it on his own. He settled with relatives in Guanajuato. But the farming state felt too small and eventually he returned home to Mexico City, where he rented his own apartment, working as a bartender and later as a mechanic. He did a stint as a car

salesman and a cab driver; he washed cars and, lately, drove around journalists like Jorge Ramos, the Univision anchorman, and his sister Lourdes.
He also chauffeured the girlfriend of a cartel boss to his jail cell outside
Mexico City. She'd fly into town for conjugal visits; Samuel would wait at
the jail, then take her to the mall and back to the Mexico City airport.

Now he was twenty-seven years old, and his girlfriend, soon-to-be-
wife, was pregnant. He had returned home and made amends with his
family.

"The traffic is horrible today," he said.

I reached for the radio dial. "Maybe you should find a more boring,
safer customer."

"Alfredo," he said. "If I could make a peso or two for every threat I've
ever received, I don't know that I would necessarily be a rich man, but I
wouldn't be so *jodido*. I would be approaching 'middle-class' status, that
label the government promotes these days. I wouldn't be working so hard
to put food on the table."

"Who's threatened you?" I asked.

"Customers, strangers. Threats happen all the time in Mexico. That's
how Mexicans communicate with one another. That's the only thing that
works. They threaten you for everything and anything. Fear works better than taking someone to court, or calling an attorney. Corruption
always gets in the way—when you try to do it the right way, you come
out without a peso. That's ridiculous, a waste of time and money. Instead,
we just pick up the phone and say, '*Hey, hijo de tu puta madre, me la vas a
pagar, o te voy a matar.*'"

"You've done it?"

"Just this morning when I saw my stepdaughter's boyfriend, I chased
him out of the house and told him if I ever see him again I will bust his
head against a rock," he said. "And then I would put his head on the road
so everyone would see it."

"Would you?"

"Nah, but the threat worked. It saved me money and time."

"So you think these threats from these so-called cartels are bullshit?" I asked. "I shouldn't take them seriously?"

"Only you know what you have done," he said. "Just don't do it again. Mexicans, at times, forgive. Look at me—I've forgiven."

"And you're not afraid?"

"Frankly, I forgot the last time I ever felt fear," he said. "Whatever fear I ever had was extracted from me when I was a boy."

"How so?"

"A witch doctor performed a cleansing on me when I was four or five years old and eliminated all the fears inside me," he said. "Just like that. I haven't felt any fear since then."

I couldn't tell whether he was being serious. He reminded me of my mother. She had performed a similar "cleansing" on me when I was a young boy.

"But, Alfredo, you have to believe," he said. "You can't just go and tell a *curandera,* 'Here, fix me.'"

"Stop talking like my mother," I said. "The *curandera* will have to wait. Angela is waiting."

He steered through Paseo de la Reforma, pushing cars out of the way, his eyes always fixed on the road. He made a sharp right on the corner of Sevilla, past the nude statue of *La Diana Cazadora* perched on a fountain and originally modeled in the 1940s after a secretary who once worked for Mexico's state-owned petroleum company.

Angela was already waiting on the sidewalk. We walked in the lush park that anchors La Condesa. Stately homes in art deco style stood guard around an oval of trees and gravel paths. The stone benches lining these paths served as vestiges of the 1861–1866 French occupation that ended with the execution of Maximilian by firing squad on a bare hillside outside the city of Querétaro in 1867. Today La Condesa is the neighborhood of foreigners and artists, diplomats and journalists, writers, designers, actors and movie directors. Angela and I walked hand in hand and then found seats at our favorite coffee shop, Café Toscano, overlooking the park. We ordered cappuccinos and wheat toast slathered in strawberry jelly.

"So tell me all about it," she pleaded. "Every detail."

I stumbled over my words, knowing she wouldn't approve.

"I need more time, at least one more day," I said. I needed to wait for details from informants, sources needed to verify information.

"The last time I checked we also have telephones in the United States," Angela shot back.

She listened to me, her gaze wandering to the side as I rehashed my conversation with Miguel. I told her I wanted to go to the west coast state of Nayarit, near Puerto Vallarta, and finish reporting on the migration of Americans going south. If I had to leave Mexico for a while, I would at least have some stories to write. I was convinced I would be fine.

Whoever is behind this thing, I said, just wants to send a message. The peace pact is on. Besides, what if this isn't about me, but about the U.S. investigator himself?

She started shaking her head.

"I promise I will take a direct flight in twenty-four hours to Dallas from Puerto Vallarta," I said.

She cringed. I saw anxiety coming over her face—her eyes narrowing, furrows in her forehead, her lips tightening. Even though Miguel wouldn't say explicitly whether or not the government itself was behind the threat, Angela saw it a little more clearly.

"Alfredo, the signs have been there all along. Even the Mexican drug czar told you to lay off and write about tourism stories—anything but this. What more proof do you need? You're running out of time. You damn well know this isn't the first time.

"What part of 'the Mexican government is behind this' don't you understand?" she asked.

She took a sip of her coffee, grimaced and put it down. She stared across at me.

Angela had opened the door to the mysteries of our homeland and Mexico City years before, when we were still good friends but when I was already starting to fall in love with her. She and I had taken an old, piss-stinking train from Ciudad Juárez to the place she called home, Mexico City. She took me through "her city," showing me neighborhoods like the trendy Zona Rosa, Coyoacán and the grandiose Centro Histórico. We ate *chilaquiles* for breakfast at Sanborns, decorated with beautiful tiles from Puebla. Later, we walked the Plaza de las Tres Culturas, where a small Aztec pyramid, a colonial church and modern buildings stood— all the modern juxtapositions and pretenses displayed for the world to see. We spent our time reading tourism guides and survived on street tacos, mangos from fruit vendors and cheap beer. I loved every minute with her, and she had no trouble convincing me that working in Mexico could be a reality for both of us. It felt like our destiny.

A little more than a year earlier, Angela and I had done a story about allegations that the government's drug czar was on the payroll of a cartel. The day the story ran, Angela received a message from a trusted source: "Leave Mexico. Go on vacation—a long one—you and your boyfriend."

For Angela, the vacation became permanent. Her company decided it was no longer safe for her to report from Mexico and changed her assignment to the border, where she would cover issues like immigration.

Weeks later, we had headed north to the border with Angela's stuff in tow. She cried softly as an enormous moon guided our road out of the city, her two dogs and half her belongings crammed into a Ford Expedition. Samuel and his now pregnant wife followed us in a minivan with the rest of her things. We didn't say much. We traveled Mexico's countryside, through the fertile land of Guanajuato, the flatlands of Aguascalientes and hilly Zacatecas, and finally reached the open blue skies and barren desert region of my Durango—the most beautiful of all the states and cities, I told Angela. She disagreed. Nothing like Mexico City, she declared. For once, I didn't argue.

"The only thing that makes me happy," she said then, "is the thought that you will stay in Mexico City, and with that, the possibility of my return. If you leave too, I'll lose my connection. You're my anchor. We'll make it work."

Now, at the coffee shop, Angela was no longer patient, or nostalgic.

"We're paid to tell stories, to tell people the truth, but how can we do that when we can't even be honest with ourselves?" she said. "I adore Mexico, every bit as you do, but it's not the same country we once knew. That Mexico is being destroyed, falling apart. The journey is over, at least for now. You have to get out."

I couldn't tell her I was wrong, not at the moment. How do you tell someone that everything you thought you knew was really a lie? That this was the only home I ever yearned for, that leaving Mexico was like leaving myself behind, just as I had done all those years ago when I was just a boy.

I reminded her of 1986, the summer of discontent, when angry, hopeful protesters marched across the northern state of Chihuahua demanding free elections. Mexicans trace the origins of democracy to either the 1968 student rebellion or the 1985 earthquake. For me it was 1986, when I was a rookie reporter and witnessed how Mexicans armed with idealism gave life to the movement that would bring the downfall of the political party that had long governed Mexico. Young and old took to the streets to remind Mexicans of the unfulfilled promises of the revolution decades before. Protesters rallied around a tall, handsome man named Francisco Barrio Terrazas, an accountant and dynamic speaker from Juárez who represented the opposition PAN party—which had never won an important election against the PRI.

"*Pancho Villa vive, cabrones*," became a rallying cry, a reference to the revolutionary leader who once used Juárez and El Paso as his bases of operation. He'd meet with revolutionaries hiding in El Paso, and in his free time would shop for clothes, bullets and weapons for his troops, who were trying to topple a dictatorship that had ruled Mexico for more than thirty years. Barrio Terrazas was part of a movement known as Los Broncos del Norte—people, largely in the north, who believed in a more democratic Mexico, one in which the opposition party wasn't cowed, as the PAN had been accused for decades, but was competitive enough to win.

The protesters condemned the federal government for the taxes they paid to Mexico City but that never seemed to make it back up north. Along the border, economic development was strong, but infrastructure lagged. Many people were also furious at a series of peso devaluations, especially in 1982, when the Mexican elites lost their fortunes and Mexico's middle class saw its savings disappear.

Among the most ambitious protesters was an idealist named Felipe Calderón. Decades before he became Mexico's president he was an up-and-comer in the PAN party along with his then girlfriend, Margarita Zavala. He had a full head of curly hair and wore enormous round glasses that covered his cheeks. He and the other protesters carried posters and screamed for the PRI to leave power: *"¡Ya basta!"* Enough!

My mother had been there too. When one day that summer the protesters took over the international bridge connecting Ciudad Juárez to El Paso, she was handing out burritos from Freddy's, which was just a few blocks away. Petite in sweatpants, white socks tucked inside flat shoes, her apron stained with red and green salsa and streaked with refried beans, my mother would walk with her sack filled with burritos. I was reporting on the protest, and I hoped she wouldn't see me. But I felt proud.

"¡Tenga, ánimo!"—Here, courage!—my mother had said as she pulled burritos from the sack. She'd made sure no one went hungry that day.

I took a deep breath. The progress we had seen couldn't be a lie, I told

Angela. I couldn't be wrong. Mexico, the conquered nation, had come too far.

"Angela, I can't leave. Not now," I said.

She shook her head.

"Stop talking to me like I'm some naive, stupid shit," I blurted, straining to keep my voice low.

"Look, I know you wanted to prove everyone wrong about Mexico—beginning with your parents—but this is no time to prove anything," Angela retorted. "This isn't about winning an argument. It's about saving yourself."

"It's about understanding who's behind all this crap that's bringing this country—our country—to its knees," I interrupted.

She shook her head even more furiously in disgust. I sighed and looked away.

"Tell me the truth," Angela begged. She looked at me the way a stranger would. "Are you staying to find some kind of truth, or purely out of selfish reasons, trying to find a scoop to beat the competition?"

"I'm no closer than you are to understanding what it is anymore," I said. "All I know is that I need to find out what's going on. I need to be sure. Otherwise I will always wonder whether everything I grew up believing was a fucking lie."

"Tell me what you find out when you're six feet under," she said and grabbed her bag.

"Six feet under?" I asked sarcastically. "But I told you I want to be cremated, my ashes spread from Mexico to California and on the border between El Paso and Ciudad Juárez."

"This is bullshit, and you know it," she screamed. "How can you follow a story—how can you expect to get at the truth—when you can't trust anyone?"

Beside us, passersby walked the corner of México and Michoacán. Customers looked at her and then at me. Angela abruptly walked away, leaving me behind. I ordered the check and hurriedly, nervously walked home alone. Parque México's trees might come crashing down on me at any second. Everything, everyone—shadows included—seemed suspicious.

The next day Angela barely said a word. She locked the bedroom door as she packed her bags alone.

I pleaded with her to come out.

"You have stopped being a reporter," she said, opening the door. "You're part of the story now. You're so close now that you can't even divide the lines, and that's putting you and everyone close to you in danger. I can't believe you can be so selfish."

When she walked out of the bedroom with her bags, I stopped her and gave her a long hug.

She didn't resist.

"For no one else but yourself, get out," she said softly. "Don't be afraid of being scared. A little bit of fear is a good thing these days. Be fearful of not being alive. That also takes courage."

Samuel knocked on the door. He took one look at us and promptly took Angela's bags and left.

"*Te quiero, güerita,*" I said, putting my arms around her again. I love you, blondie.

She looked at me, hesitating. Her face marked by weariness. Her eyes filled with defeat and emptiness.

"Take care," she said and headed for the door, slamming it shut. She would be in Texas in a few hours. At that moment, I knew I should have gone with her.

FIVE

Puerto Vallarta glistened with whitewashed walls, a sparkling board-walk at the ocean's edge and towering cruise ships. A days-old news-paper lying around at the car rental place by the airport carried the story of a new batch of killings and the U.S. ambassador's concerns about the threat against an American journalist. I picked up the paper and threw it into the backseat of a white Jetta. The peace pact didn't seem to be working.

I drove north out of Puerto Vallarta, and as the road to the neighboring state of Nayarit narrowed, the tourist gem faded and gave way to Bahía de Banderas, natural beaches speckled with tiny concrete houses and palm-roofed huts. I popped a mix CD into the car stereo, and the song "México en la Piel"—"Mexico Under My Skin"—by Luis Miguel began playing. It is a love song and an homage to the many Mexicos: the north with its hot, barren desert and mountainous terrain, the south with its colorful folklore and endless beaches. I raised the volume and sang along.

I understood Angela for being angry. I knew I sounded like a lunatic. I couldn't seem to explain to her that I needed to get my head around this thing.

Driving the winding road alone, I felt a sense of control, pride even, that I could not be frightened into running. I tried imitating Luis Miguel, the way my youngest brother, Mundo, did when he would take his hands and, with a deep stare, dramatically slick back his hair as he belted a tune. Mundo, then studying to be a prosthetics specialist, was one of my four siblings born in the United States, and I loved watching him imitate Luis Miguel and Juan Gabriel, signs that assimilation hadn't completely washed away his *mexicanidad*. I laughed out loud.

Suddenly, out of nowhere, two enormous pickups sandwiched me on the road, a red Dodge Ram roaring ahead and a faded blue Ford tailing me behind. Both had tinted windows, with men in cowboy hats, just like the narcos in the movies. This is how they fence you in. I looked nervously for a place to pull over or make a U-turn. Was the guy in front checking me out in his rearview mirror?

I spotted a Pemex gas station. Without putting on my blinker, I swerved into the parking lot and skidded to a stop behind the pumps. The trucks stayed on the highway. I realized I'd been holding my breath and exhaled. Jesus, what a chicken shit I am. So much for self-control. Everyone drives trucks here. You thought you were so brave, goddamn it! I suddenly felt very alone without Angela.

I stopped in at the convenience store of Mexico's state-owned gas monopoly and bought a Coca-Cola. I snapped off the cap and took a long swig. It was cold and sweet, made with cane sugar, not that awful corn syrup they use in the United States. I took out my cell phone.

"Hey, just calling you to tell you I'm fine," I told Angela. "Everything is great," I lied.

"Be careful," she repeated curtly. "I'll see you tomorrow. Love you too."

I got back in the car and headed on to San Pancho.

Condos were going up along the highway that turned into a two-lane road once I crossed into Nayarit. Narco money. The billions of dollars from drug proceeds have to be laundered somehow. Real estate was big;

so were banks, casinos, horse racing, dollar exchange houses, even mom-and-pop shops. I could see dirty drug money and traffickers everywhere. The drug trade amounts to up to 4 percent of Mexico's $1.5 trillion annual GDP. Was it my own paranoia?

San Pancho remained an old fishing village, even as Americans were coming in droves to buy condos. Signs on the road boasted: "Live on $15 a day or less. Maid included. Gardener optional." One million Americans, mostly retirees, were living in Mexico. Maybe this was Mexico's future economic growth: old Americans and surfers lured to Mexico's beaches. I checked into a forty-dollar room at the Hotel Cielo Rojo, the Red Sky Hotel. I dropped off my computer and changed into shorts and flip-flops. A woman across the street ran a stand where she flipped quesadillas and fish tacos. I had some tacos and a second Coke. I thought of my mother, who had sold *gorditas* stuffed with *chile verde* from her own shop at the age of thirteen.

With my stomach full, I headed to the beach. The sky was red with dark, low clouds moving in from the western horizon. A few rays peered through the mosaic, the sandy beach giving way to a mirage of blue waves beyond the palm trees. I walked along the empty beach and saw no one. I kicked off my flip-flops and ran on the sand. Luis Miguel was now blasting from a stereo, his version of one of Mexico's iconic tunes, "La Bikina," about a lonely, beautiful, scorned woman struggling with a pain of betrayal so deep it provokes a river of tears. The guitar is upbeat, but the violins seem to weep with loneliness.

Sick of running, I dropped down onto the beach at the ocean's edge and built a pillow of sand. My body, weary from the stress of seven days on edge, sunk into the ground. I closed my eyes. The ocean waves massaged my feet. I thought of calling my mother, but what could I possibly tell her? I'd rather she not know anything about the threat. She wouldn't tell me to leave. She'd just lie awake at night praying. Besides, any argument I could make would now sound foolish. As tired as I was of Mexico, I was also sick of the pragmatic, idealistic American inside me.

My mother and I had had many contentious discussions over the same subject: Mexico's future. I'd once asked: What would a Mexican government truly of the people, by the people and for the people look like? She was quiet for a moment, thinking, measuring her words carefully.

"*Sólo Dios sabe,*" she'd replied, looking straight ahead. Only God knows.

"*Dios* is too busy in the Middle East, helping us hunt down Osama bin Laden, too busy taking care of other problems," I said, needling her. "We need to learn to hold government accountable as a people and not leave everything in God's hands."

"Don't underestimate God," my mother responded. "*Dios es grande.*"

"Don't underestimate the people," I retorted, and returned to eating barbecue beef grilled by Mundo.

My mother shot me a look that said, *Ay, mi Fredito, mi solecito. Ya no eres tan mexicano.* Oh, my little sunshine, now you are naive as only an American can be.

My mother, too, felt a painful pull. Decades in the United States had not changed her. She was Mexican, a woman of quiet dignity, integrity and humility, with a deep faith in the Virgin of Guadalupe, the brown-skinned saint of Mexico now worshipped in just about every corner of the United States and beyond. She never bothered to learn English. She spoke of her home, San Luis de Cordero, as her final resting place. She would return to our homeland one day but would do so without her children. Mexico was her destiny, her burden—not ours.

My mother loved her homeland but didn't trust the men who governed Mexico.

"The only thing I love more than our family, with all my heart," she once said, "is Mexico. Mexico is my homeland, my identity. But I won't let the government ruin my children like they're ruining my country."

My mother liked to say: "*En México, haces lo que puedes, no lo que quieres. La fe es lo único que tenemos.*" In Mexico, you do what you can, not what you want. There are always limitations. Faith is all we have.

Yet my American side believed that hard work and good intentions could change history, eradicate corruption, pave the way for democracy, create rule of law—even in Mexico. Mexico somehow always reeled me back. It gave me a sense of purpose. Just setting foot in Mexico made me happy, even though who I am and what I represent—the native and the outsider—is often met with as much rejection in Mexico as it is in the United States. I had spent years trying to shake the feeling that I was hopelessly American in Mexico and Mexican in America—never fully American, never fully Mexican, often feeling less than one, sometimes more than two, depending on the moment.

Again I'd asked my mother: *"¿Usted no cree en las posibilidades?"* You don't believe in the possibilities?

"If I did, do you think we would be living here?"

SIX

I was born in San Luis de Cordero, Durango, a state shaped like a
human heart, in my grandmother's home, in the shadow of church
bells and into the hands of a midwife. The whole family helped with my
birth. My paternal grandmother, Mamá Rosa, was the first to hold me.
My mother cuddled me, her firstborn, in her arms, while my maternal
grandmother, Nina, took the placenta and wrapped my umbilical cord
around it. Tío Delfino, a short, wiry man, dug a hole in the backyard. He
buried my umbilical cord under cactus and ocotillo shrubs, next to the
afterbirth of my *tíos,* cousins, aunts and my father. Grandma Nina shov-
eled dirt over the hole.

My buried placenta, Nina and Tío Delfino later told me, tied me to
this land forever: a shriveled root to affirm that, no matter how far I
went, one day I would come home. One day we all would come home.

Economic growth had stalled in little towns like San Luis de Cordero. The population of the country had doubled in less than a decade,
but there was little work to speak of. More and more people left for the
United States. The population of San Luis de Cordero never really fluc-
tuated much from two thousand or so because the men who were gone

would come back just long enough to get their wives pregnant. Most of the children would grow up and dream of heading north, of meeting their fathers and buying trucks to show off when they came back home and learning a few words of English.

I couldn't imagine a morning not waking up to my mother, Herlinda, singing along to José Alfredo Jiménez or Javier Solís on the radio. The music—"La Media Vuelta" ("The Half Turn")—softly floated through my open bedroom window. I can still see her outside, the shadow of her splashing water on her flowers and plants, singing. Our neighbors would say that when my mother sang, even the roosters stopped to listen. Women who shuffled into the street every morning with buckets of water to moisten their dirt-caked walkways, tamping down the dust, did so with a skip in their step, *con más gusto,* as they listened to my mother sing.

She sang for the whole town. She sang at town fairs, at morning Mass, in our own living room after dinner, her voice bursting into the night like fireworks. One song, "México Lindo y Querido"—"Beautiful, Beloved Mexico"—was a favorite of my father and the other men celebrating their last hours of fiesta before heading north to work. They were braceros, U.S. guest workers. I spent my early childhood alongside women: my mother, aunts and cousins picking corn in the morning to make *masa* for tortillas to mop up our beans and rice, patiently waiting for the perennial return of fathers, husbands, sons and brothers from their jobs *en el norte.*

During the spring, my father was never home. He was two thousand miles away in California's San Joaquin Valley, preparing the fields for planting cotton and tomatoes. My father was around so little that I would call him Señor, instead of Papá. But our house came alive when he was there. Young men would drop by and ask my father how to find jobs in the United States. How much was the pay? How plentiful was the work? What was the United States like? The way they talked sounded as if they were trying to get to the moon. My father liked the United States, and having dollars in his pockets, but he didn't imagine living there permanently. The United States was simply a temporary fix.

My brother Juan and I roamed San Luis de Cordero as if we owned the place. I was four; he was three. Our sister Lupita was still a toddler, followed by Mario, the baby. Juan and I walked alone in the summer rains and in the blistering sun. We walked past freshly painted pastel-colored homes made of adobe brick. A fresh coat of paint meant money from abroad. Every day a pickup truck would meander through the streets with a loudspeaker mounted on its roof, calling out the news of "today's special" or asking us to "please join the such-and-such family to bid farewell to so-and-so." In the afternoons the rains would begin, digging rivulets into the dirt streets. But they were ours, those streets that told stories. By day we'd play hide-and-seek with Tío Delfino, making him run after us for what seemed like miles, although it was really only a few blocks. At night, Tío Delfino would play guitar by the light of a kerosene lamp and teach me a few chords. Some days we hiked Tío Antonio's cornfields while he roasted thick ears of corn. Delfino was my father's older brother; Antonio was my mother's eldest brother. Everyone lived nearby; we were all one family.

On weekends, my cousin Rubén and I would head to the local movie house. He practiced running the projector, which later became his first job, and used the public-address system to remind locals about the upcoming fiesta or news from California or the release of the latest romantic comedy. Movies featuring the beloved actors Pedro Infante and María Félix played on weekends, comedies that pitted the poor against the rich. The poor always won in the end by laughing at the injustices they faced and the absurd hurdles they had to jump. This was the Mexican film industry's *época de oro*. I had the lucky job of stuffing bags with peanuts and tangerines. Popcorn came much later.

Our life was simple, but I didn't know the meaning of poverty. Using dollars my father sent, my mother ran a store out of our home. The *tiendita* served as a local grocery, its shelves replete with fruits, including mangos and *guayaba,* vegetables, cookies, soap, soft drinks, cigarettes and toys. When I was supposed to be in bed at night, I would sneak into the store—the room next to my bedroom—and open the boxes stuffed with toy cars, trucks, stuffed animals and soldiers that my mother brought back from the market in Gómez Palacio or the Soriana in the nearby city of Torreón to resell.

I played with them in the dark, not wanting my mother to catch me. When she discovered my secret, I reasoned with her:

"Someone has to try them out to make sure they work."

My mother would just shake her head in disapproval. But I'd make her forget my bad behavior by begging her to sing. She'd usually oblige.

At home, my mother called me Freddy, but all around town I was "Herlinda's son." Everyone—Rosa from the grocery store; Chiquis at a shoe store; Kika and Gabriel, who lived near the cinema—would wave at me when I was out about town. They singled me out because I was *el mayor,* the eldest, an honor in Mexican culture.

"Look." They'd point. "Herlinda's son. He's growing up so fast."

But on a crisp March day in 1964 my sister Lupita drowned, and our world slipped away. Weeks after Lupita was buried, I sat in my grandmother's living room, playing with my cars on the dirt floor, when I again heard my mother sobbing and whispering. In her mind, life in Mexico was over. Something was wrong—*había un mal*—in Mexico. *Mal, maldición*—a damning. It felt as if we were cursed. When my mother looked at her four boys—Juan, Mario, Francisco and me—she saw us growing up in a country with an ill-fated future. She feared tragedy awaited us.

"There's nothing here for us—nothing," she'd tell me whenever I'd protest and whimper that I didn't want to go to the United States like all the other boys in town. This was home.

"I need to give you and your brothers a real chance in life. I need to give you a life of opportunities that I never had," she'd say.

Her brother, Tío Antonio—like every generation before him—tried reminding her that Mexico was on the verge of greatness. But, like most Mexicans, my family didn't have the right connections. We didn't have the right ancestors. We didn't know people or come from privilege. The only sure thing we had was access to U.S. dollars, thanks to my father's hard work across the border.

San Luis de Cordero still did not have paved roads. There were no schools that went past the sixth grade and there was no electricity. The same was true for many of the small towns throughout the country. The so-called Mexican Revolution, the conflict that had swept up my mother's uncles to fight alongside Pancho Villa in 1910, had failed our hometown the way it had failed so many other pueblos across Mexico. Justice was a luxury we could not afford.

Had Lupita lived, my mother asked her own mother, how much of a chance would she have had in San Luis de Cordero? In a country of laws rarely enforced, ruled by a coterie of the powerful, a nation of lonely women, old men and children? So much of Mexico's energy was sucked away north. My mother would give us something better by sacrificing her love for family and her homeland. We would start all over again. There was no choice for us, she'd say, but to follow her man to *el norte*. She had decided.

"Mexico needs time," Tío Antonio would say. "You cannot abandon what's left of the family."

"Watch me," my mother would respond.

We waited outside the plaza in front of a looming white cathedral. A Virgin Mary statue watched over us. The virgin, dressed in a blue cloak and white veil, looked sad to me. We were there to receive our last blessing before heading north. The road would take us to Ciudad Juárez, a border community buzzing with opportunities. Or so said other locals who'd been up north. They painted images of prosperity, big homes with bathrooms, toilets that flushed, television sets and wide streets near cotton fields for kicking balls. American investors were building factories on the Mexican side of the border, beckoning tens of thousands of Mexicans to work. I started kicking and screaming when I saw the bus driven by a man named Don Pedro closing in. Our neighbors told us they would miss us but we were lucky.

I didn't feel so lucky. Who would care for my chickens, the rooster and the street dog that felt like he belonged to me? What about my toys? My mother's friends hugged her beside the bus that would take us so far away from our native land.

Tío Delfino got on his knees and gave me a long, long hug, forgetting to wipe the tears from his eyes. "I'll be waiting for you, *m'ijo.* I'll always wait for you here."

"*Vámonos,*" my mother said, arranging us in line, my three brothers and me, as the bus door swung open. Frank, the newest baby, in my mother's arms, Mario in between Juan and me—all under the watchful eye of our grandma Nina, who would go with us in part to reacquaint herself with the growing family in the United States that she'd never met.

Every time my eyes grew moist, Tío Delfino would remind me where my umbilical cord was buried, half a block away from where I would depart to the new world, just a few blocks from where my sister Lupita lay six feet underground.

"*M'ijo, aquí está su ombligo,*" he'd say. "*Algún día regresará.*" You're umbilical cord is here. Someday you will return.

"*Algún día regresaremos todos,*" Nina agreed.

Yes, I will return home, she'd say. We all would.

I don't remember much about the bus ride, although my mother reminded me later how much I cried and how I tried sleeping, as if hoping I'd wake up and find it had all been a bad dream.

People were coming from all over the country to Ciudad Juárez, a city with roughly 325,000 people. Juárez was the pilot city for the first maquiladora program, which promised the construction of assembly factories with American and other foreign capital that would be staffed by eager

Mexican workers laboring for low wages. With the help of the maquilas, U.S. consumers were getting their television sets and other electronics at cut-rate prices. Over the years, foreign investment accelerated. Electricity poles popped up, and roads were paved anywhere a maquila mushroomed. Water was trucked in. But the city forgot, or just didn't care, to build enough housing, schools, movie theaters or parks to accommodate the workers and their families. In the beginning few seemed to mind. Few bothered to even consider setting down roots in a *pasajera* city on their way to something better, someplace new.

My father worked in California and was getting the paperwork that would bring us legally across the bridge. He met us in Juárez and worked across the border in El Paso that winter, waiting for the rain in California to end so he could return. I kept hoping the rains would never stop so we would head home to Durango. My cousins remember me carrying on about how my town and friends back home were just as good—better, even—than the people across those mountains in front of us in El Paso. Everyone ignored me and kept staring at those mountains, where a star shaped by thousands of bulbs was lit during the Christmas season.

Within a year the paperwork arrived. I remember my mother proudly raising her right hand at the U.S. consulate in Ciudad Juárez. She firmly pledged to be a good resident of the United States—not a pledge of citizenship but a vow to obey our new country's laws. Bewildered, we, too, raised our hands, my three brothers and I standing in a neat row.

"Welcome to the United States," the woman said, and smiled, offering each of us a red lollipop. We all smiled back, not sure why.

The green cards were the prize for my father's years as a field laborer in California under the bracero program, which had earned him U.S. residency and the chance to have his family reunited legally. We kids had no idea what had just happened, but my mother was excited. We rushed home from the U.S. consulate offices, all of us holding hands.

With our papers secured, we went back to my aunt's home in Ciudad

Juárez, where we had been staying, to get our things together to join our father in California. That year, we were among an estimated thirty-eight thousand Mexicans who entered the United States legally.

My mother took me to a corner and instructed me.

Leave the toys behind. Just get your clothes ready and make sure your brothers follow your example. Okay? Don't get too attached to anything here because we're beginning a new life.

Sí, Mamá.

While we packed our bags my aunt went knocking next door to find the neighborhood's *curandera,* a spiritual woman. She would perform a *limpia,* a cleansing, on us before we departed. One by one my brothers and I lined up in a dark room, wide-eyed without saying a word. The woman blew on us the smoke of copal, a sacred pinesap incense, and then ran an egg across our shoulders and arms. The shell was cool and gave us goose bumps—it was supposed to absorb all the evil spirits, or evil eye, she said. The egg yolk, according to belief, would then rot.

"See," the *curandera* said, as if we should already feel lighter, "the evil is gone."

I don't remember the egg yolk rotting. But I do remember all of us eagerly nodding our heads. We couldn't wait to get the hell out of there, out of that eerie, smoke-filled room. My mother looked at us quietly. She believed we'd needed that *limpia* to start our new lives in the United States clean and pure, and to put the curse of family tragedy behind us.

America and its dream seemed simpler, nobler. It was just a few feet away.

SEVEN

A flash of lightning and a crack of thunder startled me to my feet. I rushed beneath a thick palm tree for shelter. I shivered, although the rain was warm. Beyond the rain, I heard a hawker's booming voice resonate throughout the deserted beach as he called out, *"Pescado con chile y limón."*

The storm quickly gave way to a light drizzle.

I mustered the courage to call my sources with contacts inside the cartels. I had been afraid of the information they might have, afraid the threat could be true. I looked around the beach one more time, wanting to take in the moment.

The first source, an informant for the U.S. government, chose to speak in code. A former federal policeman who had also once worked for the DFS, the informant lived in Laredo. He had been brought in by the U.S. investigator to protect him and his wife from hit men who had already killed his two sons. The informant kept a Mexican police scanner and usually stayed up into the wee hours of the morning monitoring radio frequencies, the movement of cartels and their secret conversations. He was searching for any useful tips for the U.S. government, because he was determined to find out what had happened to his family. Insomnia was the price he paid for getting information. He still had contacts in the cartels, particularly the Sinaloa organization. He quickly answered the telephone.

"Here, it's very hot, so hot you can't really breathe," he said.

"Here, it's raining hard," I said, writing his words into my notepad, carefully trying to understand his code.

"It's best you get out. The rain is dangerous," he said. "Come to the hot, humid weather." Get out of Mexico and make a run for Texas. "Rain is bad for you."

He had one more thing to say: *"Los de la última letra creen que estás comprado por El Chapo."* Those of the "last letter"—in other words, the Zetas—say you've been bought off by El Chapo. El Chapo is the leader of the Sinaloa cartel, archrival to the Zetas.

That almost made me laugh—imagine, the Zetas reading my articles! They had more to worry about than whatever I was writing for the *News*. If I had been writing more about the Zetas lately, it was only because of the trouble they were stirring up in Texas. Local authorities in Dallas had denied the presence of any Zetas in north Texas. Then, one December evening in 2004, as men grilled steaks and drank beer at a house in Mimi Court, a shootout erupted. One man was killed and three were injured. One of the shooters was directly linked to the Zetas. Two crucial eyewitnesses who survived the shooting were arrested on drug charges but then released from the Dallas County jail after police botched the paperwork and then set a low bail. The eyewitness who posted the $750 bond was rearrested only after the *News*, going on new intelligence, made repeated inquiries about him to police and the Dallas County district attorney's office. I'd worked on the story with two other colleagues, Jason Trahan and Ernesto Londoño. Having three reporters write about the Zetas' activities in north Texas was the paper's subtle way of communicating with the Zetas: It's nothing personal. Just the business of informing our readers on cartels operating in their north Texas neighborhood.

I thanked the informant and hung up.

The second source was Paisana, who was somewhere on the U.S. side of the border. Before she gave me any information, she had a question: You didn't write that story about the peace pact that ran in Mexico, did you?

"Yeah, that was me. Why?"

"They're pissed."

"Who? The cartels? The government? Which cartel?"

"All of them, but it's the government you should be concerned about."

She continued. "Alfredo, there's not much difference between the cartels and the government. They're both the same motherfuckers, you understand? You're a fly to them—no more, no less. They'll swat you in a second without a blink."

"How do I get a message to them?"

"What message?" she asked.

I wasn't sure. "Please lay off? I have no personal agenda against you? All one big misunderstanding? I was just doing my job?"

"These people aren't very sophisticated about messages," she said. "The only thing they understand is force, raw power. Who has bigger *huevos*? You or them? My suggestion is that it's best you get out of Mexico. That's how you'll let them know you got the message, especially after that last article. That's the only motherfucking message you need to send them."

"Okay, Paisa. Thanks." I tilted my head back, put my notepad and pen away and looked at the sky, the clouds still moist, threatening more rain.

I called another source, a Mexican American who ferried cash for the cartels to U.S. bank accounts. He stuffed so many bundles of cash in his gas tank that he had to repeatedly stop for gas along the way from Dallas, Austin, San Antonio to Laredo, where he was awaiting orders for the next bank deposit. He had just run into an up-and-coming leader in the Sinaloa cartel, Édgar Valdez Villarreal, at a convention for customs brokers in Cancún. The former Texas high school linebacker already had a reputation as a ruthless hit man whose metrosexual grooming, blond looks and green eyes landed him a rather strange nickname: La Barbie.

"La Barbie at a convention?" I asked, incredulous. *"No mames, güey."*

La Barbie was the highest-ranking American in a Mexican cartel. La Barbie's brother was a customs broker, and the hit man thought the convention would be a good chance for the two to catch up.

"I didn't believe it either," the source said. "But he greeted me in the men's room after he took a giant piss. He washed his hands and waited for me to zip up, wash my hands and then he called out my name. Just like that. I kid you not."

My source had asked him about the threat. La Barbie replied, "We're not stupid. Not us, but I wouldn't put it past the government."

Then I called the U.S. investigator. He didn't pick up.

As I headed back to the hotel, the rains cleared. I passed a church reflecting the glow of the setting sun.

The woman across from the Hotel Cielo Rojo was back, working her little stand. Now beef was on the grill, and she was turning the meat and flattening out tortillas with an iron press. I watched as American tourists, retirees and surfers strolled by—they seemed to belong more to this place, where cars were quickly replacing donkeys, than the woman making corn tortillas by hand. Maybe this was progress. Maybe these gringos were bringing the innovation and technology that this town needed, giving these kids other possibilities to look forward to other than grilling tacos or fleeing to the United States in search of dollars.

I watched her roll and press the *masa* into flat circles.

A boom box blared a *cumbia,* and a couple danced between the plastic tables and chairs. The man was heavy-set and wore a straw hat, a cowboy-style red and white checkered shirt. He seemed unable to find his step, too stubborn to follow as the woman tried leading.

The pulsating *norteño* music—accordions and *guitarrones* jamming—plus the aroma of tequila lured me over. I took a seat at one of the chairs and just smiled at the woman at the grill, who quickly brought me what she said was her first order of tacos of the night.

"¡Recién hechecitos como para chuparse los dedos!" said the woman, known to some of the locals as Doña Mari. Freshly made and so delicious you'll want to lick your fingers! Want something to drink?

She had a stash of tequila made by a *tequilero* across the border in Jalisco. She didn't wait for me to respond. She poured me a glass and handed me a couple of extra corn tortillas and a dish of green jalapeños.

She stood over me smiling, awaiting my approval—just as my mother would—as I dove in for my first bite. I raised my glass.

"Buenísimo, Señora. Just like your fish tacos," I said, patting my heart with my right hand. *"Gracias."*

She made a sign of the cross, blessing herself for luck. I sipped the tequila that had been poured from a bottle with no name and I watched the dancing couple struggle to find their rhythm.

Mexico's "democracy" belongs to the politicians, intellectuals, idealists, to the elite and the opportunists, but their vision for Mexico does not always involve consulting the majority of people who live day to day. There is no local ownership. For Mexicans, the higher one's income, the more deeply a person believes in democracy, at least on paper. Mexicans like the taco woman base their lives on Mexico's giant informal market, obeying only the laws that are convenient to obey and taking life as it comes, because *mañana, quién sabe*—tomorrow, who knows? The taco stand outside her concrete home belongs wholly to an underground economy, a shadowy world now closing in on all of us. It's the only way she and many others like her know how to get by.

The couple quit dancing and took a seat near me. The man simply looked at the woman, occasionally buried his face in her chest as she laughed and told him stories. He seemed distracted by her dark beauty and sweaty cotton T-shirt. He planted a noisy wet kiss on her lips. They seemed to care little what anyone else thought.

The woman at the grill began sifting through her pirated CDs and I eagerly shifted over to help pick out the music. I was delighted she had Juan Gabriel and immediately put on "Así Fue."

The woman threw more strips of beef onto the burning grill. *Chiles toreados*, grilled jalapeños, roasted on the side. Families crept outside onto their porches to get a peek, some glancing through open windows at their nightly TV *novelas*, trying to cool off from the humidity. Some took a seat. Others stood or sat on the concrete sidewalks outside their homes. For a minute I felt as though I had never left San Luis de Cordero.

With the party now set to last much of the night—the song "Hasta Que Te Conocí" alone plays for twenty-six minutes straight—I placed a hundred pesos on her stand, nodded at the woman, winked at the couple and left. I had an early flight back to the United States and one more phone call to make, maybe two.

I slowly walked across the street, over the puddles, and made my way up the hotel stairs. In my bare room, I changed out of my shorts, still wet from sitting on the beach. I lay down on a hard bed with a fluffy pillow and watched the fan turn. I tried sleeping, but couldn't.

The fan kept spinning, not quite drowning out the music. I got up from my bed and peeked through the window. Juan Gabriel's voice still boomed. I heard the laughter. The stubborn man seemed to have found a step, or maybe the woman had just given up and was now following him. I listened to the lyrics carefully, seeking my lost innocence through Juan Gabriel's songs.

I closed the window. I took out my cell phone and called the U.S. investigator.

"Still in Mexico, *carnal?*" he asked, using a slang word meaning "brother."

"I was hoping you would tell me whether I should be here or not," I said.

"I would if you listened to me," he said.

"Any news?"

"No solid information, but you really need to back off, at least for a while," he said, and added ironically, "The peace pact fell apart. As I suspected, it never really had a chance."

"What happened?" I asked. I suddenly felt a nervous twitch. The peace pact had me believing I couldn't be a target. My hand started tapping the bed.

"These guys don't know the first thing about trust," he said. "They want to kill each other *como perros*. They're becoming smaller groups now, *más cabrones*. It makes it harder to work out arrangements among themselves."

The Sinaloans could be monsters, but they were more pragmatic. One member of the Zetas stood out for his savagery, the U.S. investigator said. Miguel Ángel Treviño Morales was different. He had risen through the ranks of the Zetas quickly on a pile of bodies. Unlike the founders of Los Zetas, Treviño Morales had no military experience. He had never been a soldier, or a member of some elite army unit. He was a thug. We had some similarities. He was one of nine children, raised by a single mother who crisscrossed between Texas and Mexico after their father abandoned them. He'd held a number of odd jobs as a young man, including cleaning chimneys in Piedras Negras and driving his older brother's trucks stuffed with pot between Dallas and Laredo. That brother, Francisco, had served as his surrogate father, and was now in jail in Big Spring, Texas. Treviño Morales had washed the cars of a drug capo known as El Caris. He'd eventually won his trust. He later became associated with cops, even became one—briefly—which for traffickers is akin to graduating from college.

He looked for recruits who mirrored him: uneducated, street-savvy young men and women who believed Mexico rewarded only the powerful. He was angry. He looked for that in recruits as well. He wanted recruits who lacked opportunity, people who believed they had been screwed by society. He'd put a loaded gun into the hand of a recruit and then order the recruit to point at some random person in front of them. Treviño Morales would put his hand over the recruit's heart to measure how fast it beat as he yelled, *"¡Chíngatelo!"*—Fuck him over! If the recruit hesitated, he'd take his gun and either put a bullet to his head or offer him a job as a lookout. It all depended on his mood that day.

"You have to remember that the people the cartels are recruiting are those who are most pissed off at everyone. The people without a job, without an education, without a future," the U.S. investigator said. "Haven't you seen the messages in banners they put up? They can't even spell.

"One group has to emerge as dominant before the killings will stop and that could take years," he said.

So the killings were on again. The peace hadn't lasted more than a few weeks.

"That's how the game is played," the U.S. investigator said. "That's why you need to step away. It's a free-for-all and you would be just another number. The only word narcos understand is *tradición,*" he said.

Betrayal. My father had said something similar when I told him I wanted to be a reporter.

"Why would they go after me?" I asked. "And more important, what's gonna happen to this country?"

"Your name is on the stories. And you're in Mexico. Don't trust anyone. *¿Me entiendes?* You understand? Just stay in touch with me and you'll be fine."

"Okay," I said. "But what's gonna happen to this country?"

"They'll fight till someone cuts a deal with the government, or one cartel is left standing," he said. "A lot of people will be killed. You don't want to be one of them."

"Fine, I get it," I said. "I'm leaving."

It isn't worth putting my life on the line, I thought, for a bunch of punks with shiny guns emblazoned with images of the Virgin of Guadalupe who simultaneously worship Santa Muerte, the saint of death.

"Thing is, I don't think people understand how serious this is," my source continued. "Mexicans are still living in denial, convinced that this is a problem isolated on the border—a border problem—*¿me entiendes?* They think blaming the United States *les quita su responsabilidad*—it absolves them. And Americans couldn't give a shit about anything to do with Mexico, unless it affects their beach time."

I knew he was right.

"So chill out for a while," he said. "It'll do you some good. *Carnal,* be careful. Watch your back. Stay in touch and constantly change your routine. *No te pierdas.* Don't disappear."

I said good night and immediately dialed Angela. I left her a message, assuring her I would be back in Texas the following day. I wished the fan would run faster to blow away the humidity.

I opened the window one more time. Night had fallen without any stars or moon in the sky. The chatter and music outside was even louder now. I wanted to join them for a *caminero*—one for the road. But I was afraid again. I wanted to go home. I wanted to find home, more convinced than ever that it was no longer in Mexico. I crawled into bed and stared at the fan again.

That evening, as I lay in bed in San Pancho, listening to a thunderous saxophone, it became all too clear that whatever evil my mother feared when we left our country had now been released. Evil was running wild in Mexico.

PART II

EIGHT

1994

Ashes from Popocatépetl's plume of smoke rained on my new neighborhood in Coyoacán. I lived in one of Mexico's most storied and historic quarters, in a hacienda that was more mansion than house, painted white, green and cool yellow, with high ceilings, hardwood floors and a verdant backyard. Out front, white ash drizzled the red 1988 Volkswagen Gulf I'd just bought from the outgoing correspondent.

The traditional, wealthy neighborhood was surreal to me, an immigrant from a dusty Durango town. My father had headed north to the United States as a young man to earn dollars. Now I was thirty-four, having come to Mexico to follow my dream of reconnecting with my homeland after spending the majority of my life in the United States. I had gone native. I was ecstatic to be on my first official assignment as a "foreign" correspondent. But I could feel a growing bitterness around me.

That year, 1994, had been a tough one for Mexico. The country was mourning the violent deaths of two key political leaders, including a presidential candidate, and the PRI, which had represented the ruling system for more than sixty years, was showing signs of weakness, though the party was still entrenched in power. An indigenous uprising had begun in the south. The currency was in free fall as a peso devaluation wiped out savings accounts and made the few pesos in Mexicans' pockets worth far less than they had been a month before. Like the peso, the country's chance at progress—that promise that had come with the signing of NAFTA that year, intended to catapult Mexico into first world status—was shrinking.

Now a volcano threatened to erupt.

As the new correspondent for the *Dallas Morning News,* I suddenly found myself counted among the city's nouveau riche. I lived among Mexico City's elite, a small circle almost impossible to penetrate unless you had the right contacts, the right invitation or something to offer—in my case, an American newspaper. When I'd meet neighbors at the central fruit market, outdoor fish restaurant or neighborhood coffee shop, they would ask me where I was from, who my relatives were. Maybe they thought I was from a posh suburb or a lineage of diplomats and academics. Instead, I'd tell them, *"Soy hijo de un bracero de Durango."* I'm the son of a bracero from Durango. I could see the embarrassment. They saw me as a Mexican whose father had left with nothing, yet I had returned as a "foreign" correspondent for a major U.S. publication. It didn't exactly say much about Mexico's own possibilities.

While I felt out of place among the elite, I was also intrigued by them. Two former presidents, a well-known aristocrat and dozens of "limousine liberals" with ties to the PRI's top ranks lived in coveted real estate along Coyoacán's cobblestone streets. I lived on Calle Tatavasco, right off Avenida Francisco Sosa, one of the wealthiest streets in all of Latin America, named after one of the country's best-known poets, who was also a journalist. My landlord was the former president, Miguel de la Madrid, who was the first to promote the lowering of trade barriers that later transformed the nation. His family owned several homes in the area. He'd walk his dog in the plaza, and occasionally the two of us would wave to each other. *"¿Cómo está?"* I asked. I doubt he knew I was his renter, but nonetheless he was always polite.

For generations, these *priístas*—members of the PRI—had referred to us, the six million Mexicans living abroad in the United States, as traitors, or *pochos*—Mexicans who had become too Americanized and out of touch with their roots. We were branded by our broken Spanish and affinity for odd customs like trying to be on time. One dinner with a senior PRI official close to the president ended abruptly after a heated debate broke out between us over who had betrayed whom: the immigrant, like my father, who fled north in search of opportunities, or the *priísta* who put his own interests ahead of those of the nation. I felt he was gauging my "Mexicanness"—something that happened more often than I liked to admit. He believed we were the *malinchistas,* betrayers of the culture, or, worse, *achichincles,* a derogatory term meaning servants, lackeys of the United States.

But Coyoacán seemed everything that Mexico could be. Folkloric, wealthy, modern yet traditional—perfectly contradictory. The Marxist revolutionary Leon Trotsky found exile here; the artists Diego Rivera and Frida Kahlo once lived just a few blocks away from my home. Hernán Cortés, the Spanish explorer who, with the help of some three hundred men, had conquered Tenochtitlán, once used Coyoacán as his private playground.

Artisans hawked their wares from stalls around the central plaza, and vendors grilled sweet empanadas, fried churros and served Oaxacan hot chocolate near a plaza guarded by a fountain featuring two coyotes in the middle. In typical fashion, a church anchored the plaza. On the Day of the Dead, the city, and especially Coyoacán, went all out to celebrate a holiday that dated back to the Aztecs. Friends and families gathered at graves and homemade altars, sharing songs and stories to honor their departed. As the late autumn chill began to set in, wreaths of flowers known as *cempazúchitl,* orange Mexican marigolds, blanketed the area.

The first time my parents visited the neighborhood market—colored richly with ripe fruits and vegetables, herbs and house plants, red meat on the butcher block, whole chickens stacked on white tile counters—my mother nudged me nervously and nodded to the young *señoras* telling their maids which food to put in their baskets.

"Do you think they think I'm your maid?" my mother asked in an embarrassed whisper.

My mother had worked as a maid when she was young. She had a sixth-grade education and had worked in the fields of California. She had been part of a union movement and was a vocal supporter of farmworkers' rights. So she felt a particular empathy for women who worked as servants in the homes of Mexico City's rich. My mother looked furtively at the darker-skinned maid, the woman's woolen socks pulled to her knees and a checkered smock over a humble dress. The *señora* had manicured hands garnished with gold rings. It had certainly been a long time since people had looked at my mother as "the help." I could tell it bothered her that here, in her own country, others would begin to do so now.

"*Que se vayan a la chingada,*" I said, tightening my fist. "Let them go to hell—you're the mother of an American correspondent! Plus, you're *güera con ojos verdes*"—light skinned with green eyes, I said, mocking Mexico's latent racism. "Didn't my father use his dollars to seduce a lovely pale-skinned girl like you?"

After reprimanding me for my bad language, my mother shook her head.

"No one was born to be a servant. There's no such thing as destiny or fate," I told her. "It's about good old-fashioned work."

She shot me a look and warned, "Someday, someday." When I was a boy, she had tried unsuccessfully to preach to me, but the importance of faith was lost on me.

To reorient myself to my country after nearly thirty years living in the United States, I visited my colleague Dianne Solis at her two-bedroom apartment in Polanco, the rich, modern neighborhood close to the presidential residence at Los Pinos. Riding in a cab, I looked in the direction of the volcanoes towering over the far edge of the city like two shadows stirring, spewing their ash as a warning sign to all of us. Dianne and I had become friends because she helped recruit me for the *Wall Street Journal* after I graduated from the University of Texas at El Paso, which is perched on a hill overlooking Ciudad Juárez.

She, too, had grown up in California's San Joaquin Valley, and she had been working in Mexico as a foreign correspondent since 1991. When I got starry-eyed about Mexican democracy, Dianne brought me back to reality: "The revolution failed, Freddy. That Mexico is dying."

The revolution, which had aimed to overthrow the autocrats of Mexico, did not end democratically in 1920. Some questioned whether it was really a revolution or instead a series of feuds and coups not very different from what Mexico was facing now. The PRI had always been a complex system, made up of the nation's heavyweights who ran local, state and federal elections from a centralized committee. In 1929, General Plutarco Elías Calles formed local and state electoral committees into a national electoral confederation, the Partido Nacional Revolucionario (PNR), the original ancestor of today's PRI. Over time, the system took different names. In the 1930s, the presidentially coordinated coalition of parties, worker unions, peasant organizations and the armed forces came together under the banner of the Partido de la Revolución Mexicana. Eventually, in the 1940s, it became the PRI. Whatever the name, Mexicans thought of the PNR, the PRM and then the PRI as the party that would represent them and serve their interests.

The regime relied on patronage and hierarchy, artfully and painstakingly renegotiating with different factions every six years, a period known as the *sexenio*. Under the PRI regime, the military was no longer officially inside of the political system, but it remained well taken care of. The PRI tamed the revolutionary generals with promises of political power, and as the decades passed, the party kept power-hungry men in check with term limits.

While known for its authoritarian control over Mexican society, the PRI was also benevolent, using its power only when it needed to keep people in line. Under the PRI, power would not rest with one man, but with a powerful board of regents. It provided the rich with access and power, and it provided the struggling poor with whatever they needed most. For years party members gave out bags of rice and beans, just enough to get by, in exchange for votes.

Yet political repression was constant, beginning with the union strikes of the 1950s. The unrest reached its height in 1968. Young people gathered in droves that year, demanding greater transparency in government and more civic participation. Their demands were met with heightened controls and public displays of force by the authoritarian government. On October 2, 1968, student protesters met government firepower. Police forces gunned down dozens of student protesters in Tlatelolco, a public square where they had often gathered. "Tlatelolco" became synonymous with massacre. It was Mexico's Tiananmen Square or Kent State, and the wounds hadn't healed by 1994.

I had written dispatches of hope from émigrés and *norteños* in northern Mexico, Mexicans who dared to imagine something better, a new government, a democratic opening. From across the border, it had seemed a different Mexico was indeed rising, albeit with many of the same intractable problems of the past. More than half the population lived in poverty, education was an appallingly low priority and corruption was the cement that held the entire decaying system together.

In 1988, Carlos Salinas de Gortari took the presidency amid suspicion that the PRI had stolen the election from the Frente Democrático

Nacional, an alliance of former PRI members who had split with the party after their leader, Cuauhtémoc Cárdenas, was passed over as the presidential candidate. Cárdenas, the eldest son of the revered president General Lázaro Cárdenas, now led the national leftist opposition movement. Born in Los Pinos while his father was president, he was raised in privilege, and was determined to rescue the spirit of the PRI that his father had helped reorganize in the 1930s.

"Imagine FDR's son coming back to take down the Democratic Party," my friend David Brooks had once explained to me. "Now you have the son of Lázaro Cárdenas attempting to rescue the progressive principles of his father that were perverted by his party over the last forty-eight years." I had met David during the summer of 1988 when I took time off from the *Journal.* That vacation had turned into a weeks-long odyssey as I was ordered to stay in Mexico and help cover the aftermath of the election.

David and I were often the only two correspondents covering raucous election board meetings in the wee hours of the morning when opposition party members charged that Salinas's election was tainted by fraud. One evening, opposition members walked up to a podium on a platform strewn with stuffed ballot boxes, some of them burned, that had been found in a Dumpster. Shouts of *"¡Fraude!"* had erupted in the tiny chambers of the interior ministry on Avenida Bucareli, right across from a restaurant once frequented by Che Guevara and Fidel Castro as they plotted revolution in Cuba. I'd called Dianne to boast in Spanish that I was right there, alongside "a gringo reporter."

At that moment David, red haired and freckled, turned to me and asked, in perfect Spanish, "Who's the gringo reporter?"

David was born in Mexico to parents who had fled the United States to escape persecution during the Joseph McCarthy era. Mexico, thanks to its noninterventionist foreign policy, had long served as a refuge for political exiles from all over the world, including Franco's Spain, the military juntas in Chile and Argentina, and Stalin's Russia, as well as for those who had fled the Holocaust and conflicts in the Middle East.

From then on, David and I became good friends.

During those days, there was also hope. The United States would put an end to the dispute over Salinas's victory, publicly congratulating him as Mexico's next president. Salinas promised Mexicans that they'd enter the first world of prosperity. Four years later, with the signing of NAFTA, many Mexicans would believe him; they were ready to leave the memories of Tlatelolco and faulty elections behind. NAFTA would open Mexico to the world, and challenge the PRI's hegemony.

Once in office, Salinas had quickly embraced a bold, global vision and was able to fit into that new world nicely. Educated at Harvard, he was not just the first Mexican president to speak English publicly but also the first modern leader to break with nationalist rhetoric and call for closer ties with the United States.

Salinas personally courted foreign investors and the media. He privatized a number of industries, like banks and telephone companies, auctioning them to the highest bidders. Some investors became billionaires. Carlos Slim took over the sole telephone company and the country's central telecom infrastructure, thereby preventing competitors from entering the market for years—ultimately making him the richest man in the world. Salinas then asked for political donations from the new monopolies that had taken over the public companies that had once controlled more than 90 percent of Mexican industry. The new oligarchs ponied up millions. In one dinner alone, some contributed up to $25 million.

Salinas said the reasons for Mexico's misfortunes lay in its failure to create a stronger partnership with its neighbor to the north. The NAFTA agreement embodied Salinas's vision for a sweeping expansion of free trade policies. Mexico was to leave behind its insular past and march confidently into the first world.

But as it clamored for free trade, the United States was also targeting and punishing Mexican immigrants. In El Paso, the local border patrol sector chief, Silvestre Reyes, the grandson of Mexican immigrants, expanded on a buildup along the U.S.-Mexico border. He called the program "Operation Hold the Line."

I caught wind of the operation when I walked into the empty offices of the *El Paso Herald-Post* on a Monday morning in September 1993 and noticed that most of the telephones were ringing all at once. It was my last month in El Paso before heading to my new job at the *News,* and it was early in the day for reporters working on an afternoon newspaper to be at their desks. I answered as many calls as I could and realized the callers weren't complaining about their newspaper service or asking about a particular story that day. One caller after another complained: "Where is my maid? The gardener? The babysitter? Where are they?"

In 1993, many Mexicans would still walk across the dry Rio Grande riverbed, which was really just a wide concrete drainage ditch, to enter downtown El Paso and catch buses to their jobs. With his focus on the border fence, Reyes arranged for dozens of border patrol vans to line up against it to prevent Mexicans from crossing. The operation diverted crossings to other parts of the border. Business at Freddy's began to plummet; gardens weren't pruned; maids didn't show up to take care of homes, nor did nannies make it across to babysit for children.

Mexicans fumed while America stood idly by. Salinas used the moment as a wedge to persuade U.S. congressional leaders to approve NAFTA. With this trade agreement, he said, Mexico would create so many jobs that its countrymen would no longer need to migrate to the United States for work.

If Mexico liberalized its economy, political openings and opportunities would follow. Talk of electoral reform—a sure death for any authoritarian system—began to pick up momentum among the opposition party, PAN, including a successful businessman and rancher from the central state of Guanajuato named Vicente Fox. It also began to inspire reformers inside the PRI. Salinas just needed time and money to make those reforms happen.

Another of Salinas's reforms was the creation of the National Solidarity Program, or *Solidaridad,* an idea taken from his own doctoral dissertation at Harvard. It aimed to rescue a faltering relationship between the government and rural communities by promoting subsidies and winning over a new generation of leaders. The PRI needed some fine-tuning, and Solidaridad would be its answer. Salinas brought Luis Donaldo Colosio to head the program. A native of the northern state of Sonora and a graduate of the University of Pennsylvania, Colosio also became Salinas's handpicked presidential candidate to succeed him. Colosio ran what many believed was a feeble campaign. But he promised to continue Salinas's pet projects, backing NAFTA and the continued openness of the political and economic sector.

Yet many frowned on NAFTA, doubting the trade pact would change anything. An indigenous group in the country's south was one vocal critic.

On the eve of January 1, 1994, the date NAFTA would take effect, an estimated three thousand people of Mayan descent in the southern state of Chiapas took up arms to rebel against a government they believed acted only on behalf of the interests of the privileged few and that had ignored their poverty and trampled their traditions. They called themselves Zapatistas, in honor of Emiliano Zapata and his band of Mexican revolutionaries, and quietly took over half a dozen indigenous communities. Carrying old rifles, pistols and machetes—plus, crucially, a list of influential media contacts from around the world—they launched a guerrilla war. They demanded nothing less than self-determination of indigenous communities.

At least publicly, Colosio had begun to stump for real reform inside the PRI, and his speeches had become a rallying cry for political pluralism—and a thorn in the side of many party officials whose power and wealth depended on the propagation of the old system. The party was rife with factions fighting one another. Party leaders smiled for the camera as a seemingly solidified group, but behind the scenes they were at each other's throats, especially with every upcoming election. It seemed only to worsen over time, until Colosio was gunned down in the hilly Lomas Taurinas neighborhood of Tijuana. It wasn't so much the system against Colosio, but Salinas's faction against its enemies inside the system.

Declassified documents in 2000 would reveal evidence of a conspiracy—witnesses and potential whistle-blowers methodically killed in the wake of the assassination, botched investigations and widespread cover-up of evidence. But Colosio's assassination remains shrouded in mystery. Constitutional and political constraints prevented other top party leaders from running for president. So Salinas, with the prodding of PRI factions, turned to a bright, unassuming economist, Ernesto Zedillo. Born in Mexico City but raised along the U.S-Mexico border, Zedillo, the son of a mechanic, was considered an outsider, and he was suddenly thrown into a political and economic firestorm.

The party could no longer hide the gaping problems in the economy, impunity in the justice system or pervasive social inequality. Zedillo, a former student protester in 1968 and a top aide to Colosio, seemed determined to let the country take a new course, even if it meant sacrificing the party. If maintaining unity and the PRI's stranglehold on power required more peso devaluations to compensate for the party's mistakes—if it meant covering up corruption, fraud, graft or crimes—Zedillo said he'd trade it all for whatever might come.

Crusty politicians like Carlos Hank González, one of a cadre of leaders controlling the PRI's well-oiled political machine, grew nervous as rising stars within the party began to question the system, and opposition parties like the PAN and the Partido de la Revolución Democrática (PRD) grew stronger. González, the son of a German colonel, would likely have become president had it not been for laws that required both parents of presidents to be Mexican. Instead, Hank González was one of the PRI's top power brokers representing one of the many factions. He'd risen from elementary school teacher to billionaire while holding various positions in the private and public sectors, such as agricultural secretary and mayor of Mexico City. He was linked to a web of illegal activities, including alleged ties to drug traffickers, though nothing has ever been proven, and he once famously said that a "politician who is poor is a poor politician." *Forbes* estimated his wealth at $1.3 billion, but his close aides have said it was much larger. He stewed angrily over the technocrats who were calling the shots in the party and demanding a democratic opening in 1994. In his estimation, the reformers were ruining a good thing.

When I arrived in Mexico, the economy was plummeting, and the reputation of the man blamed for the economic disaster, Salinas, was in ruin. Salinas left office in November 1994. His brother would soon be placed behind bars, accused of being behind the murder of José Francisco Ruiz Massieu, the secretary general of the PRI. Salinas would go on hunger strikes, initially for a laughable four hours, and then for another twenty-four hours, to demand that President Zedillo absolve his brother (he was later acquitted after spending ten years in jail). Salinas would leave Mexico, first for Ireland and then Cuba.

NINE

I n my home, the PRI culture of patronage was strong.

Doña Carmen and Don Rafael, the housekeeper and gardener at my Coyoacán home and office, were quintessential PRI rank and file. Doña Carmen, a short, plump woman, would often arrive late to work at my house-turned-office because she "had" to attend a union meeting or join a march demanding a pay raise for fellow domestic workers. She beamed with a coy smile, slightly dragging one limp leg. I enjoyed her laughter and the way she sliced mangos in the morning, a breakfast staple along with her *huevos a la mexicana:* scrambled eggs with tomato, onion and chili.

Her loyalty wasn't so much to the PRI as it was to her family and the house workers union, which looked after her interests. The union lent its support to the PRI and guaranteed votes. The PRI in turn would make sure pay raises came, along with beans, rice, tortillas and a free T-shirt at every election. More important, Doña Carmen had the ears of a PRI representative and knew the woman would help her if she had any problems.

The PRI coerced, co-opted and corrupted everyone. Along the way, they aroused quiet disdain among members like Doña Carmen. In public she showed them respect. In private, she grew to hate them, especially after the latest peso fiasco, which had forced Zedillo to push the congress to raise taxes; meanwhile, the price of basic staples like tortillas and beans was rising due to inflation. She was suspicious of them, disliked their double-breasted suits and white handkerchiefs, resented their pretentious culture in which the *licenciado,* the guy supposedly with the college degree, is always the *mero mero,* the top boss, the man with the final say.

Doña Carmen had been working for me for nearly a year when I began to notice food missing from my pantry. My friend and newest colleague, Laurence, a tall and lanky American reporter we fondly called Lonny, would watch her wobble out of the house, her bags filled with cans. At first I ignored Lonny's reports, convinced that Doña Carmen was perhaps taking one or two cans, and maybe she really needed them. But after a while, I discovered that she had been "borrowing" entire shelves of my canned chipotle and jalapeños. I could overlook the canned peppers, but it was her dishonesty that bothered me.

"Dude, jalapeños today . . ." Lonny would say.

"Money tomorrow!" Javier, our Mexican news assistant, would chime in.

Doña Carmen often invited me over to her house to try her *tacos al pastor,* although I wasn't sure she meant it.

"Come eat with real people," she'd say. "Anytime, just come over."

I took Doña Carmen's offer and went over unannounced. She seemed surprised when she opened the door to her home in Colonia Santo Domingo, a working-class neighborhood in Mexico City's southern section, home to transplants from the poorest states in the south of the country. She had a worried look.

"I was just in the neighborhood," I said with a big grin. "Thought I'd drop by and try those tacos you promised me."

"Come in, come in," she said. "Have a seat."

She lived in a home with a small courtyard along with two other families, everyone working as maids or gardeners.

She was embarrassed when, after chatting over instant coffee for a few minutes, I walked right past her and pointed to several cans of jalapeños on her shelves—the same brand that I had bought at the supermarket.

"Been meaning to ask you why so many of my cans of *chiles* are missing," I said, aware of the uncomfortable situation I was creating. "I keep buying and buying to replace them without ever eating one jalapeño. These aren't them, are they?"

Red faced, she explained that because I traveled so much she only took my food with imminent expiration dates to give to the needy on her block or to the Zapatistas fighting in Chiapas. She played victim, finding any explanation to get out of a confrontation that could ruin our relationship.

"I swear, *mi licenciado,* that this won't ever happen again," she said. *"¡Por mi madrecita de Dios se lo juro!"* I swear it by my sweet mother of God!

I cringed at the sound of the word *licenciado.* For the average Mexican the sixth grade was as high as you got. Those who achieved higher education were the elite, and they earned the title *licenciado.* Thanks to the corrupt culture of the PRI, *licenciado* had lost its meaning—it was now nothing but a sarcastic term of deference for someone who held power. The *licenciados* were the corrupt ones who owned condos in the city, homes in the country, hired private drivers, kept a lover on the side, lived on public money without ever having to account for one peso of their lavish lives. Their burgeoning power was a symptom of impunity that had roots in power structures dating back to the days of the Aztecs, which were molded to the modern age by the PRI.

As comfortable as I felt with working-class people like Doña Carmen and Don Rafael, they saw me differently.

"*Perdón*, I won't do this again," she pleaded with me that afternoon at her house—even after continuing to deny she'd taken the cans. "*¿Sí, patrón? Sí, mi licenciado?*"

I wanted to tell her that I would gladly give her my jalapeños, beans, tortillas, even pay her weeks in advance to help her through the peso crisis. But please don't steal; just ask. And stop calling me *licenciado*! Instead, I just stared at her, shook my head and tried to remain stone-faced as I said good-bye and walked away.

I shared Doña Carmen's skin and hair color and had also been born in a small town where the dusty winds of March scattered everything in sight. I considered her to be family, and family doesn't steal from one another.

Even if at times I had felt less than welcome in the United States, I always believed I stood a chance of getting ahead on a more level playing field. Or, at least, I knew where I stood. The Mexico I confronted felt uneven, hypocritical, sad and stuck. The rich locked behind their doors; the poor working any job they could invent for a paltry handout. The Mexicans I could relate to the most were usually the ones who had fled north or who spent time in the United States, those who understood my bicultural, binational world.

Doña Carmen was polite to me, affable, but I knew she couldn't understand a Mexican in a tie who didn't belong to the PRI. Nor did she understand what a Mexican American was, someone traversing two worlds. She saw us as naive, as people with a chip on our shoulder and an accent.

I seethed in anger and nursed a frustration that I couldn't quite shake. From that day on, I rebelled by mocking the PRI culture, calling everyone *licenciado*—from my relatives in the United States to those who were still members of the PRI in my native Durango. I paid homage to the shoeshine boy in Coyoacán, the waiter at Las Lupitas, the restaurant near my home, the newspaper vendor and particularly to Javier, whom I spent the most time with and who tried in vain to explain Mexico's complexities to me. I called them all *licenciado*. Some rather liked the sound of it: *¡Licenciado!*

One morning Don Rafael, the gardener, stormed into my study as I was working at my desk and listening to Alejandro Fernández's "Como Quien Pierde Una Estrella." He asked me to lower the music in a tone that surprised me.

I thought maybe he'd actually discovered the dead man inside the well, a ghost story oft repeated in a home that everyone insisted was haunted. I dismissed their theory as Mexican mysticism, but Lonny, ever the cool, handsome American surfer dude from Santa Cruz, huddled up with me one day: "Dude, there's some weird shit in this house. I don't want to freak you out, but I think there's a ghost here." Of course I didn't believe him, but I was at a loss to explain why one morning I woke up on the floor next to the wrong side of my bed with a broken wrist. Doctors were perplexed because, they explained, the X-rays showed that the break appeared to have come from a foot stepping on my wrist. I had been alone reading.

When Don Rafael showed up that morning with a serious look, I thought he'd solved the mystery. Instead, his eyes cast to the floor but his voice firm, Don Rafael said he needed a raise. He had already failed to persuade the previous correspondent, and he didn't want to fail again, not during an economic crisis. So he had brought company. He asked me to go to the front door. I was perplexed but followed him to the entrance.

My home, as just about every home in rich neighborhoods, had a giant gated door to keep out the angry masses. With the crisis of 1994, anger had arrived on Mexico's doorsteps.

I swung the door open to find a half-dozen gardeners, sweat on their foreheads, wielding hoes and shovels, picketing outside. Don Rafael had come to inform me that they were his friends, and they were waiting—impatiently—for more money for their *compadre*. The men represented a union of maintenance workers who'd banded together whenever a fellow worker needed a pay increase.

"I hope you don't mind," Don Rafael said. "But this is nothing personal. I'm due for a raise."

I grinned, almost relieved that the hoes weren't guns. I told the men about how my parents once fought alongside union leader César Chávez in California for farmworkers' rights. Chávez's United Farm Workers union and his message of rights and justice reached the California fields where my parents worked. With few rights beyond those bestowed at whim by ranchers, farmworkers suffered at the hands of their employers. They could expect to earn a fraction of a dollar an hour. Few ranches had toilets for their workers and housing was poor, often without indoor plumbing or even clean drinking water. The average life span of a U.S. farmworker in 1965 was forty-nine years.

My parents had been reluctant to join the farmworkers' movement at first. They held green cards and wanted to do nothing to jeopardize that coveted status. But when Robert F. Kennedy stood with Chávez, and climbed on top of a car in California in March 1968 and shouted in his Boston Irish accent, *"Viva la huelga"*—Long live the strike!—my mother was sold. When Kennedy spoke, his voice ringing out from radios carried by workers picking tomatoes that hot, sad June of 1968 after he was assassinated, my mother would stop, put her index finger over her lips and motion to us to listen and memorize the words translated into Spanish.

"Shh. *Escuchen.*" Listen up, she'd say, and later reminded me daily of that quote from George Bernard Shaw after I dropped out of high school: "Some men see things as they are and say 'Why?' I dream things that never were and say 'Why not?'" Even though she didn't speak English, my mother found the words so powerful even in translation that it became her daily mantra.

I stressed to Don Rafael that I was sympathetic to his concerns. I would take care of the situation and give him his overdue raise, I promised.

And I told Don Rafael that if he needed anything, all he had to do was ask.

"No need to have your friends miss work because of me," I said.

"Sorry, but this is how we do things in Mexico," he responded, a bit embarrassed. *"La unión hace la fuerza."* Unity is power.

"I'm beginning to understand," I said. *"No se preocupe."* Don't worry about it.

When Javier and Lonny heard of my encounter that morning, they spontaneously formed "SUTAC," the Sindicato Unido de Trabajadores de Alfredo Corchado, or Syndicate of Unionized Workers of Alfredo Corchado. Whenever they wanted me to pick up the bill for a meal, or anything else that involved mustering some kind of leverage, they would look at each other and just say: "SUTAC."

Some weeks later, Doña Carmen announced she was quitting. She had found a job as an Avon representative. By suggesting she might be stealing from me, I had broken the code of nonconfrontation. Polite as always, she made up an excuse to save face, both hers and mine. She used a timeless defense used by many presidents before her: She blamed the gringos. Dona Carmen said she couldn't work under Lonny. He was too arrogant and stubborn. Doña Carmen and I bid each other farewell.

Zedillo's days-old administration got off to a rough start as the economy began to implode in 1994. A blame game between Zedillo and Salinas ensued.

Throughout the turmoil, the country's reserves were dipping dangerously. Zedillo had inherited a time bomb when he took office. The previous ten years had been marked by a liberalization of Mexico's trade and financial sectors. Some banks that had been expropriated in 1982 were privatized anew by Salinas, but with little oversight or rules to restrict lending. There were no bank reserve requirements and government backing of loans encouraged reckless lending. Between 1988 and 1994, credit from local commercial banks to the private sector rose by 25 percent a year. Circumstances were ripe for a crash. The reserves backing the nation's currency were falling. The peso-dollar exchange rate had been carefully locked in a narrow band and the currency's value didn't reflect the new realities of economic vulnerability.

Assassinations, the uprising in the south, endemic corruption and what the incoming administration called "arrogance" on the part of the outgoing administration would cause the biggest political uncertainty in more than sixty years.

On December 20, the new finance minister, Jaime Serra Puche, unwisely told a private meeting of Mexico's top businesspeople about plans for a 15 percent devaluation of the peso. When the meeting ended, many immediately went out and converted pesos to dollars. Two days later, in an effort to preserve dwindling federal reserves, which over the year had fallen from about $25 billion to $6 billion, Serra Puche halted the long-standing policy of propping up the peso to keep it in a narrow range against the dollar and let the Mexican currency float freely. Panic ensued. Investors tried to cut their losses. An estimated $8 billion in currency fled the country, wiping out any net gains in foreign investment for 1994. Real wages fell by more than half and inflation rose to 52 percent.

The results were catastrophic both in Mexico and across the border. U.S. stocks dropped 16 percent, while foreign investors feared losing the $30 billion they sank in the Mexican market. The suppressed rage against political and economic reform was like an electric current that had jumped the wire.

A U.S.-led bailout of $50 billion helped stabilize the faltering economy. Even then, Mexico stood on shaky ground. The old system of patronage and raw power was now imploding from within. No one knew what would emerge to take its place. Never in its history had Mexico become so economically subservient to foreign finance. With the economy in shambles, the monsters emerged. More corruption was exposed.

Zedillo fired more than five thousand police in Mexico City who were believed to be running crime rings, working with gangsters or were otherwise on the take. All that move seemed to do was put more bad ex-cops on the street with nothing to do in a lagging economy. Unemployment in the formal economy surged to nearly 25 percent from 10 percent. The black market and the informal economy swelled on all sides, from the illegal *puestecitos* that families ran to make ends meet, selling school supplies or socks or CDs or secondhand clothes, to criminal enterprises including prostitution, arms trafficking and—increasingly—kidnappings and drugs.

Zedillo brought the military to the streets of Mexico City to replace the cops he had fired. They took over avenues in my Coyoacán neighborhood, jamming up traffic with military trucks. I saw them as I'd travel on weekends to shop at the new Walmart. The military quelled the violence in the short term. The camouflage green military tanks, packed with helmeted soldiers carting rifles, rolled around the city and offered a show of force.

But petty and violent crime had become rampant in the city. Kidnappings for ransom and "express kidnappings," in which the perpetrator forced the victim to withdraw money from half a dozen ATMs until funds dried up, became more commonplace. Everyone had been a victim at one point or another, including friends and colleagues. Dianne was assaulted and robbed twice. Getting into a taxi was especially dangerous. Many of us turned to private drivers, and began leaving home without credit or debit cards. Some stopped wearing suits, high heels or jewelry, afraid that even the faintest hint of wealth would bait criminals. We'd leave our business cards at home, afraid the thieves, if they kidnapped us, would know the address of our homes or offices and put the lives of loved ones at risk. A few of us got new ones made without addresses.

One afternoon I got into a VW Beetle street cab, gave the driver the address and then realized we were going the wrong way, heading south on Revolución and not toward Coyoacán.

"Señor, I think we're—"

Shut up, the driver barked.

I looked behind me and saw another car with three men tailing us. I was being kidnapped. At the busy corner of Revolución and La Paz the driver slowed down, and I shoved open the door and jumped out. The driver swung a crowbar and partially hit my back. I stumbled and hit the curb. Both cars sped off as some onlookers ran to help me and others started yelling after the drivers. I thanked them, stretched my back, patted off the dust from the ground and walked home. Surely, democracy would overcome this too.

Past the southern edge of the seething city, Popocatépetl kept spewing ash.

TEN

It took a trip to the past, to my hometown of San Luis de Cordero and a visit with Tío Antonio, to better understand the shadows moving over Mexico, even after spending several years reporting on the country from my new vantage point on the ground. I drove down from El Paso with my parents and fourteen-year-old sister, Linda, in 1999.

One late afternoon, as the sun began to set, we strolled through the streets of San Luis de Cordero. The streets seemed emptier than ever, as if every house, street, plaza and church had shrunk with time. If NAFTA was supposed to be the savior of Mexico, I didn't see it in my hometown that summer. Most of the men were absent and increasingly so were many of the women. The 1990s were economic boom years in the United States, and the demand for Mexican workers was greater, but this time the U.S. government didn't bother to create a bracero program that would bring Mexican workers over legally. San Luis de Cordero felt desolate and the people there were little more than shadows. Unlike my father's era when workers followed seasonal labor patterns, there was little flitting back and forth across the border. With tighter security along the border, people left and rarely came back. They populated new states from California to Texas, Colorado and beyond.

Rumors swirled that violence was growing in the mountains beyond San Luis de Cordero, in the Golden Triangle, where marijuana fields had flourished for decades. Our town was still quiet, though. As if in sleeper cells, criminals had entered San Luis de Cordero, but they kept quiet.

Even as the economy tanked in the 1990s, the drug trade brought billions of dollars into Mexico. Many federal authorities, including soldiers and customs and port authorities, remained on the cartels' payrolls. The cartels offered employment while the formal economy continued shedding thousands of jobs. The nation continued to wait for that entrance into the promised first world.

That afternoon, half a dozen of us gathered on the dirt-floor patio of my grandparents' home, a small hacienda-style house made of adobe with a stucco facade and a tiny courtyard, living room, kitchen and three bedrooms, built by my grandfather Arcadio years earlier. My cousin Lucia and her husband, Alfredo, now owned the home. Both had returned from working in Chicago and were determined to raise what was left of their family in San Luis de Cordero by operating a grocery store and butcher shop. They were getting by, but their children were already dreaming of heading north. The countryside was dying and Tío Antonio angrily blamed NAFTA, which gradually brought down prices for basic staples, forcing businesses to be more competitive. Beyond the grocery store, the benefits for the struggling workers didn't spread much beyond Mexico's tiny elite and U.S. businesses.

How could the two million Mexican corn farmers ever compete with Iowa farmers, for example, who were subsidized for crops like corn? he asked.

Even before NAFTA, much of the Mexican agriculture sector—with the notable exception of corn—was already unprotected from U.S. imports, thanks to previous Mexican government concessions. NAFTA would soon liberalize corn, not only a crucial crop in Mexico but also the symbol of the nation, which was the birthplace of the grain some seven thousand to ten thousand years ago. NAFTA meant a decline in small-scale maize production for farmers who were unable to compete against the influx of heavily subsidized corn from the north. Both farmhands and small farmers began to emigrate illegally, heading to places like the meatpacking industry of Nebraska, the cornfields of Iowa and the shrimp industry of North Carolina. Others would end up in the underground economy.

In this changing economy, the PRI was in free fall. By 1999, parts of Mexico were governed by one of two opposition parties, the PAN or PRD. In Mexico City, residents elected their own mayor for the first time in 1997. They picked Cuauhtémoc Cárdenas of the PRD. The PAN governed our hometown.

These changes were hard for Tío Antonio to stomach. A stout, muscular man with light skin and hazel eyes, always in his familiar white straw hat and leather shoes, he had become the family patriarch and was a die-hard *priísta*. He was the town's strongman. At sixty-seven, he was just three years younger than the PNR, the predecessor to the PRI, and he was one of the few in my family to have returned permanently to Mexico after having worked in the United States—a point of pride that he often brought up. He and Tío Delfino both served as PRI mayors of my hometown and often visited us in California to work the fields temporarily and solicit money to run the municipalities back home. They always seemed to be out of cash for basic services, like paying the local policeman, or for fixing up the church, building a school or fixing potholes.

"Don't forget the land where you came from," Tío Antonio would say. With the help of money he'd collected from San Luis de Cordero's expats, he was able to begin work on a road connecting the town to the city of Gómez Palacio. His biggest accomplishment was the building of a secondary school that he said would lead to more opportunities and eventually close off the gates that led to the United States, a fickle country that discarded Mexicans like yesterday's trash when their services were no longer needed. An educated population, he said, meant a brighter future for Mexico. Yet, I'd ask him, where would the jobs come from?

My *tío* didn't like arguments. Hundreds of thousands had died during the revolution; their deaths wouldn't be in vain. When he spoke he commanded attention, and everyone listened as he and I debated the political climate. He was worried about Mexico's future, he said. The PRI *was* the nation, he argued. He would remind us of how, at times, the PRI had achieved remarkable feats. During the 1930s and 1940s it had solidified a national political identity under then president Lázaro Cárdenas, who'd pushed agrarian and oil reform. He'd confiscated nearly fifty million acres, or 80 percent of Mexico's arable land, from hacendados—wealthy and sometimes despotic landowners—to distribute to the working class. In 1938, he'd kicked big foreign oil companies out of the country, alienating two of the world's greatest powers and its biggest stakeholders: the United States and Great Britain. He'd generated a deep sense of nationalism.

Later, Tío Antonio reminded us, in the 1940s the government of President Miguel Alemán had undertaken infrastructure projects throughout the country, putting Mexicans to work constructing dams, highways and electrical lines—not unlike Franklin Roosevelt's New Deal. The projects had given people hope. Foreign capital had poured in, particularly into Mexico's music and movie industries, which were celebrated throughout the hemisphere.

"The PRI is the Mexican way, *m'ijo,* my son," he told me, speaking with his deep voice and measured speech that seemed designed more for a political rally than a casual conversation with his nephew. He repeated a refrain often heard in Mexico, but he said it without cynicism, with a heartfelt confession and pride in his voice: "Every Mexican has a little PRI inside them, some more than others."

The PRI system, he explained, was a reflection of the Mexican himself. The PRI created the stability, he said, that kept Uncle Sam and his mighty military from meddling in its internal affairs. The more stable Mexico was, the less Mexicans would feel subordinate to the Americans, he reasoned.

Lowering his voice to a warning, almost sinister tone, he continued, as I wrote in my notepad:

"These changes you speak of and write about have the hand of the U.S. government all over them. We should beware of the consequences— because there will be consequences."

He sounded like the hounds of hell defending the PRI. I nodded out of respect. He is just frightened to lose his way of life, a life steeped in paternalism, I thought. If I could, I'd vote for the man in boots promising change—Vicente Fox—the candidate who now campaigned in both Mexico and the United States, including California, where Tío Antonio's children now lived. Fox kept my *tío* awake at night, worrying about what lay ahead. But I said nothing. We just sat there in silence until my mother spoke up—something that didn't happen much, especially around her older brother, whose stern manner sometimes bordered on intimidation.

"What has the PRI done but look after itself and its own interests?" she challenged. "Look at our town. Everyone is gone. Look at our family—your sons, your daughters, your brothers, sisters—most of us live in the United States. Wake up, Antonio. Stop being stubborn. We have to try something new. Otherwise, Mexico will empty itself out."

My *tío* wouldn't hear it. He spoke rapidly, without pausing, and grabbed a tree branch to make his point. He scribbled the word "PRI" in the dirt and slashed an *X* across over it, mimicking what voters had been doing for nearly seven decades. The end of the PRI was akin to the death of a father who would leave millions orphaned. The PRI had been the architect of much of Mexico's twentieth century. How would the country survive? Yes, anyone can talk about change, even a cheap politician in boots, he argued. But what will replace the PRI? Who or what would fill the vacuum? U.S.-backed candidates? The United States? Please, *¡m'ijo!* The Americans aren't satisfied with taking half of Mexico's land. They wouldn't rest until they controlled the entire country, he insisted.

"Change will kill Mexico, break it apart into tiny pieces," he told us confidently but with an edge to his voice. *"Tengan cuidado*—be careful what you ask for. Once it's broken it will be gone forever." My sister Linda looked on, puzzled by her *tío's* unease.

ELEVEN

Not long after that visit, Angela and I pulled out of the Los Angeles International Airport as the sun was beginning to cast its morning rays over the Pacific Ocean. We were trying to catch up to Vicente Fox, who was hunting for votes and financial support in California—not from the migrants directly (that we knew of), which was against Mexican law, but from their families and friends back home. We had rented a red convertible and were driving up California's Interstate 5, which turned into Highway 99, the mouth of the San Joaquin Valley.

On that Sunday morning, as the dew evaporated and our car cut through the San Joaquin Valley fog, I could sense that Mexico's renewed sense of possibility and nervous anticipation had reached the immigrants in California. All anyone talked about was whether it would be possible to topple the PRI. There were more than ten million Mexicans now living in the United States, and Fox's people were encouraging them to call home.

The *News* took a special interest in the elections. We were one of the only, if not the only, U.S. newspapers conducting polls in Mexico for the presidential race in Mexico. The largest newspaper in the Southwest, we also had the largest foreign bureau in Mexico, with a staff of twelve, including reporters, editors and administrative staff. By then Angela and I were a couple and she was officially part of the bureau, having moved down in 1999 as the foreign correspondent for the television arm of the newspaper's parent company, Belo. We were living together in Coyoacán and, whenever possible, working together on stories that took us around Mexico or, now, into the California of my childhood.

Memories came back to me of that first American home, our trailer house in a melon patch. All along the highway I imagined scenes from my youth: a boy, his brothers and mother stooping in the fields; my father on his tractor, wearing his white cowboy hat, dust clinging to his weathered brown face as newly plowed rows appeared below the tractor blades; my mother moving across the fields with a short-handled hoe, the kind that was later banned because it required the worker to stoop for hours, causing crippling back pain that haunts her to this day.

Every morning before dawn, my mother and father would haul Juan and me out of bed before the *shh shh* began—the sound of men and women thinning weeds from the surrounding melon fields. As our parents made their way to other fields, they'd drag us groggy eyed to the school bus stop at the edge of a cotton field. Our parents, like millions of Mexican immigrants at that time, had little or no education, but they knew that education was the only way out of poverty. It was the key to everything, they believed, even if they didn't have the slightest clue what we did in school.

After school, the bus would drop us off and our father would pick us up. Juan and I would skip as high as we could so that Papá could see our heads bobbing up and down amid the rows of cotton. When I was in elementary school in Oro Loma, we moved from that clapped-aluminum trailer to Eagle Field. Once a concentration camp for the Japanese during World War II, in the 1960s Eagle Field became a housing complex for hundreds of Mexican migrants, my cousins included. The fields surrounded the camp like a sea, and we felt as if we were stranded on an island, deserted except for other unlucky families like ours. At night, mice would terrorize my brother and me as they scampered in from the fields.

And if it wasn't mice, it was border patrol agents. Even though we were in the country legally, we panicked at the sight of them. Once, my father arrived home unexpectedly from work, accompanied by two agents. He had forgotten his green card and had come home to retrieve it. The men led him away in the back of a van, transported to some station to verify his identity. A fan of Superman, I tied a sheet over my shoulder and threw myself at them, thinking I could muster superpowers and really fly. They chuckled and left with my father, who returned late that evening.

Despite our hardships in California and how much I missed Mexico, I couldn't help but become American. I played basketball in the afternoons, pretending to play for John Wooden at UCLA, threw a football at dusk and jammed to "Sugar, Sugar" at night. I pretended to be Jughead, the drummer for the Archies.

Even so, I always longed for Mexico. I would lie awake at night dreaming of how to get back home.

All I could see in my future were fields, until one day a television crew, doing a story on exploitation of underage workers, asked me how I felt about working conditions. I wasn't so much struck by the question itself as by the fact that someone had wanted to give me a voice. How cool it would be to be the one asking those questions!

But everyone who looked like me planted, irrigated, picked, busheled, baled. Sure, I had learned English—in part with the help of a bilingual school assignment that called for the Mexican kids to stand up and sing the song "Ben," a Michael Jackson tune that I later found out had been inspired by a rat. It also helped that I was a B student. But all the book work wasn't going to prepare me for the highest position I could imagine attaining: a field foreman. I dreaded school and dropped out my sophomore year, though it wasn't long before a teacher I remembered as Miss Miller came knocking on our door.

It wasn't unusual for my teachers to show up. They seemed convinced that I could make something of my life. Miss Miller had been my English teacher, and every once in a while when I was sick or skipped school, she'd check in on me, making sure my excuse was real. Normally I didn't mind. Miss Miller had the best legs in town. I was a pimply faced, hormonal kid and couldn't really keep my mind on anything else. I'd just watch her walk, my eyes locked on her hemline. But when she showed up after word had spread that I'd dropped out, I feared what was coming.

At the time, Hispanic kids were dropping out by the dozens. Miss Miller seemed to want to save at least one of us. She chose me.

"¿Quiere quedarse a cenar, Miss Miller?" my mother asked. She always asked any guest to stay for dinner.

But even though she didn't speak English and Miss Miller spoke no Spanish, she quickly read the worried look on our guest's face.

"¿Qué pasa, Freddy?" My mother looked at me hard, desperate now for a translation. She turned to Miss Miller. "Me . . . no speaky English."

Miss Miller looked at my mother and slowly said, "Your son—" There was a lot of pointing and hand gestures at this point. "No more school."

My mother's face fell as she registered the meaning of those words.

"No!" she yelled, sadness deep in her eyes. "No—you can't! No!" She was shrieking in Spanish, not even pretending to be civil in front of Miss Miller. My cheeks burned with embarrassment.

"This is not about you," my mother said desperately. *"It's about my sacrifice and your father's sacrifice to give you and your brothers a chance in life. You're the firstborn. You have to set the right example. No, Freddy! You have an obligation, a responsibility that's bigger than you. You can't do this. It's not your choice."*

"Alfredo, what are you doing?" my teacher challenged me. "You want to work in the fields your whole life? You could do something with your life—anything you want, Alfredo."

Yeah, right, I thought. Only the white kids do well. They go to Stanford, Berkeley, UCLA, I said defiantly. We go on to the next field.

Two years passed and I didn't go back to school. But my mother wouldn't give up on me. Finally, Mamá offered me a bribe: Pick any car, and she and my father would make the down payment and first few monthly payments. I had to agree to three things: Leave California and head for west Texas, where Mexican Americans wore ties and had possibilities beyond the fields; enroll in school again; and avoid getting married until I completed my education. I liked the rancher's daughter at the time, and for a week I debated the question: car or girl? I was smitten, but at seventeen the lure of a 1978 Camaro felt more like true love.

Angela and I steered off the highway into Bakersfield for the first of two Fox rallies that day, pulling the convertible into the parking lot of a small baseball field where a few dozen people were waiting. The Fox campaign had predicted thousands would show, but the small turnout did not discourage Fox. He joked with the sparse crowd, at times furiously kicking his boots into the dirt. He was practicing, he said with a wide smile, for the "ass kicking" he was about to give the PRI. He campaigned in California in blue jeans and black snakeskin boots, drawing a sharp contrast with the PRI men in suits. He was a broccoli grower and a former Coca-Cola marketing guru. He'd also served as governor of the wealthy state of Guanajuato. He was a towering, charismatic figure with ancestral roots in Spain, Ireland and the United States. His Irish grandfather, Joseph Louis Fox, had immigrated to Ohio and then moved to Mexico, where he'd fallen in love with a criolla, a Mexico-born Spanish woman. He'd stayed permanently, raised a family and built a ranch in Guanajuato called San Cristóbal. Fox and his brothers owned the land now, and the candidate projected an image of himself as a tough rancher who wouldn't take crap from anyone. Mexican immigrants in the United States seemed enamored with Fox, who proclaimed his veneration for them and their contributions to Mexico.

There was another politician in the crowd closely observing the scene. On leave from the Mexican congress, Felipe Calderón was a Mason Fellow at Harvard University's Kennedy School of Government, and he was studying the PAN's presidential campaign. He no longer had the long, shaggy hair from his days in Ciudad Juárez, when I'd first met him. The large round glasses were gone too. He peered through his rim-less glasses, looking every bit the scholar, scribbling words on a yellow legal pad.

He was also dressed in a light blue oxford shirt that had become a trademark for PAN politicians. Sporting a baseball cap to cover his receding hairline and protect him from California's searing sun, Calde-rón studiously took notes. He had been hinting for years that he might one day run for president. We were never close, but any time I'd see him I would approach him and shake his hand. Like any politician, he greeted me as if he remembered me.

What do you think? I asked.

Very interesting, he replied and kept on writing.

Fox ended his speech with a triumphant call to "Mexico's heroes"—the immigrants who worked so hard to support families back home. The crowd went wild with whistles and shouts of *"¡Viva México!"* Fox had promised in his speech, as he usually did, that if elected, he'd find a way to return to the days when men like my father could work legally in the United States and restore the circularity that had long been a hall-mark of the U.S.-Mexico labor market. That would put an end to coy-otes, the smugglers who, along with more border patrol agents, were making it harder—and more dangerous—for workers to cross. Some three hundred migrants were dying every year as workers took increasing risks to make it across the border, from taking isolated routes through the deadly Arizona desert to dangerously cramming inside vans or railroad cars with other migrants like themselves, often with tragic consequences.

"Mexico is grateful to you," Fox said, his voice booming over the sparse crowd. "Mexico misses you."

A much larger crowd greeted him at the annual county fair in Fresno. I wasn't sure whether they were there to support Fox or to dance to the *norteño* music.

Again, he called his supporters "heroes."

Fox's campaign promises once seemed less far-fetched. Between 1942 and 1964 the United States and Mexico had jointly managed labor migration—a circular pattern—between their countries on a massive scale. Under the bracero program, the U.S. government agreed to pay Mexican workers the same wages as U.S. workers, provide unemployment benefits and pay for their round-trip bus tickets. Mexicans like my father, *tíos,* aunts and cousins picked cotton, oranges, sugar beets, broccoli and grapes here. In Chicago they repaired railroads; in upstate New York and in Washington's Yakima Valley they picked apples. In Pittsburgh they worked in the steel mills. Almost anywhere an unfilled job came up, the men and women from Mexico arrived to help. They were the unsung heroes of the U.S. war machine in World War II. Some towns, like Lorain, Ohio, were so grateful they organized welcoming committees to meet the Mexicans as they got off buses and trains, even urging them to stay on and bring their families with them. Many *paisanos* were shocked by the warm reception, especially because years before, following the market crash of 1929, busloads of

Mexicans—some half a million—had been shipped back to Mexico, no questions asked.

Over the course of the bracero program, the number of Mexicans working and living in the United States doubled to five million. They were some of the most ambitious Mexicans the country had to offer. Around a hundred Mexican communities—the majority of them in the states of Michoacán, Jalisco, Guanajuato, Zacatecas and Durango—were sending their young men to work abroad. Initially, they were taking over jobs left by men who'd entered war industry jobs elsewhere, or the war itself. In 1940 in Nevada, for example, there were about one million white Americans working in the fields, but by 1942 that number had dwindled to about sixty thousand, the majority of them replaced by braceros. Along with their sweat and muscle, they brought with them their culture, their food, their religion. Slowly, they began transforming the United States.

The experience of working in the United States transformed the braceros as well. As they gained the financial independence to buy new vehicles and homes, their viewpoints changed too. Braceros piped money back to impoverished communities that had relied on little more than the earth and rain to provide for them. After World War II came the Korean War, and the United States again needed more laborers from Mexico, especially when the baby boom generation increased the demand for food. That second phase of the program, which began in 1954, had lured my father north.

Juan Pablo Corchado worked the cotton fields of west Texas and the chili fields of New Mexico and southern Arizona as a bracero, one of an estimated 430,000 Mexicans who entered the United States legally as guest workers in 1957. He had decided as a young teenager that he wanted to be like his brothers and the older men who would roll into town with new Tejano hats and rolls of dollars in their pockets. He was a wiry, cocky seventeen-year-old who, during outings at the cantina, liked to wear a borrowed gun in his belt. He sat for weeks in the plaza of San Luis de Cordero, in front of the white church with other boys his age, joking, smoking, drinking and waiting for someone to change their lives. One day—finally—a slow-moving blue pickup with a speaker atop the hood stirred up the dust. A voice boomed:

"The United States needs men. If you're interested, meet tomorrow with your documents in hand."

He and dozens of other men—*tíos,* cousins—scurried home and dug out their birth certificates as proof of Mexican citizenship. They visited girlfriends and promised eternal love and marriage upon their return, when they hoped to be flush with cash. They received their worried mothers' blessings, the first of many. They hugged their fathers, who gave them a few pesos to make sure they had enough money for food and a place to stay until their first payday.

The evening before he left, Juan Pablo did his chores on his mother's ranch for the last time; his father had died when he was a boy. He counted the chickens, pigs and two dozen heads of cattle, as he had done every morning and evening for years. Although he had his sights set on making money in *el norte,* the life he envisioned was back in Mexico. He dreamed he would double the cattle on the ranch, start a general store, maybe even get married.

His oldest sister, Felicidad, or Tía Chalá, as we knew her, advised him how much money he would need once he touched U.S. soil: one quarter. That would be enough to cover a phone call to her, a soft drink and a bus ride to her home in central El Paso. My father was stubborn but listened closely and obeyed every order she gave him. Juan Pablo and his pals hopped on a train to Ciudad Juárez, then headed for the border, where they crossed on foot. Across the river they got a glimpse of El Paso, civilization curled around a bald mountain range.

In the morning they arrived at the customs office in El Paso, where U.S. health officials ordered the men to strip. Juan Pablo closed his eyes and, like the men around him, muttered a few choice curse words before stripping naked; he hesitated only before taking off his boots and his white hat. He waited to be sprayed with insecticide and checked for lice, like a cow. The process was humiliating, but he knew it would pay off. He already liked the city lights, the cars and pickup trucks on paved roads, the houses in neat rows, the orderliness of it all. Texas ranchers came to study them, walking quietly around, making comments among themselves in English. They examined the men's hands and biceps, looking them over as if they were horses. Juan Pablo did not have much meat on him and certainly no bulging biceps. But he had a look of fearless determination. Nothing scared him, certainly not a new country, the boss he couldn't understand or even the English-only documents he signed without ever knowing his rights or the conditions of employment.

My father and tens of thousands more men eventually settled in California's San Joaquin Valley, where work was interrupted only by the rainy season. By the early 1950s, Mexican laborers made up the majority of farmworkers in California.

And now here was Vicente Fox, calling these men and women heroes. What did he know? I got the chance to ask him just that after the rally. Fox was lounging in a Fresno hotel room as one of his campaign aides ushered in Angela and me. This region, Fox told me, had become home to many of his neighbors from his hometown. I told him I had many relatives here too.

"Are they voting for me?" he asked.

"I don't know, but I'll ask," I answered.

"Your relatives are heroes," he said.

"If you really think we're heroes," I told Fox, "prove it by granting me the first interview if you're elected president. Give this Mexican hero the first interview."

The two campaign aides in the room fidgeted and looked nervously at Fox, as if I had overstepped my bounds. But Fox didn't hesitate.

"Your polls show I'll win, right?" he asked.

"Anything is possible," I said, taking notes. "As you know, our polls show the race is very close."

He looked at me and grinned.

"Yes, you can win," I offered.

"I need you to do me a favor: Call me with the poll results before they're published."

"Sure," I responded. "You and the other two candidates. We'll give all of you a heads-up." This was normal practice, because the *News* wanted reaction from the candidates to include in our stories.

"*Hecho,*" he said.

We had a deal.

"Don't forget," I said. "Politicians shouldn't break their campaign promises."

"I won't—and I'm not a politician."

We shook hands, Fox's pizza-sized hand squeezing mine. He kissed Angela on the cheek, and they swapped stories of their Irish ancestors as I waited impatiently. I wanted to get a head start on Fox's caravan to have time to visit my family.

Later that day, my aunts and cousins ran outside to wave to the passing caravan. I don't remember whether Fox even returned the greeting, but it didn't matter. Here in front of them was the bus carrying the candidate who represented an alternative, a nation that didn't fear, that didn't think it was condemned to its paternalistic past but believed it could generate the kind of possibilities my family thought they could find only in the United States. Angela and I raced to Fox's next stop, veering the convertible onto Route 152, with the Doobie Brothers' "Long Train Running" blaring. The California sunset was spectacular, red as a tomato. I looked at Angela and liked the way the sun shone in her green eyes. I felt it too. We had an overwhelming hope for Mexico.

On a gray day, July 2, 2000, the rains seemed to collapse over Mexico City. I ran around the Zócalo looking for shelter from the storm. The Catedral Metropolitana tilted, having sunk into the soft earth from the weight of its stones. This majestic sixteenth-century church, studding the heart of Mexico City, had been sinking for centuries. The bells ringing inside its two towers echoed off the palaces enclosing the Zócalo, the central square, twenty-five bells singing their melancholy song, swinging between hope and dread.

I received a call from Juan Hernandez, an aide to Fox. His lead was irreversible, the aide said. Come now. I raced to the PAN campaign head-quarters, sure that Mexico's historic moment was imminent. I arrived at their base in Coyoacán, and Hernandez ushered me into a room adjacent to where Fox was meeting with his team. I walked toward a small window where I could see the crowd growing outside. Although there was a lot of commotion, people weren't celebrating outright. Many just stood on street corners. They had waited a long time for this moment. Some seemed petrified that the PRI wouldn't recognize the results or that some kind of fraud would once again blacken the day. A vendor riding a squeaky old bicycle with a large basket filled with sweet bread shouted, "*Pan, pan.*" Many laughed and applauded him. Others wolfed down steaming tacos stuffed with steak, cheese and jalapeños, freshly cooked from food carts moving through the crowd. Everyone wanted to get in on the action, including the vendors selling fruit, hot chocolate or T-shirts with Fox's beaming face on them. The rain fell gently as I waited for Fox.

That evening was the culmination of a democratic movement years in the making, from the first days that I'd witnessed protests in Ciudad Juárez in the 1980s. The movement had spread across the country like a slow-burning fire, finally reaching Mexico's capital on a soggy, rainy July night.

Strange, I thought, to see ordinary Mexicans, young and old, shoulder to shoulder, the rich rubbing elbows with the poor. Why were they so willing to believe in Fox and—if it came to that—defend their vote? Fox swung open the door and crossed the room in a single stride. He sat down across from me.

"I told you I'd remember what I promised," he said, even before I turned my recorder on.

"I didn't think you would," I responded honestly.

People were coming in and out of the room, smiling and celebrating, but Fox remained calm. He stretched his long body, spiking the heels of his boots on the floor. I asked him about everything, from the promise he'd made to immigrants abroad, to how he planned to usher in democracy. In Fox's typical hyperbole, he responded by assuring that his win that evening had provided him with the kind of political capital to pass long-awaited reforms that would transform the Mexican system. Congress would have no choice.

I asked how he thought he would meet the people's sky-high expectations. What did he want his legacy to be? His answer was blunt—and worrisome.

"People will remember that I was the man who kicked the PRI out of Los Pinos," he said confidently.

His work was already done.

The interview lasted no more than thirty minutes. He had other reporters waiting, including one from a national newspaper that was angry because I'd gotten the first interview. I made my way to the crowded exit and stepped outside. After an exclusive interview like that, the first thing you do is call your editor, talk about the interview, figure out the substance of the material, work out the lead and debate the story length, asking for more space but knowing you'll get less. Instead, I called my mother. She was in bed already, watching the moment live on television from our home in El Paso. My father was next to her.

"I didn't think I would live to see this," she said.

"Well, I'm glad you did," I responded, "because your son was the first reporter to interview President Vicente Fox."

She sobbed as she passed the phone to my father, who didn't say much. He, too, was in shock.

As I wrote that evening, the somber, determined face of President Zedillo suddenly appeared on the office television. He was seated at his presidential office in Los Pinos, dressed formally, wearing the tricolor presidential sash across his chest. Behind him were two icons of Mexico: the gigantic national flag and a portrait of nineteenth-century president Benito Juárez. Zedillo spoke deliberately and clearly on a television network—Televisa—long manipulated by the PRI. Without hesitation, Zedillo boldly congratulated Fox on his election as president of Mexico and pledged that his administration would cooperate fully during the upcoming five-month transition period. He called upon the PRI to be proud of a long record of accomplishment. They, too, had transformed Mexico, he said. In that spirit, they must respect the outcome and support Mexico's new president. In less than ten minutes, between Zedillo's speech and the concession speech of the PRI candidate, Mexico's democracy had arrived, solidified by the Federal Electoral Institute, created to ensure votes were respected.

Near midnight on election night, Angela and I stood at the foot of the Angel of Independence on Paseo de la Reforma as Fox addressed a gathering of several thousand supporters. Maybe this was the long-awaited revolution, the one we thought had died. Fox would change Mexico, I told Angela. The electrified crowd listened eagerly to his speech, but didn't respond with the usual victory cheers.

They pleaded with him instead: *"¡No nos falles! ¡No nos falles!"* Don't fail us! Don't fail us!

The morning after, nothing happened. No one protested, not in the streets, not through official channels. The all-night celebration had ended, and people simply returned to work or resumed their summer vacations. All seemed orderly, so much so that one longtime PRI *tricolor* member called to tease me: "How boring. An election just like in the United States—boring."

TWELVE

On a hot, miserable September afternoon in 2003, I was driving my old black Toyota 4-Runner into the mouth of Ciudad Juárez. I had spent the three years since the historic Mexican election in Washington, D.C., covering what I believed at the time would be a game-changing relationship between President Fox and President George W. Bush, a former Texas governor. But everything had changed following the attacks of September 11, 2001. The ties between my two countries loosened. My editors finally gave me the green light to go home to Mexico City with a stopover in Ciudad Juárez, where narco violence was growing amid decade-old questions about what was behind the murders of so many women.

The growing problems in Juárez reflected what was going on in the rest of the country. The PAN was struggling to replace the old system with a new one. The *priístas,* those in the congress, clawed, schemed and plotted their return to power. They quickly adopted a strategy of gridlock, halting proposed major reforms. Mexico's historical legacies hadn't been undone by electoral democracy. The Fox administration seemed determined not to deal with the past, but seventy-one years of authoritarian government had left its mark. Mexico's endemic corruption wasn't going to disappear.

People in Washington were learning more about the cartels, which were growing exponentially unchecked in the early 2000s, often with the quiet support of Mexican authorities. One intelligence official–turned–diplomat, Crescencio Arcos, shared with me a pile of reports that detailed corruption inside the Mexican government. I pressed him about why Washington didn't share more of what it knew with Mexico City. He just shook his head and left a rhetorical question hanging over the table: "Who can we trust in Mexico?"

The parties had changed, thanks in part to the people of Juárez who'd been fighting for real democracy for decades. Yet Juárez became the poster child for Mexico's troubled transition to democracy. Two governments seemed to run parallel to each other there: one run by elected officials and the other run by highly organized, faceless criminals, or so they seemed. But it was becoming increasingly clear who actually held the power in Juárez, and power meant deciding who would live and who would die.

For years, bodies of women had been turning up in the desert outside Juárez, one after another; by some estimates, the death toll reached more than three hundred. Young women were being systematically picked up, raped and murdered. Years passed, parents demanded answers, but the guilty were never caught. Some investigations, while begun in earnest, ended with assassinations of agents and witnesses. The murders continued. Many of the women killed were petite and pretty, dark skinned with long black hair. They were almost always poor. Some worked in the maquilas, the assembly plants that had cropped up in Juárez over the years.

I had followed the story of the killings, of bodies found in the desert— it was impossible to ignore. But I had avoided reporting the story myself. The *News* wanted answers, and so I finally went, even though I knew that in Mexico the likelihood of solving a crime of this magnitude—most crimes, in fact—was small. The unsolved murders reminded us of the demons that lurked, and Juárez reminded me how utterly wrong I was that there was even a remote possibility of justice being served, or worse, that democracy was the overnight cure for Mexico's ills.

I quickly learned that official investigations were shoddy; evidence routinely went missing. Once, a dress worn by one of the murdered women was washed and not tested for clues because, according to the Mexican authorities, it was dirty and had a strong odor. It was impossible to know how much was due to incompetence and how much was a cover-up. Theories of the murders ran from organ traffickers to Satan worshippers to witches and blood sacrifice, one soul for the death of another. This could explain why, theorists said, if you plotted the locations where the bodies were found, it made the shape of a diamond.

I drove past tacky billboards, advertisements for dentists, lawyers, restaurants, nightclubs and more dentists. A trail of pink crosses and ribbons lined a busy avenue, putting the government to shame. The city reflected the sun with concrete and metal: brand-new industrial parks and urban sprawl, shantytowns of tin and cardboard, shacks filled with the destitute, people on their way to the American dream who got stuck at the border.

I parked under a skinny mulberry tree in a dust-whipped neighborhood, a squatter's domain dominated by unpaved roads and houses bearing the bland colors of the aluminum sheets and concrete blocks with which they were built.

I was at a domestic violence center to speak to a mother whose daughter had been one of the victims. In a small room I stared at her eyes blotched red from permanent sadness. She spoke to me of her final memories of her fifteen-year-old daughter—the last meal they'd shared together, the Virgin of Guadalupe medallion that her daughter put on every day before leaving for her factory job, how she'd never returned. Her mother felt tremendous guilt because they had had an argument on the last day of her daughter's life. She didn't even remember what they'd argued over, just that she hadn't told her daughter how much she loved her. The next time she saw her was at the mortuary. Her daughter was so disfigured that she'd opted for a closed casket—rare in Mexico. She'd cried so much then, she said, that she hardly ever cried anymore.

"There is no more life left for me," she told me. "I just want justice for my daughter, but where do I even begin?"

Her story echoed those of other mothers and fathers. Their daughters had disappeared; the authorities could never pinpoint how or from where. The victims were likely shoved, or possibly lured, into a car, but no credible witnesses or investigations followed. When anyone spoke up, they'd quickly go quiet again.

The woman who ran the crisis center, Esther Chávez, said she had no idea who was killing the women and she made it clear she was not an investigator. Her role was to bring awareness to what she referred to as the "broken democracy" Mexicans inherited, and the injustice it bred.

"If you want to know what happened to the daughters of these women," she said one night as we traveled the roads of Chihuahua, "if you want to know what Juárez has become, you must talk to Dante. In Juárez, he's known as the devil's lawyer."

Sergio Dante Almaraz, originally from the state of Guanajuato, was a lawyer for the Juárez underworld. He'd been lured to Juárez's dark side, he later told me, because that's where the money was. His clients included robbers, drug traffickers and car thieves, and he was rumored to know more about the slayings of these women than anyone else. But the word on the street was that he had run afoul of the cartels.

"Dad is very busy," Dante's daughter and receptionist would explain to me over the telephone. "He will get back to you. Be patient."

Finally, after three months of hounding, Dante called me back. I immediately took out my notepad.

"You want to talk?" he asked.

"Yes, very much so. I'm—"

"Be in Juárez tomorrow morning, eight a.m.," he interrupted. "I'll call you at seven forty-five a.m. and tell you where to meet. Okay?"

Perfecto, I responded.

He had one condition: He'd ask the questions.

At precisely seven forty-five a.m., Dante called. I answered as I was driving across the international bridge into Juárez from El Paso.

Sanborns, he announced. See you there. I'm wearing black, sunglasses, and I'm carrying a brown briefcase.

Click.

Sanborns? I thought, disappointed. This was Mexico's International House of Pancakes, but with a department store and bad coffee.

I crossed the border into Juárez and made my way. The movers and shakers of Juárez usually had their morning breakfast meetings at Sanborns. I recognized local lawyers, politicians and a table of journalists—people I knew from previous stories. Some of the reporters had given me tips on my investigation; some I had known since the days of the Juárez marches for democracy. I slid into a table and ordered a hot chocolate. I wouldn't dare taste the coffee. I browsed through the day's newspapers. I kept peeking over the paper looking for a man dressed in black—but that was practically half the room.

Dante, built like a football linebacker, sauntered into the diner half an hour late, dressed impeccably in black. He looked like the devil. His jet-black hair, obviously dyed, was slicked back from his forehead. He had a dark complexion and high cheekbones. As he made his rounds at other tables, he looked over at me, pulled down his sunglasses and winked. He pushed his sunglasses back into place and shook hands with some of the journalists sitting or standing not far from me.

At last he took a seat across from me and scoffed at where I'd chosen to sit.

"This is too public. Why not something in the back?"

"It's packed," I said. "Unless you want to wait?"

"What the fuck—there are no secrets in Juárez anyway," he responded in Spanish and took a seat.

"I don't trust anyone who drinks chocolate," he blurted.

I smiled, hoping he was joking.

"You need to drink our bad coffee—the worst in Juárez," he said, turning over his coffee cup as the waitress approached, rustling her ankle-length skirt striped like a roll of Life Savers, a pale imitation of a Mexican *folklórico* dress. I turned over my cup as well, determined to suffer through the bitter coffee if it would loosen up Dante. We talked for a long time, almost two hours, mostly about nothing. He pointed at the journalists near us.

"The sight of them makes me want to puke," he said. "Some pretend to be gossiping, but they're just watching us—you to be exact. That's why I wear sunglasses here," he continued. "I can keep an eye on my enemies."

"Yeah, but they're journalists—harmless," I answered. "I've known some of them for years."

"Don't be naive. Some are the eyes and ears of the cartels," he said. "They're paid weekly for information, and right now you're their prize. In other words, you're fucked."

I glanced up at men who just seconds ago I had seen as friends.

I tried keeping my poker face. But I could feel fear churning inside me. Time and time again, reporters had minimized Dante's importance. When I'd asked for Dante's cell phone number, some balked. They said I was wasting my time interviewing a mafia lawyer, a man with outlandish stories and a dubious reputation. Had they been protecting me?

"Those motherfuckers have the power to literally kill you with the information they provide their fucking bosses, you understand?" Dante said.

"How do you know this?" I asked.

"I ask the questions, remember?" he said.

He paused, looked at his watch. He finally got to the reason why I'd wanted to see him. But first, he had something else to ask.

"So you knew Mario Escobedo?"

My face flushed. Caught off guard, I replied reluctantly. "Somewhat."

"Tell me—" he insisted. "Remember, the rule. I ask the questions."

We were now looking for each other's weak spots, waiting for the other to blink or grow tired. I didn't tell him then, but I would later confess what he already knew: Mario Escobedo was my sister-in-law's cousin.

Mario had been working with both his father, Mario Escobedo Sr., and Dante on a case in which two bus drivers were falsely accused of killing eight women in a 2001 incident known as the "cotton field" murders. The bodies had been uncovered in an old cotton field right across the street from the Twin Plant Association, a group representing foreign-owned factories, or maquilas, that employed tens of thousands of women. The two drivers, Víctor García Uribe—El Cerillo, or "The Match"—and Gustavo González Meza—La Foca, or "The Seal"—looked to police like the perfect scapegoats. When they showed up to meet the media, they had been beaten badly. And what about those burns? Well, investigators said, they were "self-inflicted" cigarette burns, to sensitive parts of their bodies including their genitals.

They would eventually be exonerated, but it would take many years. La Foca would die in prison.

The younger Mario had been vocal in his criticism against the government and police, publicly accusing them of fabricating evidence. One afternoon he'd stopped for gas and a soft drink in Juárez. He saw two policemen, each in his own car, and he gave them a friendly wave. As he left the convenience store, he noticed the two police cars were following him. He sped up and they did too. Then they started shooting. Frantic, Mario got on the phone with his father and screamed he was being chased. He drove with his cell phone glued to his ear and begged his father to do something.

"Call the governor—call anyone!" he pleaded. "Father, they're going to kill me. Help me!"

Mario senior took off in his car and headed toward his son, hoping to rescue him. But the car chase ended with Mario's vehicle crashing against a wall. A witness later said at a court hearing that one of the policemen had calmly gotten out of his car and fired a bullet into Mario's head.

At a subsequent press conference, the police explained that Mario had been a victim of mistaken identity. They thought they were chasing a criminal who had escaped from prison. They shot at Mario because they were returning fire; they said he'd shot first. To prove they'd been shot at, the investigators showed a police car with several bullet holes on the right side. But those bullet holes had not been there at the time of the chase—a photographer from the Juárez newspaper *El Norte* had taken pictures at the scene of the incident that rebuffed their explanation.

Dante had vowed to Mario senior that he would take the case and help find justice for Mario. He'd also handled the case of the two bus drivers on his own. I would learn this was Dante's turning point. Dante knew he was declaring war on the cops and the cartels they worked for. The very ones he had once represented as their lawyer.

Dante waited for me to answer his question.

"First let me clarify the rules," I said defensively. "I won't talk about sources. I never talk about sources, and I think you can respect me for that."

"Except that Mario wasn't just a source, right?" he said in his accusatory tone.

Seeing that I had clammed up, he continued.

"Okay, we can talk about that later," he said. "So you want to know who's killing the women of Juárez, right?" I turned the tape recorder on.

Dante told me several stories, his theories, his investigations. One account by an eyewitness had me hooked. We talked for weeks about a client of his, a witness to the murders. The man, Dante said, had been involved with the Juárez cartel, which included members of the local and state police force; the feds, including the military; and the governor. The man later crossed the cartel, claiming a load of coke he and others were protecting had been stolen, when in reality he and his friends had stolen it. *Sicarios*—hit men—retaliated by ambushing the truck he and other traffickers were driving outside Juárez, in the town of Zaragoza. He survived by hiding under the bodies of his murdered friends—friends who knew about the women. He knew about gang rapes and murders too. He had witnessed at least one scene, and he had told Dante everything he knew.

The man had been put in a prison by Dante himself to protect him until his identity could be changed or until the cartel forgot about him, whichever came first. For now, he sat in jail with stories that he wanted to share just in case someone knocked him off, even within the prison walls. It wouldn't be hard: The Juárez cartel ran the place, which was like a community all its own, with food stands, even mini factories where prisoners made clothes and other goods. Parts of the prison essentially mirrored a roach-infested hotel stocked with rum and condoms for conjugal visits.

Many of the women—perhaps the vast majority, the witness told Dante—had been victims of domestic abuse. Husbands and boyfriends got rid of their wives and girlfriends by killing them brutally—in the most horrible of ways—to make it look like the work of serial killers. Other victims had been involved in the drug trade as pushers, distributors, collectors, even *sicarias*—hit women. But some were victims of nothing more than the new power that controlled Ciudad Juárez. For some members of the Juárez cartel, killing was a sport. Newly empowered and flush with money, these men operated without any rules; they were men turned cops turned cartel members.

On nights after successful drug runs, there were parties, the witness said. In collusion with the cops, narcos would lure or kidnap women—or the cops would just do it themselves. The cops would first identify potential victims, study their routine, find out whether they had boyfriends or parents and whether anyone would notice if they were gone. It wasn't hard to lure the women—police would stop them on the street as they got off work and tell them that a family member was missing or something had happened to their child, and wouldn't they please get in the backseat of the police car? The cops would then transport them to the parties, where they would be gang-raped. By the end, the women always knew too much, and they were killed. They had to be discarded. The savage murders sometimes involved obscene mutilations. The cops, or other lackeys on the payroll, got rid of the bodies, dumping them in the desert.

"This isn't exactly news," Dante said as we drove one morning along the wide Eje Vial Juan Gabriel boulevard on our way to the border. Seeing the amazement in my eyes, he added, "Don't pretend to be so surprised."

I didn't say a thing. I had heard similar stories, but hearing about someone who'd claimed to be a witness caught me off guard.

"How can it be?" I asked. "Isn't Juárez the laboratory for democracy?"

Dante couldn't help but smile.

"Why are you looking at me like that," I demanded. The mountains of El Paso got closer. "Weren't you part of the citizen demonstrations for democracy?"

I reminded him of Francisco Barrio Terrazas and the young students, and the old men and women walking with canes, the younger women teetering on high heels, all of them shouting slogans for democracy, everyone carrying candles as they demanded an end to the one-party rule, as they dared imagine a more just and equal country.

"For Americans, everything is black or white, demons or angels. This is Mexico. You know that," he said. I took out my notepad and began writing.

"What are you saying?" I asked.

"Don't worry," he said. "You worry too much. The more you Americans insist on democracy, the more sewage you will find. This country has illusionary institutions and it will take decades to even begin to clean the shit."

"I thought you were fighting for justice."

"I'm just trying to get even," he said. Dante had a habit of evading questions.

As we reached downtown, Dante explained, "The cartel's henchmen are called 'La Línea.' That term is prohibited here. No one says it and yet everyone knows it. La Línea is the shadow that's growing over Juárez."

La Línea. The story, coming from one source—who would have to be nameless—would never get past my editors at the *News*. But I had something solid to work with.

"Tell me more about La Línea," I asked.

He put his sunglasses on and looked straight ahead, a sign he wasn't going to touch the subject for now.

It took weeks to verify the tip. Phil Jordan, the former agent in charge of the regional office of the DEA in Dallas, was from El Paso. He had worked with Kiki Camarena, and his own brother had been killed by what he suspected were drug traffickers intent on sending him a message. He had a score to settle. He showed me confidential reports listing a group known as "The Gatekeepers," the American name for La Línea, he said, who were working as drug distributors for the Juárez cartel. La Línea provided the muscle to protect the Juárez cartel and managed their distribution network.

"These guys are so powerful, they have immunity to kill anyone they want," Jordan told me. "Because they run the show. They are the show."

My colleague Ricardo Sandoval also helped me check out the tip using his mine of sources in Mexico City. Sandoval had well-placed contacts in the federal government, especially the prosecutor's office, run by President Fox's drug czar, José Luis Santiago Vasconcelos. Ricardo had been trailing Vasconcelos for weeks, jockeying for a seat next to him at a meeting, where he'd slipped him a note saying, "We need to talk." He'd responded, "Yes, very soon."

One late evening the three of us sat inside his office right off Paseo de la Reforma and talked about every cartel in Mexico except—conspicuously—the Juárez cartel and its enforcers. As we got ready to leave his office, I nudged Ricardo.

"What about La Línea?" Ricardo asked.

"Yes, we've heard of La Línea, but they've been quiet and haven't given us much trouble," Vasconcelos said, without elaborating. "It was great seeing you guys."

"So there is a La Línea?" I asked.

He tried to hurry us out the door.

"Wait, *licenciado,* please," Ricardo protested. "Just one more question. *Un ratito más.*"

"Your American counterparts have Juárez cartel capos listed as enemy number one. The U.S. is hunting down Juan José Esparragoza Moreno, 'El Azul,' " I added. "There is a billboard with his mug on it next to an El Paso mall on Interstate 10."

"You can't always believe your neighbors," he said, with his hand on the door. "Be careful, and don't get into trouble."

"*Así lo dejamos. Muchas gracias,*" Ricardo said as I wrote on my notepad and waved. "*Pero quisiéramos seguir el diálogo.*" We'd like to keep the conversation going.

Back at the border, I called Vasconcelos's man in Juárez, the federal prosecutor. Over lunch at a popular local chain restaurant, Barrigas, we'd check the facts of what I'd uncovered so far. The lunch crowd was noisy as I cut into a steak and washed it down with fresh lemonade. I told the federal prosecutor what I kept hearing over and over again about La Línea. Who were they? Did they have a role in the killings of those women?

The prosecutor looked at me and his face flushed. He said he had to get to another meeting. He abruptly got up and left the table, more than half his steak still steaming on his plate. I gestured to the waiter that I would be back and hurried behind him, calling for him to stop. I reached him as he was turning the ignition in his car.

"Be careful where and how you use that name," he said.

"So they do exist," I responded. "Talk to me about them."

"Just forget them," he said. He yanked the gearshift into reverse.

M others screamed, activists marched—the outcry directed at the crimes against women was deafening. But the government seemed unwilling to do anything: The traffickers were in charge here.

My stories generated attention in the United States and in Mexico. We even used "La Línea" in the lead of a story Ricardo and I coauthored. Still, no one was caught; no one was prosecuted. The day our story ran, a man dropped by the newspaper offices of El Norte in Juárez, which ran our story as well, and left a manila folder marked with block letters: MUY IMPORTANTE. EL SADAM SE LLAMA . . . The colleague said the message was probably one of Sadam's men mocking us and challenging us to write about him. We did. Nothing happened.

Sadam was one of the top hit men for La Línea. Some of the Mexican criminals liked to appropriate names of Middle Eastern strongmen—I presume, to mock the United States. I shrugged it off, even as a Mexican colleague warned me to be careful. Some of his reporters had been threatened before.

At a panel in Juárez sponsored by one of the dozens of NGOs that became involved in advocating for the women, I spoke about my newspaper's investigation into the murders. Following the presentation, a group of Mexican reporters came up to me and peppered me with questions about La Línea. Who were they? A group of rogue cops, hit men, gang members? Did it really exist? Had I made it up? Why was I giving Juárez a bad name?

I stared at them and didn't know who was more naive, them or me? Why were they asking me questions when they surely knew the answers? As I walked out of Juárez's old city hall, my phone rang and a man with a deep voice I had never heard before told me exactly where I was.

"Aquí voy detrás de ti por la dieciséis . . ." he said, then mentioning the street name, corner, the building. I could hear a radio in the background, as if the voice was coming from inside a car. The cell phone screen read "Unknown." I panicked, hung up and ran to Dante's office, which was nearby, across the street from a police station.

When I walked in, I was relieved to see him there and told him what had just happened. He leaned back in his chair, ran his hands through his shoe polish hair and stared at me, for the first time, with lines of concern on his forehead. He called in his son Irving, also a lawyer working there, and repeated the story. No big deal, they agreed. Irving told me it was likely someone trying to scare me, and then he left for a meeting.

It was a big deal, I thought.

Dante said La Línea must now be on to me, which meant the underworld of Juárez was on to me. The city of my youth was on to me. "Look, you have disturbed their universe," he said matter-of-factly. *"Ahora si ya te chingaste"*—Now you've really fucked yourself. "They're pissed and they will come after you to either kill or scare you, or your family," he said. "Somehow they'll send you a message."

"My cousin is a Juárez cop," I protested.

"I hope they don't know that, 'cause then he's fucked too," Dante said. "You're at least American. He's not."

The more I listened, the more I ached to return to El Paso. I had left my vehicle on the U.S. side because the speaking engagement was just blocks away in downtown Juárez. Now I was too afraid to walk out on my own. I stalled and asked more questions, hoping my heartbeat would slow down. I listened as he gave a litany of names of people who he said were in the pocket of the Juárez cartel. Dante's hands had been as dirty as anyone's. But at least he admitted it, and for some reason his honesty made me trust him.

This was the first time I had come so close to the cartels, listening to one of their voices on my phone. If they knew my cell phone number, what else did they know?

"Hey, I can drive you to the bridge," Dante said.

"But the police department is right next to your office—" I responded. "What if they see me?"

"You can lie down in the backseat," he offered. "You'll be okay."

He drove an SUV, so it was more like a back compartment. My instructions were simple: We would drive a few blocks past the police department, and then he would pop the back just short of the Santa Fe international bridge connecting Ciudad Juárez to El Paso. I would make a dash for the American side of the border.

We left his office. Dante popped open the liftgate and I crawled in. I suddenly thought—a bit too late—what if Dante is lying and he's planning to deliver me to the cops working for La Línea? Before I could say anything, he slammed the compartment door and got into the SUV and turned the radio on. He drove. I stared at the ceiling. He was now on his cell phone, talking to a client, catching up on a case.

The vehicle moved quickly, navigating streets right, left, right. As I lay motionless in the back of the SUV, I could see storefronts and guessed a familiar route—the same journey I used to make years before when I dreamed of being a musician by day and covered huge political rallies late into the night. I suspected we were driving through barrio La Mariscal, along Mariscal and Ugarte. The area was once synonymous with prostitution, because when revolutionary Francisco Madero and his men rode into Juárez, on May 10, 1910, prostitutes followed closely, cheering the men. The street was known then as Calle del Diablo, the Devil's Street.

I thought back to when I was in college, when Juárez had been a romance to me. I would sling my black guitar case over my shoulder, pop a Juan Gabriel cassette into my Walkman and listen to "He Venido a Pedirte Perdón"—"I've Come to Ask Forgiveness"—as if seeking forgiveness from the world I left behind. I'd make my way over the international bridge and the same song that had started me off in El Paso would still be playing when I reached the Strip in Juárez, an avenue packed with bars and brothels and hole-in-the-wall attorneys' offices for getting a quick divorce.

I would mostly avoid the Strip and detour toward El Noa Noa, the bar where Juan Gabriel got his start. There I'd make a right and then a left onto Avenida Mariscal, lined with smugglers, street jugglers, musicians, strip dancers and more prostitutes, and hotel rooms you could rent for the hour—just like the one across town where I had lost my virginity with a girlfriend I'd met at the community college I'd enrolled in after my mother had bribed me to get an education.

I'd head to a home that musicians had turned into a recording studio. I'd knocked on the black door, and a thirtysomething musician named Danny, his light-colored hair twisted into a long braid, swung open the door to let out a gust of marijuana smoke. He always seemed stoned. Inspiration, he called it. It was at that house studio where my friends and I laid musical tracks that we planned to record, led by our front woman, a tall, blond, blue-eyed, typically cute *güera* from Chihuahua. I played guitar and wrote the songs. Jacobo played percussion and guitar. Selena was not just our sexy singer but my inspiration—she'd wink at me when she sang.

When we weren't in Juárez recording, we would hunt for stories for the college newspaper. One day in early fall we drove up to the hills where new neighborhoods were sprouting indiscriminately and faster than the city could contemplate providing basic services like paved roads, lighting and water.

The loud, cracking sounds of construction were overwhelming. Houses built with the waste of other construction projects—concrete bricks if the owner was lucky; slabs of aluminum, plywood, even cardboard for those with less—bloomed in the desert beyond the city limits. In Juárez, the rich lived in high-walled compounds in the heart of the city, while the poor were relegated to the hills that climbed toward the mountains marking the city's western boundary. Thousands of people— up to fifty thousand per year, by some estimates—were flocking to Juárez for jobs in the booming Mexican border town and the possibility of work in *el norte.*

Yet something had felt wrong even back then. There was no plan for this kind of growth. The city had swelled from some three hundred thousand when I arrived in 1965 to more than a million, and there was no new visible infrastructure, no new parks, no movie theaters. Juárez was still the city of concrete in the middle of the desert that attracted investors, workers, smugglers and stragglers of all types. We interviewed a political leader in the community who was busy trying to organize the out-of-control growth. It's too late for Juárez, he'd told us. What we're doing is damage control.

It was 1983.

Dante was still glued to his cell phone, nonchalantly talking to his client, when he popped open the back door without leaving the driver's seat. I got up on my knees, looked around and saw nothing out of the ordinary. As I hurriedly stumbled out I couldn't remember feeling happier to see blue skies. I slammed the back door and waved back at Dante. He shouted:

"*Hay que tener huevos*—you've got to have balls. Don't let the intimidation get in the way of trying to find answers," he said. "Remember, you're an American." Then, unable to contain his sarcasm: "*¡Eso, cabrón! This is Juárez, chingao!*" he said, giving me a thumbs-up through the window as he drove off. I saw him pick up his phone again.

"I'll see you soon," I said wearily, and quickly jogged toward the Mexican customs station. I took a deep breath as I stepped onto the international bridge, with concrete embankments on either side. I took out my blue U.S. passport and my black iPod and scrolled to the song "Día Cero" by the Chilean rock group La Ley, turning the volume up full blast. I looked at the dried-up Rio Grande below me and, where the waters should have been, saw a graffiti portrait of revolutionary icons like Che Guevara and Pancho Villa telling the *migra*—the border cops— where to stick it. I glanced from the steel fence that lined the bridge. I felt an inexplicable high. Dante was right: I wouldn't let them scare me. But as I crossed the border and felt the fear evaporate, sadness set in. Juárez, like the rest of Mexico, felt foreign to me.

I talked to Dante many times after that day, but I never saw him again. Once he called to say he was in Mexico City and needed to talk to me. He sounded frantic; he believed assassins were after him. He was visiting federal agents to talk about the threats, to seek protection. His nephew had gone missing. I wasn't sure what I could do for him but offered to meet him at a local breakfast place down the street, Los Bisquets Obregón in Colonia Roma. I waited for an hour, and he never showed.

Days later he called again, proposing another meeting. He sounded like a man awaiting his death sentence. We agreed to meet again in Juárez. Despite all he had seen and knew, I heard panic in his voice. Fear. I wanted to remind him of the words he had said to me: "*Hay que tener huevos. This is Juárez, chingao!*" But he sounded so devastated that I thought it would be insensitive. Instead, I muttered:

"Are you okay? What's wrong?"

"I have some things I have to tell you," he said cryptically, words I scribbled in my notepad. "But not over the telephone."

I proposed we meet at a bar near the bridge where he'd dropped me off before. He agreed, but reminded me of an old rule: Touch base fifteen minutes before in case he had to change the location or time. Maybe we'd meet at his office?

Dante's anxiety made me nervous about meeting him there. I remained noncommittal but promised to call as planned. That day, he didn't answer at all. Still, I showed up at the Kentucky Club and waited more than two hours, nursing a tequila. I then walked back across the bridge, more worried than annoyed that he hadn't come.

Days later I took a flight back to Mexico City and heard the news: Gunmen driving a Ford Expedition with New Mexico plates had gunned down Dante with a 9-millimeter and AK-47. Witnesses reported the make and plates of the car; the cameras on the Juárez road where he was shot, which could have helped identify his killers, were suspiciously out of service.

I called friends in Juárez as soon as I heard. They said he might have been in some trouble with the Juárez cartel. A relative had gone missing, and Dante had gotten vocal about it, going so far as to mention La Línea on a radio program just a few days before he was killed. They didn't know why he had been killed, but it was enough, they said, to know that you don't mention La Línea in public.

I didn't have much time to mourn his passing. Mexico was coming undone.

THIRTEEN

U.S. Highway 83 in Texas is a lonely, curving corridor dotted with abandoned villages and fast-food joints. One of the main arteries of Los Caminos del Río—the River Roads—it cuts alongside the Rio Grande and through the city of Laredo. Founded in 1755, Laredo once served as a capital of the independent Republic of the Rio Grande, which was set up briefly in opposition to General Santa Anna.

In 1848, Laredo residents faced a decision. Following the U.S.-Mexico War, the United States gave residents in Laredo the choice either to stay on what was now U.S. territory, the north side of the Río Bravo, or to move south of the river to Mexican territory. Some stayed north, not so much out of loyalty to the United States but because they felt attached to the land. Many headed south to start fresh. They brought their belongings, their horses and cows; some even went to the cemetery, dug up the remains of their loved ones and brought them along to be reburied in Mexico in "Nuevo" Laredo. The region became known as Los Dos Laredos.

In the spring of 2005, I went to Laredo often to file dispatches of Americans kidnapped in Nuevo Laredo. I would usually avoid Nuevo

Laredo, even as I tried to dig up information about how the Zetas were changing the trafficking business model. I was foolish to think that the danger would keep to the south side of the border.

The economy in Los Dos Laredos depends on trade. It is the largest inland port on the U.S.-Mexico border, with four international bridges and one railway. The border faces the entrance of Interstate 35, "NAFTA Highway," and the giant U.S. market. Everything—from fruits, vegetables, TVs and blow-dryers to stoves, refrigerators, vehicles and drugs—makes its way from Mexico to the United States at this crossing point.

The two Laredos quickly became a hot spot for Mexico's cartels—especially the Zetas, which, in the fifth year of Fox's term, began consolidating their power in the region.

The Zetas began as an elite security detail for the leader of the Gulf cartel, Osiel Cárdenas Guillén, and as a paramilitary force to protect the cartel's business interests. Cárdenas Guillén, a former federal policeman, took over the legendary cartel after the U.S. government locked up his predecessor, Juan García Ábrego. Cárdenas Guillén didn't want to take any chances and assigned his trusted deputy, Arturo Guzmán Decena, the task of organizing a highly trained group of elite bodyguards to protect him and expand the Gulf cartel's reach beyond the state of Tamaulipas, which borders south Texas. Along the way he rid himself of smaller rivals across the region and declared war on the Sinaloa cartel, which had been expanding its distribution route in the Nuevo Laredo area.

Guzmán Decena was a Mexican army special forces soldier who defected to the cartels in 1997. He turned first to former soldiers, some of them from the Mexican special forces unit known as the Grupo Aeromóvil de Fuerzas Especiales (GAFE). The training the Mexican recruits got from the Americans wasn't comprehensive because there was some concern among top U.S. military officials that such extensive special operations training could one day backfire. So the United States limited what it taught the recruits. But the Mexican soldiers did learn intelligence gathering and infiltration techniques they would need to fight the cartels.

With his men, Guzmán Decena built Mexico's first narco army. Many of his soldiers came from impoverished backgrounds. The army had offered jobs; the cartel offered money and power. The three most trusted men within the Zetas were Guzmán Decena (Z-1), Rogelio González Pizaña (Z-2) and Heriberto Lazcano (Z-3); the Zs were code names denoting their ranking and seniority in the organization. These three men, along with new recruit Miguel Treviño Morales (Z-40), embarked on secret missions into cities and towns across Tamaulipas, including Nuevo Laredo. This was Treviño Morales's hometown and he knew the targets intimately. He gained the reputation of a traitor. They were there to execute Cárdenas Guillén's rivals and ensure that the Gulf cartel remained the most powerful drug trafficking organization in Tamaulipas and along Mexico's Gulf coast.

On a hot August morning in 2004, the gunmen rolled into Nuevo Laredo sporting powerful military-style weapons, some smuggled by veterans of the Gulf War, like AR-15s and .50 caliber machine guns. People were paralyzed. If you frighten your enemy enough with firepower, you may defeat him without having to actually fire so many bullets—just get the message across. From that moment, the Zetas controlled Los Dos Laredos.

One afternoon in 2005, I sat with the U.S. investigator along the border. We had met earlier that winter and quickly developed a bond. We had California in common. He was the son of a Mexican who had volunteered to fight for the U.S. government in World War II, which won his father U.S. citizenship. As a teenager, the investigator played linebacker and halfback for his high school football team. He had dreamed of becoming a U.S. agent, just like his hero, Kiki Camarena, the fallen DEA agent.

He was now a veteran investigator for the U.S. government. The Zetas—especially Treviño Morales, who went by the name El Cuarenta—dominated his attention. Cárdenas Guillén had been arrested in 2003 (he would eventually be extradited to the United States) and Guzmán Decena was killed in 2002.

The investigator had been following drug traffickers throughout Mexico for years, and he had studied the fraternal Sicilian model of organization that the cartels modeled themselves after. But the Zetas were different. They weren't businessmen. They were more militaristic, and they practiced unprecedented acts of barbarism with total abandon. They fed live victims to tigers; they chopped off heads and delivered them to doorsteps; they mutilated bodies and left them in public places. Rivals were trying to imitate them, recruiting and matching the Zetas in both brutality and violence. If the Mexican government did not confront them, the cartels would send the country over the edge, the investigator warned.

New rivalries between employer and employee, he predicted, would emerge between the Gulf cartel and the Zetas. At the time, the Zetas didn't have the contacts they needed with the Colombians to really move merchandise, but they could control distribution routes with force and charge a fee for anything that passed over "their" border, including migrants and drugs. The Zetas were like aliens in the world of organized crime, unpredictable and unknown. It was difficult to say what would come next from them.

The sun set over the Rio Grande as the U.S. investigator told me how deep the corruption ran between the Zetas and the Mexican government. Yes, the parties had changed, but all too often the same bureaucrats remained in their positions, their connections and fraternity with cartels virtually unchanged. Except for one big difference: The Zetas were more generous with payoffs and bribes, often paying as much as 30 percent of their earnings to key government officials. The U.S. investigator felt particularly frustrated with the Fox administration. Oftentimes he'd pass along tips to military generals and federal police about key criminal figures, but the tips went nowhere, or worse, got shared with the criminals themselves. Sometimes instantly.

As always, he was suspicious of the friendly waiter who wouldn't even let us finish our tequilas before he refilled our glasses. I needed to go, I said; I was meeting some friends.

Will Ramón be there? he asked.

Maybe, but he won't meet with you, I responded.

El Mañana is a family enterprise that includes my friend Ramón as publisher; his brother, Heriberto, a columnist; his sister, Ninfa, who worked as an editorial consultant; and his mother, also named Ninfa. She is an elegant representative of the paper's old guard and one of the most powerful media moguls in Mexico. Ramón was waiting for me at an upscale sports bar in Laredo called the Agave Azul. The bar counted among its clientele businesspeople, federal agents, congressional aides and a growing number of Mexican exiles already running away from the troubles across the river. Cecilia, my friend who'd been with Angela and me the night of the threat in Mexico City, was in town and joined us. At the time, she was living in El Paso, doing a research project in Juárez and writing magazine stories.

We found a table and were looking over the drink menu when a group of male twentysomethings sauntered in. They were dressed ostentatiously, like midranking henchmen, with their long black hair, baggy pants and gold chains. They walked toward a table near us and sat down. One got up to use the restroom; on his way back, he looked straight at me and pointed his finger as though he was cocking a gun. I wasn't sure I had seen correctly, so I asked Ramón, "Did he just do that?" I imitated the gesture. "That's probably the new greeting in Laredo," I joked.

No one laughed.

"I should go check on that," Ramón said.

Cecilia didn't like the idea of confronting the men and told us so. She warned Ramón that if he got up, she would leave. He stood up anyway.

"Alfredo, we should leave," she said.

"Cecilia, I'm starving. Plus we're on the U.S. side of the border," I responded. "Nothing is going to happen."

Ramón walked toward the bathroom, stopping first by their table. He extended his hand to the man I had pointed out. The man shook it. They exchanged a few words. Then Ramón continued on to the men's room.

"*No hay pedo,*" he said when he slid back into his seat. He seemed quieter, keeping any concerns to himself.

"Great," I said. "Let's order."

Cecilia was upset. She asked Ramón if he'd give me a ride. I handed her the keys to the car rental. She beelined for the door and left.

A moment later, the manager of the restaurant came over and politely suggested we leave. Ramón, annoyed, demanded to know why. He was well known in Laredo and not accustomed to such treatment.

"For your own good," the manager said. He tightened his jaw as if to say, "You know these guys as well as I do—now go."

I wished I had listened to Cecilia, followed her instincts. I tried to calm down Ramón.

"*Güey*, let's go. We'll catch up with Cecilia and grab a couple of burgers somewhere else," I said.

I grabbed my coat. Ramón was angry, and he followed me grudgingly toward the exit. I headed for the door, but Ramón was stopping every few feet to greet someone he knew—and he seemed to know everybody in both Laredos. Before I could grab Ramón and get us out of there, a waiter carrying a tray with two shots of tequila intercepted me.

"These are for you, Señor," the waiter said.

"You have the wrong people," I responded. "We didn't order any drinks. We're leaving."

"They are courtesy of the man in the corner," the waiter said, pointing to a man sitting at the bar, someone I had never seen before. The man gave a small wave, then started to make his way over. For a moment, I thought perhaps the tequilas were meant for Ramón, given his popularity. I told him the tequilas were probably his, but before he could answer, I felt a hand slapping me on my back.

The man, shorter and stockier than I am, which is all I can remember about his appearance, greeted Ramón briefly but kept his arm around my shoulder. Ramón got pulled into another conversation with a group of women standing next to us.

"I'm glad you're here again," the man told me in Spanish. "We appreciate your interest in our two Laredos. As you can see, there's a lot going on here. We're a friendly city, with great people and beautiful women. *¡Para que veas que tantas viejas guapas tenemos aquí!*" he said, nodding toward a group of women chatting with Ramón.

"Yes," I agreed, not sure who the guy was or whether I was supposed to know him.

"We treat outsiders well," he continued, "until they begin to ask questions about the Zetas."

I had been breaking news about the Zetas' brutality and ties to north Texas, their increasing violence and confrontations with local police. The man's grip on me tightened. I took a sip of tequila. Ramón caught on that this was more serious and moved closer to try to listen. I said little, just nodded my head, trying to keep my expression blank.

"Things can get crazy around here," the man went on. "Let me tell you what happens when people begin to ask too many questions: They pick you up, torture you, and then they slice you, a piece here, a piece there, and then they put your body inside a barrel filled with acid and watch you dissolve."

Disturbed, Ramón interrupted and told the man to stop.

"*Ya no chingues, compadre,*" he said. Stop fucking with him, man.

"Ramón, I'm just here to deliver a message," the man said.

The man looked me in the eyes and insisted.

"*¿Me entiendes?*" You got it?

I said I did, but added that my wife was waiting for my nightly call, and if she didn't hear from me, she had instructions to alert authorities. At that moment I wished I had a wife and a bunch of kids too, and dogs and a big yard to throw a football in. I wanted a normal life.

"Listen, if they want to kill you, no one will be able to help you, not even your U.S. government friend," the man said. The group of men who'd sat near us were just outside, he warned. I realized I had been so focused on this stranger that I missed their exit.

Motherfucker. I'm in Texas, for Christ's sake!

I quickly said I understood. I told Ramón I'd be right back. I walked toward the door, where the bouncer confirmed that a group of men were sitting inside a black Escalade in the parking lot.

I immediately spotted the SUV and saw the man who'd pointed his finger at me sitting in the front seat. I thought of calling Angela, but what would I tell her? I would only worry her. So I walked outside the restaurant and called Cecilia. Luckily she picked up.

"Cecilia, we have a situation here," I said. "I may need you to call the police, but not quite yet."

"Goddamn it, Alfredo, why didn't you leave with me?" she responded. "What's going on? I told you guys to leave. I knew this wasn't going to turn out well. What happened? I'm freaking out, Alfredo."

"I can't get into details now," I said. "But if I don't call you in ten or fifteen minutes, call the cops and send them here, okay?"

"Alfredo, what's going on?" she asked.

"Just give me fifteen minutes."

She urged me to call immediately.

When I went back inside the restaurant, the man was waiting for me. He had ordered another round of tequilas. Ramón stood next to him, looking at me with concern in his eyes.

"I hope I was clear," the man said. I told him he was. We stood there without saying a word. He sipped his tequila and quickly walked away. Ramón and I watched warily as he greeted other customers. The band Quinta Estación blared from the speakers, "Algo Más"—Something More.

We waited a few moments. I asked Ramón what we should do.

"Let's get the fuck out of here," he said.

I told him the men from earlier were parked in a black SUV outside. We waited a few more minutes and then saw that the women Ramón had been talking to were about to leave. We followed them out and chatted as if we were old friends—everything normal, routine. I lost sight of the mysterious man on our way to the door. Outside, I looked for the SUV but it was gone too. Ramón and I climbed into his white Chevy SUV and pulled out of the lot. I called Cecilia to let her know we were fine.

"Shit, you had me so worried, Alfredo," she said.

"Sorry," I said, trying to remain calm. "Everything is fine. Wanna eat?"

She said no and urged me to return to the hotel.

"Now what?" Ramón asked. "Want a burger?"

Clearly hungry for something normal again, I pointed to a burger joint on the next street corner.

"Yeah," I said. "There's a Whataburger over there."

Fear had morphed into adrenaline and hunger. We ordered jalapeño burgers, then headed out on Interstate 35 south to the hotel. A car pulled into the lane next to us. I looked suspiciously at the driver, who kept glancing at us. His right hand reached for what I thought could be a gun, and I cringed, yelling for Ramón to slow down. He hit the brakes, and so did the driver. I dropped my burger and the jalapeños. Then the man smiled at us as he put his cell phone to his ear and sped off. My heart felt as if it were beating out of my chest.

We got off at our exit and drove around the hotel parking lot to check for anything unusual, but everything seemed normal. We went into my room on the ground level. Ramón stretched out on the rug in my room, while I took a chair. We washed our burgers down with Dr. Pepper and talked some more, trying to piece together what exactly had happened, what the message was, if there was one. Ramón was still living in Nuevo Laredo and didn't want to cross back into Mexico just then.

I peeked out the hotel curtains to look for anything suspicious. Just trucks hauling goods on Interstate 35, heading north to Dallas, Minneapolis, the Canadian border.

The conversation turned philosophical as Ramón pondered how his country was changing. Not democratically, as we'd once imagined, but for the worse.

"Under the PRI," Ramón said, "we were censored but had enough freedom to make ourselves believe we were practicing real journalism. No one was threatening us or killing us, or targeting our families. There were rules that everyone respected. There weren't so many criminals, and if there were they didn't act the way they do today."

"We just didn't know, because they were part of the system," I said. "Now they don't fit so neatly anymore."

Ramón's grandfather, Don Heriberto Deándar Amador, had founded *El Mañana* in 1932. He was a communications pioneer in Mexico who'd served as a telegrapher during the revolution and later operated one of the first independent newspapers in Mexico. Once, fighting government censorship, he resorted to printing the newspaper across the border in Texas and distributing it in Nuevo Laredo.

It was easier then than now. Ramón had agreed to censor his family newspaper out of concern for his staff and his family after Heriberto was briefly kidnapped by the Zetas nearly a year before. Of the two brothers, the younger Heriberto was known as the thoughtful one, a serious editorial writer with big ideas. Stocky, handsome and confident, he had a clean-cut look that contrasted with his brother's bohemian air. He saw himself among the next generation of Mexican leaders. Ramón, on the other hand, made no secret about the fact that he oversaw the newspaper not so much out of a passion for journalism, but as a commitment to his family and his grandfather's legacy.

When Heriberto was kidnapped by the Zetas, Ramón secured his release with a call to a man he knew who was active in the cartel. The man made some calls and told Ramón that his brother would be freed shortly, but the new top bosses wanted a word with him. Ramón promised he'd show up at a meeting—once his brother was returned. Ramón wanted to send the message that his family was not afraid of the gangsters and had nothing to hide. Heriberto was returned that evening. Soon after, the two brothers got in their SUV and drove to a park, where the meeting had been arranged. After midnight, a dozen SUVs, pickups and cars pulled up.

The cartel men introduced themselves one by one. They wanted a deal, and the terms were simple, they said.

Number one, *El Mañana* was to become a mouthpiece for the Zetas. Two, *El Mañana* would no longer investigate drug traffickers.

Ramón, scared but keeping a straight face, told them: "*No chinguen*— don't fuck around. If I agree to become your mouthpiece, I'm signing my death sentence and that of my entire family. If you don't kill us, your rivals will. I'll agree to number two and that should take care of your first concern."

From then on, an "official" spokeswoman of the Zetas would communicate through a police reporter, dictating which stories about crime could run in the next morning's newspaper. The spokeswoman also warned reporters of consequences for bad behavior. Reporters, even within the paper, began to grow suspicious of one another.

I must have fallen into a deep sleep, because when I woke up, it was early morning and Ramón was gone. I called, woke him up and invited him for pancakes at the hotel. Cecilia joined us, relieved we were fine, but still angry we hadn't listened to her.

"We were really brave—*pendejos*, but brave! Until we realized we shit our pants!" Ramón said. He tried joking about the evening, to no avail.

Cecilia wasn't laughing. The three of us debated how these men knew who we were or that I had spent the afternoon with the U.S. investigator. The Zetas' lookouts were everywhere, I mused. Could have been anyone. The waiter?

I headed for the airport that morning. My editor wanted to see me in Dallas. On my way there, I called the U.S. investigator, who was frustrated that I hadn't called him during the incident.

"Call me next time, okay? That was a wasted opportunity. We could have picked up some of these guys, *carnal,*" he said. "Someone who could have led us to a bigger catch—El Cuarenta."

"Okay," I responded. "But don't you find it unusual that the whole thing happened on the U.S. side of the border?"

"Not at all," he responded. "This is their backyard. I'll check my sources, but it was probably Cuarenta's people."

A few months later, Ramón had swallowed his Mexican pride and moved to Laredo for the safety of his family after the threatening calls from the gangsters increased. They had even stopped at his house to check up on him or left him warnings at his office. They owned the city.

"Come see my new place," Ramón invited.

I did and also found he had a new toy, a dark gray Porsche, a reflection, he said, of his growing awareness of his mortality. Plus, he had opened a new location of his Nuevo Laredo bar in Laredo to follow the exodus of his clients. He offered to take me for a ride, destination: Padre Island. We sped down that lonely, curvy Highway 83, hugging the border, zooming past the spot where the U.S. highway almost dipped into Mexican territory.

Ramón drove quietly. He rubbed the small scar underneath his right eye, a reminder of when one of the Zetas had struck him with the butt of a rifle after Ramón tried telling them to behave at his Nuevo Laredo bar on New Year's Eve.

The Zetas wanted increasing control of the paper, he said. They also wanted control over photographs. In one instance, the picture of a Mexican federal investigator suspected of being associated with the rival Sinaloa cartel was printed in the newspaper—which the Zetas loved. But gunmen, likely from the Sinaloa cartel, retaliated by shooting up the *El Mañana* offices and throwing two grenades inside the building. Three bullets hit a reporter, paralyzing him. If the news of the day happened to please the Zetas, it pissed off Sinaloa. Ramón couldn't win. It is dangerous to be perceived as favoring a cartel because a rival cartel might kill you and blame the other side, Ramón lectured me. Then there was the issue of publishing real news. Ramón suspected that the accusation against the Mexican federal investigator had been leaked to a reporter in cahoots with the Zetas, who wanted to embarrass the Fox government. He fired two reporters and suspected others.

On the way to the island, every now and then Ramón would lower the music of Los Intocables to share his grief, the horror that had befallen his family and the pain of abandoning his hometown. Now everyone in his family—other than his mother, a stubborn, fearless woman—lived in Laredo. He felt at times he had betrayed his country, but what choice did he have?

"We're buried alive," he said. "We're still alive, but buried in some black hole."

We arrived in Padre Island that evening. He floored it as we crossed the Port Isabel bridge, watching the galaxy of stars above us. Jim Morrison howled "Roadhouse Blues" and Ramón pumped his right hand with his index finger pointed to the sky. The waters surrounding the island trembled in the darkness.

FOURTEEN

I picked up some beef tacos and brought them upstairs to the *News* office on Álvaro Obregón in the Colonia Roma neighborhood. We had a bona fide office—no more working out of our living rooms. I let my tacos steam in their aluminum foil as I sifted through my mail. I had been gone for weeks reporting in Laredo, and the stack of correspondence was tall.

A thick envelope stood out. I expected mail from someone I had been talking to for much of that year, a man who spoke fluent English and said he worked on "financial" matters for the Zetas. He'd alerted me he'd be sending a package in the mail. He often called when he was in Dallas or Houston, always teasing about meeting for coffee, with a message from El Cuarenta. Once I actually waited at a mall in Dallas and he never showed, explaining later that he thought I was an undercover fed.

"So why call me?" I asked.

"Keep your enemies close, like friends," he said.

"What's in the package?"

"Wait and see," he responded.

"Just don't send me a bomb," I said, and hung up.

As I drizzled salsa on my tacos I noticed that the return address on the envelope was from a newspaper in Tacoma, Washington. I brushed aside the bills and opened the package: a DVD and a note from the editors. No one spoke Spanish in the Tacoma newsroom, but they had been able to make out a few words on the video. They searched those words online and ran across my stories about the Zetas and Gulf cartel. They thought I might be able to decipher the material.

I popped the disc into my computer. In the video, four men stared at the camera. They'd been badly beaten. Off camera, other men accused and interrogated the four—apparently hit men for the Sinaloa cartel, according to the accusations. Black trash bags covered the wall behind them. One of the four, a smooth-faced young man wearing a red T-shirt, with close-cropped hair and a soul patch, looked straight into the lens and was the most animated. One by one they all calmly confessed to crimes, including the killing of a Mexican reporter who had doubled as the cartel spokeswoman, the same one who used to call Ramón's newspaper. She'd apparently threatened them she'd work for the competition, the Sinaloa cartel, if she didn't get a raise. The men, all Zetas, had pumped more than a dozen bullets into her. The confessors also identified future targets, including the Nuevo Laredo police chief, who by the time I watched the video had already been killed in a blaze of bullets, just seven hours after he took the job that no one else wanted.

The confessions suddenly ended. Someone off camera cocked a gun to the head of the man on the far right of the screen. His eyes were still until a bullet shattered his brain and he toppled forward. The three comrades quickly glanced at their fallen man, blood spilling from his left temple, then darted their eyes back to the camera.

My stomach churned as I watched the video, wanting desperately to stop it but knowing I needed to see it to the end. I pushed away the untouched tacos. I leaned my face toward the screen and rubbed my forehead.

The three remaining men poured out more secrets and named names, including planned assassinations and those already killed—some of whom had also been executed since the video was taped. The talkative one in the red shirt rambled on, as if he knew those would be the last words he ever spoke. Before they were shot, they also named moneymen for the cartel, those who paid cash to government contacts, including the man they said was responsible for keeping everyone else looking the other way, the one who made sure they were tipped off about raids or operations against them: Vasconcelos, Fox's top drug czar.

The video was postmarked from San Antonio. The men had made their last confessions from a beach in Acapulco.

I ran to Angela, who worked at the far end of the office, and told her about the video. Should we do a story?

Yes, she said, although somewhat hesitantly she asked, "What if they chop our heads off?"

"This isn't the Middle East," I responded. "It's Mexico."

"Okay, I'll work my sources," she said.

I immediately called the U.S. investigator. Too explosive, he said. Not over the phone. The editors gave me the green light to travel anywhere, anytime to verify it. Days later, the U.S. investigator and I met along the U.S.-Mexico border. He had seen the video, knew the contents by heart. But he wasn't interested in talking about who was behind the killings as much as he was about warning me about getting too ahead of a story that could have deadly consequences. It was an unusually brief meeting.

"Not telling you how to do your job," he said. "But *esto está carbón, amigo.*"

"Why?"

"This one I can't touch. Not now," he said. "I've been trying to hint at this for months. The shit is inside, and everywhere."

"Just tell me, is the video authentic, real?" I asked.

"It's on the mark," he said as he left. "Keep me out of it."

Angela and I worked hard to confirm the veracity and origin of the video. Now all I needed was for Vasconcelos to answer to the charges against him.

But for weeks he'd been dodging my questions. Three times his secretary had set up a meeting, and then he'd canceled. The more he stalled, the more convinced I became that he had something to hide.

He was the only source I needed to talk to before the story could run. Finally I tracked him down on the phone, bypassing his secretary, and I convinced him that the matter was urgent.

Someone says you're taking money, I told him.

He agreed to see me the next day.

I arrived at seven p.m., as instructed, and waited outside his office. He was usually worth the wait. The drug czar answered my questions head-on most of the time, except, of course, when he wouldn't discuss either the Juárez cartel or La Línea. But, generally, Vasconcelos was one of the few officials who wasn't afraid to go on record with information. It seemed he liked getting press almost as much as he enjoyed wearing tailored suits. There was a photograph of him and a supreme court team that had handled a corruption case against one of his predecessors. I waited nervously, fidgeting in the lobby while his secretary served me weak lukewarm coffee. More than four hours passed. I wasn't waiting alone; I had informed the president's office that I was working on a sensitive story about corruption inside the government, and I needed Vasconcelos to answer to charges. To make sure Vasconcelos didn't cancel for a fourth time, President Fox's office had sent a top press aide as an emissary, and he waited with me. I passed the time thumbing old magazines, alternately drinking the bad coffee and chewing gum.

When he finally opened his office door near midnight and invited us in, four of his close associates surrounded us. They were like goons, their eyes were trained on me. Vasconcelos, stocky and broad shouldered, looked serious; he wasn't cheerful, bantering the way he did other times.

He looked clearly bothered by the circumstances and perhaps by the hour. This is the last meeting of the day, he explained, so get to the point.

The DVD player had already been set up. Vasconcelos obviously knew what I had and he seemed prepared. Apparently he'd had the video for months. I wondered whether he'd seen it before the killing of the police chief.

Were the assassins members of the federal police?

Still under investigation, he said.

He pressed play and the faces of the hit men appeared. When the men in the video accused Vasconcelos of receiving tens of thousands of dollars in monthly bribes from a cartel, I asked Vasconcelos to stop the video. He did, then gave a brief lecture on the lack of validity of the charges and pressed play again.

"Total lies," he said, as I wrote his words into my notepad.

He had barely heard the accusation and began talking over the tape. The four Gulf Zetas in the video had been picked up by rivals of the Sinaloa cartel after they'd been discovered encroaching on the Sinaloans' territory, Vasconcelos explained, verifying a story I had heard from the U.S. source. I interrupted him and asked him to play the accusation again. He scowled at me. I told him politely that I wanted him to listen closely to the man making the accusation. I needed him to listen to the charges before he defended himself.

He fumed, met Fox's spokesman's eyes and replayed the charges against him. Vasconcelos paused the disc, took his round glasses off and gave me another lecture.

"They will say any lie, especially when they're being tortured," he said. "This is nothing new."

I stared at him, incredulous. In Mexico, the preeminent investigative strategy is to pick up, beat, torture and force people into confessions, and the top cop was now denying the practice.

Vasconcelos ended the interview and took me aside. His goons had disappeared. Fox's press aide waited by the elevator. Otherwise, we were alone.

"Corchado, this isn't a story for you," he said. "Why don't you focus on tourism stories. They're safer."

"Are you threatening me?"

"No. I'm trying to help you stay safe. I know you were born in Mexico," he said. "But don't bother yourself with the problems of a country that isn't yours anymore. You're an American now. Focus on other stories."

"Thanks. I'll be fair," I said. Was he genuinely trying to protect me?

I left the interview and headed to my car, jumped in the front seat and told Samuel to step on it. A white car was trailing us, Samuel warned, shaking nervously. He zigzagged through unlit streets, descending further into darkness. He drove until we couldn't see their headlights anymore. Samuel was convinced the pursuers decided to leave us alone after it became clear we'd received their message.

Vasconcelos's words haunted me on the ride home to Coyoacán and long after I'd gone to bed. I wanted to call Angela, who was traveling on assignment. But it was too late, and I didn't want to wake her. I walked over to make sure Betty and Zorro, her dogs, had water, then returned to our bedroom.

Angela was scheduled to return to Mexico City in the morning, and she planned to head straight to the drug czar's office to interview Vasconcelos on camera for the same story for her television audience in the United States. I slept late because I wasn't feeling well. I had the first signs of the flu, a raspy throat, and I noticed I had missed Angela's call. I heard the message she'd left as her plane was about to depart for Mexico City. I looked at my watch and realized she would now be in the middle of her interview.

"How was your interview?" her message said. "Hope it was worth the wait."

I began to write the story. Hours later I heard the dogs bark, a sign Angela was pulling in. I walked outside to greet her.

"How did it go?" I asked.

"He hated every moment," she responded. "But I got him on tape. He was sweating profusely. Story still running tomorrow?"

"Yep, I'm almost finished," I responded.

"All right, I'll finish my story too."

That evening, as we prepared to go to bed, Angela remembered to give me a message from Vasconcelos.

"He said, 'Tell Corchado to dedicate his time to other stories, like tourism,'" she said. "He told me to tell you to 'leave this story alone.' What did he mean by that?"

"I don't know. He said the same thing to me."

The next day, December 1, the story ran in the newspaper and Angela's version ran on Belo TV stations across the United States. The *News* also put the video, editing out the gruesome scenes, on our Web site. We knew it would be a big story, but neither one of us was prepared for what came next.

"Are you getting this?" Angela asked as we listened to a morning news show on the radio hosted by Carmen Aristegui, one of Mexico's most respected journalists. Our story dominated the newscast.

"Yeah," I replied. "Don't worry. Let's just keep a low profile."

"I just got a call from a source. He wants to see me as soon as possible," she said. "It's about the story."

I felt weak, tired. My bones ached.

"I'll go with you," I offered.

"But you don't look well," she responded.

"I'll ask Samuel to come along," I said. "I'll be fine."

We drove to the neighborhood of La Condesa, where I grabbed a table outside at a restaurant and drank hot tea. I stared at the joggers going round and round in the park under the bright December sun, while counting every second Angela was away with her confidential source at a nearby restaurant.

She returned half an hour later, her face solemn. I was eating chicken soup with avocado and red chili on top. Angela asked for a bowl too.

"What's wrong?" I asked.

"This is serious," she said, explaining that her source advised her to leave the country as soon as possible. "They—the military, the government or both—could make life difficult for us. They're capable of anything," she said. "And they'll make it look like a car accident."

"What are you talking about?" I asked. "The government, the military?"

Were we faced with a situation like the one faced by Manuel Buendía, the Mexican journalist gunned down in the eighties by Mexican intelligence officials after he'd disclosed ties between alleged CIA-blessed cartels and the military?

"That's what I'm told," she said. "The guy asking the questions and executing the men on the video was a cartel member, working with members of the military or the federal police. I don't know, I don't know. What did we get ourselves into?"

Maybe the sources were right—they were feds and soldiers working for one of the cartels, something we had been unable to substantiate, but would be confirmed later.

I put my hands to my face and rubbed my temples, trying to rationalize the situation. My soup suddenly didn't look very appetizing. My cell phone vibrated, interrupting our conversation and the moment. A blocked number. I answered anyway. A voice on the other end growled, "Eat your soup now or eat your soup later. We like our soup cold—or hot, motherfucker."

The line clicked.

I told Angela what they'd said. She winced. My eyes darted around at the park. Could it be the man sitting on the park bench or the jogger slowly passing by? Or the guy selling mangos, jicama, watermelon? The man walking his dogs, or the one parking cars? Or was it the man who'd glanced at us suspiciously and quickly walked away. I asked for the check.

While we waited to pay, I called a private investigator we had previously consulted with on personal security issues. He asked us to call his contact at the U.S. embassy. I got a busy signal. Instead I called Samuel, who was just a block away; he picked us up and we sped toward Coyoacán. Angela watched the rearview mirror. I called my editors in Dallas. They ordered us to leave Mexico as soon as possible—on the next flight.

On our way home to pick up our suitcases, I told Samuel to keep his eyes open for anything suspicious, and if anything seemed out of order to head straight for the airport. We made it home. Angela made arrangements with our cleaning lady to care for the dogs for an indefinite amount of time. I packed our bags and we rushed out within minutes. We were suddenly headed for Cambridge, Massachusetts, to attend a nonfiction narrative writers conference that our editors, at the suggestion of a colleague, had found for us. It would be safe to detach, my editor explained, until we could come up with a plan for what to do next. Stay away for a while. Christmas was coming. Take a vacation.

Vasconcelos's words pierced through me again as I pulled out my U.S. passport at the airline ticket counter: *This is not your country anymore.* Maybe it isn't. Maybe it never was.

In late summer of 2006, I accompanied Vicente Fox on his last presidential trip across Mexico. After the threats that had sent Angela and me running, I returned to Mexico and kept investigating stories that would all point to one direction: the rise of organized crime. Fox and I had maintained a cordial relationship throughout his administration. He was a likable man and I found his candor, no matter how brash or raw, refreshing. During the end of his term, however, he repeatedly balked at the *News*'s crime reporting.

Fox didn't want the story of drug violence tarnishing the image he was trying to establish for Mexico: that of a rising democratic nation. Foreign coverage of Mexican drug cartels' growing power had angered Fox, his staff and law enforcement officials. During meetings with reporters and editors of the *News,* including me, Fox insisted that Mexico was humming along. The growing menace of criminal organizations was something Fox either couldn't or wouldn't see.

Journalists were making way too much out of small pockets of violence, Fox contended. Sure, a few outlaws had gained power replacing Colombian drug traffickers, but they would soon be put in their place. Mexico was no monster—just another country grappling with political change, a transition in process, like so many other emerging democracies around the world. He helped professionalize the federal police, created a national police force modeled after the FBI, and continued a long-term trend to militarize domestic security by appointing an army general to attorney general. He brought down Osiel Cárdenas Guillen in 2003 and later the brothers Rámon Eduardo Arrellano Félix—killed in a confrontation with police—and Benjamin Arrellano Félix, captured in the state of Puebla. Both were leaders of the Tijuana cartel. He'd also sent out the military to control disturbances by organized crime before recalling them back to the army barracks right before the July 2006 election. The action against cartels only led to increased violence.

Now in the airplane cabin, Fox sat alone, staring out into space. I took a seat next to him. Fox's tone had changed. He seemed humbled, somber, no longer wore that bravado I had known for more than a decade. Fox seemed tired.

"How's Dallas?" he asked.

He seemed to perk up talking about Dallas, a city that many of his friends from Guanajuato now called home. "I like Dallas. You know, the people I grew up with ended up going to Dallas."

He usually repeated the same story. I'd nod my head and wait for him to stop. I asked how he felt about leaving office.

"I look forward to returning to the ranch," he said. "I miss the ranch."

I put my notepad away and sat with him, finishing up a shot of tequila he had poured. He stared at the clouds outside the presidential plane and lamented the growing uncertainty in the country. The story wasn't just a caprice of the foreign press but increasingly the Mexican media too. This was no longer bloodshed isolated along the border; it was seeping into corners of the country. The violence couldn't be overlooked anymore.

I asked him whether he worried about the violence spreading throughout northern Mexico.

Fox said, in Spanish, "Dark clouds await Mexico."

"What took you so long to realize it?" I asked.

Fox simply shook his head.

"The country's transition, the democratic consolidation is under way," he added, his eyes on the land below.

I returned to my seat next to the correspondent from the *Financial Times,* and from our view above I could see Paseo de la Reforma, the magnificent boulevard modeled after Paris's Champs-Élysées, and got a glimpse of the Zócalo, the central square where I had wandered on the desolate New Year's Eve in 1994 when Mexico's economy was falling apart and I had first come to Mexico as a correspondent. I had spent so many hours in that ancient square, marveling at the majesty and mystery of Mexico's culture, walking through the excavations of the Templo Mayor, the Great Temple of the city the Aztecs called Tenochtitlán.

Now, as the plane approached the runway, we could see how that avenue and that same square were packed with protesters demonstrating their discontent with the incoming "illegitimate" president, Felipe Calderón. The protests were signs of the deeper divisions growing across the country.

History had finally caught up, if not with Mexico, certainly with me.

FIFTEEN

At his first press conference as president-elect in September 2006, Felipe Calderón looked like a man with a plan. Short, balding, forty-four years old, the son of one of PAN's founders, Calderón was supposed to consolidate Mexico's democracy and finish the job Vicente Fox had barely begun. After sixty days of suspense, he had been formally declared the winner in the closest presidential election in Mexican history. He'd won by less than 1 percent of the vote. Twenty years after he'd protested in Ciudad Juárez over stolen gubernatorial elections, Calderón was now the second consecutive PAN candidate to win the presidency.

At that press conference, Calderón talked about his plans for Mexico and reiterated his efforts to reach out to the losing candidate, Andrés Manuel López Obrador, from the PRD, the left-leaning third party. It was clear López Obrador had no intention of stepping aside. He started calling himself the "legitimate president" of Mexico and refused to accept Calderón's triumph.

But another story was dominating the headlines.

The night before the press conference, six men covered in black hoods had walked into the Sol y Sombra bar in Uruapan, Michoacán—Calderón's home state. Carrying canvas sacks dripping with blood, the men stepped inside and abruptly turned the music down. A hush came over the lively bar filled with men and prostitutes. Then, like bowlers in a bowling alley, they opened the sacks and rolled five severed heads onto the dance floor. People screamed.

The men left a banner: *"La Familia no mata por paga, no mata mujeres, no mata inocentes. Se muere quien debe morir. Sépanlo toda la gente: Esto es Justicia Divina."* La Familia does not kill for money, does not kill women, does not kill innocents. Those who die are those who need to die. Let everyone know: This is Divine Justice.

La Familia was a criminal organization in Michoacán that had been formally allied to the Gulf cartel and was now demonstrating its independence in the most unusual way. The leader, known as "The Craziest," carried a bible of his own beliefs and preached a divine right to eliminate enemies.

When a reporter asked Calderón what he thought about the heads rolling on the dance floor, he looked as though he thought this was his chance to put the election dispute behind him. Calderón acknowledged publicly that something was indeed threatening the country's security. Organized crime had to be stopped. The Mexican state had to reclaim territories threatened by drug traffickers.

Past Mexican presidents had vowed to fight crime and corruption and never did much beyond the rhetoric, but Calderón seemed genuinely determined to do something. Would someone finally push for real change in Mexico? An end to official corruption and collusion with drug traffickers? The way Calderón was talking, it certainly sounded like it.

I scribbled in my notebook: "He gets it. He really does."

Calderón had to act fast. Police agencies would have to up the ante and earn respect as law enforcers, not as thugs; judges would have to follow the law and not set a revolving price for their services. Reforms were needed to revamp the judicial system to ensure suspects would be considered innocent until proven guilty and that the practice of imprisoning scapegoats would end.

Unlike his predecessor, Calderón sounded defiant, stubborn, angry. For real democratic change to happen in Mexico, for Mexico to reach a new stage of economic and political development, the country would have to face down its demons, create a judicial system that functioned according to the rule of law and rid itself of the culture of impunity that had reigned since the country's cry for independence nearly two hundred years earlier.

Calderón echoed the revered Mexican president Benito Juárez, Mexico's first indigenous leader, who believed in making Mexico a country of laws. The nineteenth-century liberal favored democracy, individual liberties and the separation of church and state, and his legacy shaped the thinking of Mexico and Latin America. Unlike Juárez, Calderón had a Catholic streak. Friends described him as doctrinaire, a man of deep convictions and principles, a man distrustful of his own shadow.

How Calderón would face the narcos cut to the core of Mexico. What good was sovereignty when drug traffickers gradually and deliberately held the country hostage? Corruption in the system was endemic. Mexico would need its neighbor to the north.

While the United States might be admired for its efficiency, democratic principles and entrepreneurial spirit, the country was difficult to trust when it came to Mexico's business. During the revolution the United States had sent troops to the border, and they'd crossed into Mexico twice: once to chase Pancho Villa after he'd invaded Columbus, New Mexico, and a second time to occupy the port of Veracruz. The U.S. flag had flown over the Palacio Nacional once. Asking the United States for help would be anything but an easy sell in Mexico. Mexicans, unlike Americans, have a long memory. Even when polls showed sovereignty was losing its importance for sectors of the Mexican population, the political establishment still used the issue to generate nationalist fervor.

. . .

Two Americans would be key for Calderón in overcoming this history: Tony Garza and Roberta Jacobson. The two couldn't have come from more different backgrounds. Garza grew up in Brownsville, Texas, and, like most border residents, had spent his childhood crossing back and forth. His parents were from south Texas, but his grandparents came from Mexico. Garza's father served in World War II and owned a gasoline station just around the corner from the international bridge that led to the border town of Matamoros, a city named after Mariano Matamoros, a young activist priest who fought during the War of Independence and was later executed by the Spanish Crown. Garza was proud of his Mexican roots but often repeated that "only in Texas can the son of a filling station owner grow up to be chairman of the commission that regulates an $80 billion energy industry; and where else but in the United States can the grandson of immigrants return to their home country as U.S. ambassador?"

Jacobson came from a long line of Jewish public servants in New Jersey. A frustrated dancer and student of political science, she became fascinated with Latin America in the 1980s. Jacobson spent a summer in Argentina as a twenty-five-year-old graduate student from Tufts, and she became hooked on Latin America. Through her career in the State Department, she had worked in or studied countries from Colombia to Peru to Cuba. As head of the Mexico office at the State Department, Mexico was the latest challenge—and, she would find out, her most important one.

Jacobson was a Northeasterner and Washington insider. Garza was a border boy, a Texan whose name was periodically whispered as a possible gubernatorial or senatorial candidate. He didn't like Washington, but had the ear of the president. Garza worked in Mexico City, and occasionally made trips to Washington. "He hated Washington," said Jacobson. "I knew that and asked him to engage only when I needed his political advice; he appreciated my navigating Washington for him when I could. We each appreciated the other's irreverence."

Garza was pleased with Calderón's speech. Garza had been alerting authorities on both sides of the border about the cartels' menace to Mexico since he had become America's top diplomat in the country. The information came not just from his own intelligence sources along the U.S.-Mexico border and in Mexico City but also from his childhood border buddies. The situation was worsening. The United States had to step in, the way it did in 1995 when the Clinton administration led the massive bailout to rescue Mexico's economy.

"A major initiative could be to security what NAFTA had become to their economy, and when you combine security and growth what you have is a shot at prosperity," Garza shared with me.

Not a week after Calderón's first press conference, Garza, accompanied by his wife, Maria Asunción Aramburuzabala, at the time the wealthiest woman in Latin America and owner of companies like Corona, visited Calderón and his family at their home in the Pedregal section of the city. They spoke late into the evening. Inauguration was still months away, but the president-elect already faced questions of legitimacy as well as of narcos running amok. His rival, López Obrador, continued to mock him, calling him "Presidente Espurio," or "the false president."

Garza and Calderón were fond of each other. Garza had followed closely his boss and friend, George W. Bush, during and after the legal challenges following the 2000 U.S. election. He felt empathy for the murky situation facing Mexico and Calderón. That evening Calderón asked about Bush: What was he like?

"He's direct. He's honest and he values that in others," Garza told him.

As the night wore down, the two men talked over tequilas about the violence engulfing Mexico. Garza cut to the chase.

"Look, Mr. President, I want you to know that the president of the United States will stand firmly behind you. And if you ever need anything, you can call me at anytime," Garza said.

Calderón thanked him and walked him to the door.

In a follow-up meeting at PAN headquarters, the two men again talked about Mexico's deteriorating security situation. Calderón was being briefed by consultants, U.S. and Mexican experts and intelligence officials, including the man who would become his ambassador in Washington, Arturo Sarukhán. The message: Police departments, city halls, civil society, the press—just about every functioning institution in the country—were being increasingly infiltrated by the cartels. Washington would listen if he took the fight to the narcos, the advisers told him.

The president-elect himself had received warnings that he was at the top of a hit list. Intelligence had revealed that a cartel had accessed the president's personal medical records and schedule as they searched for his weakness. Calderón later acknowledged that, following a threat to his life, he'd taped a message to his children "in which I assured them that in case something happened to me, they should be sure of knowing that their father was carrying out work which he felt to be necessary."

Now, at PAN headquarters, Calderón immediately cut through the pleasantries.

"What does American help include?" Garza recalled Calderón asking. The president-elect was particularly worried about his family.

"Whatever it means for your family to be safe," Garza responded. "We want to make sure that you know we're doing everything possible to ensure that your family is safe."

On November 8, 2006, Calderón flew to Washington for his first meeting with President Bush.

That brisk autumn day, I had followed Calderón to Washington and waited outside the White House with other reporters. The last dead leaves had fallen on the lawn. I had heard speculation that Calderón would ask for help on security matters, but I was prepared to write the typical story about Mexico's call to protect its sons and daughters living in the United States without documentation.

But it became clear that the days of calling for better treatment of Mexican workers in the United States and comprehensive immigration reform—something virtually every Mexican president had insisted on since Lázaro Cárdenas in the 1930s—were over, for the moment. At least publicly, Calderón wouldn't push the issue aggressively, as his predecessor had.

He envisioned a new chapter in the bilateral relationship. Mexico and the United States were about to be more than "distant neighbors," as *New York Times* correspondent Alan Riding had suggested years before in his book of the same title. The visit was supposed to be symbolic, a standard first meeting between two democratically elected presidents of neighboring countries, despite the enduring doubts; a chance to pose for photographers, swear cooperation and shake hands. It became anything but.

In the Oval Office, Garza stayed within earshot as the two leaders spoke. Calderón got directly to the point. He described the situation in Mexico in blunt terms. He compared Mexico to opening a body, thinking that all he had to do was find the tumor and surgically remove it. Instead, he'd found a body rotten to the core from years of corruption. The cancer had spread. He proposed the unimaginable. Breaking all protocol dating back generations and swallowing his own strident nationalism, Calderón told Bush that Mexico needed the U.S. government to partner with Mexico to restore security.

"I'm ready to do my part," the president-elect told Bush, a line he had practiced with Garza beforehand. "But I need a partner."

Bush looked Calderón in the eyes.

"I'm ready to be that partner," Bush responded.

Bush read Texas newspapers and had been briefed by close aides, particularly Garza, that drug traffickers were bullying Mexico. But even then he hadn't expected Calderón to be so bold. Bush, aides said, instantly took a liking to Calderón because he was direct and exhibited none of that wishy-washy diplomacy he had grown weary of in Fox and his advisers. With this historic opportunity to deepen the bilateral relationship and reflect the growing demographic and cultural bond between the nations, the former governor of Texas said the United States was prepared to help Mexico in whatever way Mexico needed. He asked Calderón to draw up a plan. What exactly did Mexico have in mind? Calderón told Bush he would get back to him with details. Calderón, Garza recalled, jokingly added, "If Jack Bauer's got it, I need it." The two men shook hands and agreed to meet again, formally, and with more specifics.

Calderón departed, and President Bush called on his friend Garza to hold back. Bush knew Garza from the days when Garza was campaigning as a Republican for county judge of Cameron County in south Texas. On trips to the White House, Garza often stayed as a guest and the two men talked politics over cigars and drinks—nonalcoholic beer for Bush, single-malt scotch for Garza.

"Is this Colombia-like?" Bush asked Garza, after Calderón left.

"Yes and no. It could be just as serious and get there real quickly, Mr. President," Garza recalled, adding, "Colombia on the Texas border."

Just days before his inauguration, on his last flight as president-elect from the northern state of Sonora, Calderón and his team huddled. Calderón asked his military advisers to give him a demonstration of their weapons and asked a litany of questions, including which weapons worked best under an assortment of circumstances, like at night or in rough terrain. He was headed for war.

A month later, Calderón wore the commander in chief's army cap—it seemed too big for him—days after he deployed 7,000 soldiers and agents, 29 helicopters, 17 planes and 240 vehicles to his native Michoacán. More states and more troops—as many as 45,000—would follow.

American officials were blindsided by the news. They had expected a follow-up meeting with Calderón to discuss strategy, ways the United States could assist. While the Americans were eager to help, they had their hands full in Iraq and Afghanistan. They were reluctant about committing to another conflict, especially one next door, and especially without proper preparation, with decades of deep mistrust between the partners.

The two governments came together in March 2007 in the colonial city of Mérida, in Yucatán, to talk strategy. Bush had just arrived from Guatemala, where the president had pleaded with him to send U.S. special forces; the narcos were threatening to bring down the government there. The situation in Mexico was not much better, despite Calderón's continuing show of force. Bush conferred with his people, as Calderón did with his own aides and ambassador. Both men were preparing to discuss privately U.S. assistance to Mexico. Garza approached Calderón and said, "Can I have a moment with you?" He walked him over to Bush, grabbed the two presidents' arms and brought them together.

"I thought the moment right there and then would set the tone for so much of what would follow and I wanted to make sure they looked each other in the eye and they understood each other and we got the language of the partnership right," Garza said.

After the two governments had met in Mérida, Garza and Jacobson went to work.

I broke the story in May 2007 after hearing it from a source during a White House Correspondents' Dinner. I checked with sources on both sides of the border and wrote my piece about the initiative before it had been made public. Soon, Mexico's attorney general, Eduardo Medina

Mora, was on the phone, calling from Madrid, where he was on official business. He wouldn't say much, but the fact that he was calling from Europe at midnight confirmed a lot. I had lunch with Jacobson, but she downplayed the story. Something was up, I figured.

Foreign minister Patricia Espinosa had a meeting with her counterpart, Condoleezza Rice, accompanied by the Mexican ambassador and the head of intelligence. Espinosa gave Rice a PowerPoint presentation in May that covered three areas: what the Mexicans would do, what they thought the United States should be doing and what both governments could do together. From the Americans, the Mexicans wanted a ban on assault rifles, plus provision of heavy artillery, helicopters and planes. It was, essentially, a shopping list. Espinosa looked unprepared, stumbling over her words so much that she turned the meeting over to the two other members of her team. They explained what Calderón had essentially told Bush months before: The cancer of organized crime had spread across Mexico. They needed arms to fight it. The meeting, over tea and coffee, lasted no more than an hour.

Days later, a group of State Department officials, including Jacobson, were dispatched to Mexico City to meet with key counterparts who were to lead the strategy of recuperating areas that had been taken over by cartels. The meeting took place in the afternoon in a colonial home in Coyoacán. The rainy season hadn't arrived yet, but the humidity was high. It didn't take long for Jacobson to realize that the Mexican officials were all coming in shifts, and no one knew what the others were doing. No one really trusted anyone.

Garza had already gotten a glimpse of the mistrust firsthand. When Calderón wanted to communicate with him, someone from the president's office would call and ask where he was. "I'd tell them and then suddenly a member of Calderón's most trusted security team would show up with a secure radio phone and hand it to me to talk to the president," Garza explained. "What I saw was a guy who didn't trust anyone going into a situation where he shouldn't trust anyone—I'd say his wariness served him well those first days."

Jacobson didn't like the compartmentalization of information in the new administration, but the United States didn't have a choice. In July, the State Department hosted an interagency meeting with over one hundred key players from both countries in Washington to talk equipment and judicial reform and more important to work on building trust not just between both countries but among the Mexicans themselves. Soon after, Jacobson was assigned to put together a supplemental aid package, working late hours to do so. She quietly lobbied key members of Congress, like Christopher Dodd, all the while pressing everyone to keep it a secret from reporters.

She appeared in eleven congressional hearings and walked around Capitol Hill with a crumpled map showing the 235 U.S. cities where Mexican cartels were active. She cornered congressional leaders in the cafeteria, the elevator—anywhere she could. She especially stalked members of appropriation committees and key legislative directors, pointing to cities in their district. "I had to go see all of these members and staff who had never paid attention to Mexico, and in a way it probably helped to have a Northeastern woman trying to explain to them why this mattered," she said. "I wasn't Mexican American. This wasn't actually my life. I didn't grow up on the border, but it still matters. And in a way I had extra credibility to explain to them why this matters, because I didn't grow up there. Because part of what we were trying to overcome was the notion that essentially this is a provincial problem, it's a border problem, but in fact what we had to demonstrate was that it's a national problem."

Garza and Jacobson faced a barrage of questions from members of Congress and the Bush administration. Was the problem that serious? What would U.S. assistance mean, and for how long? Are we putting money into a corrupt country? Where will it end up? Was Mexico strategically prepared?

On one occasion Garza visited Bush and questioned Washington's resolve to help Mexico. Bush immediately picked up the phone and called his senior advisers. When he was on the phone with Rice, Garza recalled, the president asked, "Condi, my man Garza is here and I want to know, are we focused on this, or not? Are we doing all that we can?"

Garza added: "Bush was heartfelt about Mexico. I knew this was important to him. Without Bush's commitment, we would have been pissing in the wind."

Jacobson also spent hours talking to Mexican foreign ministry officials in Washington, particularly Sarukhán, the ambassador, a favorite among many on Capitol Hill since his days as an embassy official. He stood out with the British accent he'd acquired at Oxford. He loved quoting Dickens, using the line *"It was the best of times, it was the worst of times"* to describe the bilateral relationship.

Jacobson made sure her counterparts knew what Mexico was getting into.

"Make sure you ask the Colombians first what it's like to receive U.S assistance," she'd warned Sarukhán and others. Be careful what you ask for. After all, Mexico was loath to meet any U.S. demand—simply because those demands came from its neighbor to the north. Any financial help from the United States would come with strings attached—subject to strict rules and oversight by Congress. The $8 billion in aid to Colombia since 1999 had been overseen by prickly U.S. congressional committees that questioned everything from corruption to human rights violations. Mexico would have to agree to uphold human rights and strengthen police training, judicial reform and the rule of law.

Then there was the issue of trust, as always.

"The Colombians were not only never ashamed of their relationship with us, they were damn proud of it," recalled Jacobson. "They wanted as many Americans in there, and to hell with sovereignty. They were going to take their country back—they weren't worried about being seen with us. Mexico is still ambivalent: 'We want to be seen with you, but could you stand over there?' People here in Washington understand that. And most people are sympathetic to that—the political culture that would not respond favorably to being in your face. We have a history with Mexico that we don't have with Colombia. But every once in a while you have to realize that American officials wonder, 'Do the Mexicans want our help or don't they?' "

B ack in Mexico, according to Attorney General Medina Mora, the president lived up to his micromanaging reputation. At times Calderón personally cleared the press statements. He'd call to inquire which, if any, big capo had been caught the night before. The administration seemed determined to make splashy headlines. Medina Mora had other worries. He was particularly concerned about the country's ability to gather intelligence. Before serving as attorney general, he had been head of the nation's intelligence agency; under Fox, that agency had been gutted, because agents had been involved in political espionage against Fox as a candidate. And now the country had little intelligence to help in its fight against the cartels.

Óscar Rocha, a Mexican intelligence official, sat through some of the most crucial meetings to discuss the country's security situation. He came to one conclusion: The threat from organized crime was real. For years, voices had been lobbying for the federal government to take a greater role to combat corruption and cartel members. This cancer had been there for so long that the patient was virtually dead. Yes, they needed to revive it, but it would take years of rehabilitation to fully respond to the treatment. Often Rocha wondered whether this was a real war, or just the beginning of a tragic miscalculation by a young administration seeking legitimacy. Rocha cautiously hoped for the best, but he also knew the chances of any success against the cartels and the broken Mexican system were slim to none.

He later noted: "As we shouted 'Charge!' and headed up that hill, I realized we weren't riding on horses, but on donkeys. Forget our weapons—we didn't even have a saddle. And when we looked in back of us, the cavalry was headed in different directions."

PART III

SIXTEEN

July 2007

Tentative rays of sun reached across the ocean horizon at dawn, shining on streets covered by puddles from the rain the night before. It was the morning after what had felt like a farewell party—the cowboy and his girlfriend dancing on the sidewalk near the porch of the woman grilling tacos, our impromptu sing-along inspired by Juan Gabriel. I was leaving Mexico for what I feared in my heart would be a long time. At the first light of dawn the year of my fourth threat, I was checking out of the Cielo Rojo in San Pancho with a ticket to Texas in my green duffel bag.

Before sunrise I sped to the Puerto Vallarta airport and caught a flight to Dallas, where I connected to El Paso. From above, I watched Mexico's colorful countryside grow distant, the ravines, the green fields, the volcanoes, all quiet now.

My parents met me at the airport. My father, who generally seemed to talk less the older he got, seemed especially inquisitive about the situation in Mexico. My mother stood at his side, happy as she always was when I came to stay for a few days. I knew she'd probably already planned meals for a week—*huevos a la mexicana* for breakfast, *fideo* or *enchiladas verdes* for lunch, without the cream, the way I liked them.

I had no plans to tell them about the past seven days, my fears, my discontent and my sense of betrayal. But I didn't consider that they would have already heard the news. The threat against an unnamed Texas journalist had made headlines in the United States.

"Who was it?" my father asked.

Talking about Mexico wasn't in the cards. I put on my poker face.

"That's still under investigation," I responded, not sure what to say without outright lying.

My father knew better. I saw the disappointment in his eyes.

"You remember what I told you, right?" he asked. "The promise you made me?"

I didn't answer immediately.

I could feel his eyes on me as we walked out of the airport, but I avoided his gaze and ushered my mother toward the parking lot. I changed the subject.

"Hmm, how about a burger with jalapeños? Just as a snack," I said, careful not to offend my mother. I drove us out of the airport and headed for the border. I had no plans to cross, but just a few blocks from the bridge on the U.S. side was our favorite Mexican bakery, Bowie's. We could pick up some *pan dulce* there, and swing by to get burgers on the way, I pleaded. She agreed.

It was afternoon, no clouds whatsoever in a deep blue sky. I turned onto South El Paso Street. I glanced at a storefront Chinese takeout place: The old original site of Freddy's Café made me nostalgic—my mother carrying bowls of *menudo,* my baby sisters wiping plates with rags, my brothers and I taking orders from faithful customers. The block had changed, but it still swarmed with shoppers, especially from Mexico, carrying large plastic bags.

That was the border economy right there: moving products across the line between El Paso and Juárez, between the United States and Mexico, between—as Mexicans say—idealism and realism, hypocrisy and reality.

I thought then, as I waited to turn left onto Paisano Drive, that the border seemed so artificial and forced. I thought of all those nameless Mexicans, of us, of the *paisanos,* some of them members of my own family, who'd passed through these streets on their way into the heart of the United States. They'd brought with them little more than hope and courage to uproot their entire lives, and the stories they had heard back home—the promises of wealth and opportunity, and of a second chance.

Some of Mexico's lost sons and daughters return in brand-new cars purchased with money earned from picking crops, waiting on tables, painting homes or cutting grass in cities and suburbs across the United States. We disembark from airplanes in Tuxtla Gutiérrez, or Guanajuato, Morelia, Puebla or Durango, wearing souvenirs: Texas cowboy boots; Dallas Cowboys, Philadelphia Eagles, New York Yankees, Denver Broncos or Oakland Raiders caps; designer jeans, pockets stuffed with cash. Some, like my friend and tequila producer David Suro, return with big dreams realized—owning a business and a home, earning U.S. citizenship—and enough resources to become a philanthropist in his former homeland. We are American on the outside and Mexican within. We try to reclaim our past, seeking forgiveness from our abandoned home, which is resentful we ever left in the first place.

Others return in coffins, victims of the border's hot desert, stifling railroad cars, rough currents of the Rio Grande or ruthless smugglers growing deadlier by the day, never having entered the promised land of *el norte.* Some die up here in the north, their dreams of a triumphant return to their homeland forever buried.

I glimpsed the monuments by the Rio Grande that mark the border, discounting history, geography and the people who see it for what it really is: an illusion forced on us by far-away governments. These are frontiers shaped over centuries, by explorers who go back to the Spanish Inquisition, further back, before the Mayans and Aztecs, back before the lands divided good and bad, not necessarily the United States or Mexico, but something else, always evolving.

I looked at my mother at my side and my father in the back as they unwrapped their burgers and kept one eye on the border highway. Mexico rose to our left, a maze of *colonias* dotting the hillside across a muddy river, across the looming buildings of my alma mater, the University of Texas at El Paso, with its striking Bhutanese architecture. The colorful houses were trapped in a dust cloud from the wind and the exhaust of rattletrap buses. I had seen some of those same houses back when I was twenty-three, riding around with my musician friends. Only now there were hundreds more of them, all lured by the proximity to America.

I drove quietly, trying hard to ignore my father's stare, caught between the rain of Mexico City and the drought of the border desert. I drove past the exit to Porfirio Díaz Street, built in 1909 to mark the meeting between Mexican strongman Porfirio Díaz and U.S. president William Howard Taft. Here in El Paso, Americans would climb up high-rise buildings and watch Mexicans kill each other in their revolution, beginning in 1910. The violence had led to an influx of Mexicans—as many as 10 percent of the population—entering into the United States. The majority of them settled in Texas, including El Paso—the Ellis Island of the Southwest—where the Segundo Barrio and Sunset Heights neighborhoods became the heart of that diaspora, with its concentration of clerics, business leaders and intellectuals, and its schools, theaters and movie houses, and more than forty Spanish-language newspapers, all supported by the new "Mexican American" middle class. The Jesuit order established a network of schools catering to the children of the Mexican community. From the base of El Paso, revolutionary refugees plotted insurrections against the Díaz dictatorship.

A battered mountain topped with a cross stands guard over the west side of El Paso. The statue of Cristo Rey, a smaller replica of the one out-side León, in Guanajuato, honors the Catholics who fled Mexico. The statue looks over Smeltertown, on the banks of the Rio Grande, a site marked by a towering 826-foot-high defunct smokestack. A century ago many Mexicans labored there as skimmers, punchers or machinists for the American Smelting and Refining Company, ASARCO, and they'd settled around the factory.

Fluorescent lamplight glared across the windshield. A black truck rolled by blasting a *norteño* song probably telling the story of one famous drug trafficker or another. We were just a few minutes away from home, where the TV blaring its endless flow of *telenovelas* would hopefully dis-tract my parents.

I looked in the mirror and saw my father's long stares. He'd stopped eating his burger. He knew. When he finally spoke, he did so without commas, without hesitation, with anger and frustration. He broke the silence and finally asked what my mother, too, wanted to know but didn't have the courage to ask.

"*Fue contra ti, ¿verdad?*" he asked. The threat was against you, wasn't it?

"*Nadie sabe*—no one knows who the real target is," I responded. "No one really knows who made it, or whether it's even credible."

"*Estos cabrones no andan con chingaderas si recuerdas lo que te dije, ¿ver-dad?*" he said. Those guys don't fuck around. You do remember what I told you, right?

"Juan Pablo," my mother said. "Let's get home, eat and talk. He's probably tired."

"Yes, Papá, I do remember," I said. "More than I care to."

I couldn't ignore him anymore. Nor did I have the guts to tell him this wasn't the first time. I wished I could scream, vent my frustrations, tell him that I had gone to Mexico all those years ago determined to claim my homeland and cover the news as anywhere else, as if that were possible. I had been determined not to focus on drugs or crime but cover other real-life issues: immigration, education, the economy, entertainment. I would try to help bridge my two countries. But we had all unwittingly become crime reporters, covering *la nota roja*—"the red note," as the beat is known in Mexico.

"*¡Sí, Papá!*" I wanted to scream. "Mexico remains a vulnerable nation because two hundred years after its independence it's never been able to strengthen its judicial institutions or create enough jobs to employ a restless youth who face few choices. Worse, for those who choose a life of crime—they can love the country because Mexico never punishes its wayward sons. Look at the impunity rate! Mexico is just as you left it when you were seventeen years old, Papá, and the United States was desperate for you to come north. The Americans were so happy you and your fellow braceros came to pick their cotton, tomatoes, sugar beets, grapes and oranges that they organized a barbecue in your honor. Remember? Well, guess what, Papá? They couldn't give a damn about you today, especially you with your cowboy hat and pointy boots. Hell, they probably think you're a narco too. That's the fickle side of your adopted homeland, isn't it? Isn't that what Tío Delfino, Tío Antonio tried telling you years ago?"

But I didn't say any of that.

"*Sí, me acuerdo, Papá*," I repeated. I do remember.

I waited for my father to unleash his anger on me. And if it hadn't been so hot outside, he probably would have noticed I had turned a bright watermelon red, angry at myself more than anyone, or anything, else. Part of me felt like burying my head and not coming up for air for hours. I just wanted to cry. But my father doesn't like tears. He doesn't know what to do with them. I waited. I knew I couldn't tune him out anymore.

He reminded me about the businessman who'd wanted to invest in Freddy's Café. In 1986, a Mexican man approached my father at a bar.

He loved my mother's cooking and wanted to invest, he said. If my parents would consider opening a bigger place—Freddy's was crammed into a tiny room—he and his partners would put up $30,000, maybe even $100,000. My parents would pay back a certain percentage, 10 percent to 25 percent over five years, and then the restaurant, maybe even a chain of restaurants, would be ours. My father said he would think about it.

At first I was thrilled. Thirty grand, I thought. We were going big time! I dreamed of opening a chain of Freddy's Café all along the U.S.-Mexico border. This was the American dream, the one I'd read about in books. I started to tell people about it, ask what they thought. A few friends nodded, congratulated us or wished us luck; they, too, loved my mother's cooking and wanted to see us succeed. Then I ran into El Neto, the neighborhood drunk and, like Paisana, a smuggler of all kinds of contraband—TVs, wines, refrigerators and God knows what else. He was also a notorious lover of women. He would love every *mujer* who would let him. I told him about the sweet deal.

"*Si quieres meterte en esas transas, Freddy,*" he'd said, "*tienes que asumir las consecuencias.*" If you want to get involved in those kinds of deals, sooner or later you'll have to face the consequences. The minute you touch that money, he said, they own you.

I listened to him in disbelief. Then he started counting off the restaurants and businesses in El Paso that were known money laundering outlets. Restaurants where we knew the owners, places we shopped. Sure, we knew that there were gangs in Mexico, that drugs crossed the border, that money got laundered on both sides. But so many? Really? Seriously?

Look around, he'd said. Freddy's is a few blocks from the Chihuahuita neighborhood, where La Nacha once lived, the woman who ruled the Juárez smuggling business for nearly fifty years. She shaped the drug trade, taught small-time smugglers lessons that were then passed on to the new generation—to those like Neto, who knew every which way to sneak drugs into the United States. One common trick involved sliming the wheels of a car with marijuana so that dogs would sniff it out. While border agents were preoccupied with one vehicle, two or three more packed with bricks of weed would pass with relative ease.

This is the border, Neto said. Open your eyes.

El Neto was always the first one at Freddy's for breakfast. He'd stagger in at six a.m. just about every morning as my mother was just heating up the ovens. He spent nights loading mysterious bundles onto trucks headed for Los Angeles, using the business next to ours as storage; occasionally, when he needed extra space, he'd store his bundles in our restaurant without telling us what was in them. I knew that the southbound bundles were filled with used clothes from California. But what the heck were they shipping from Mexico north? One day I asked Neto that question.

He shook his head, pressed his index finger to his mouth and kissed it. Tattoos painted his forearms. Neto was also my guide, and took special interest in my passion for journalism, teaching me the limitations of what would be my new profession. "Freddy, don't ask questions you don't want to know the answers to, especially if you want to be a reporter." He gave me a line in Spanish, gently reminding me that curiosity killed the cat: *"Porque aquí hay gato encerrado."*

After my chat with Neto about the "investor," I'd walked away crushed and disillusioned about my plans to open a chain of restaurants with dirty money. I needed to tell my father.

Then the news about Clavi came in. Clavi, the man who had passed us Freddy's through a lease transfer, was found in Cancún, his body chopped to pieces. His corpse—or parts of it—had been uncovered in a swamp. Clavi was a nice man, a great tipper; beyond the sale of the restaurant, we'd had no dealings with him. His murder suggested something dark was simmering on both sides of the border.

That night, I pulled my father aside, worried. But he already knew.

He had done his homework. He had gone to meet the investor. He'd asked again to hear the terms of the deal, which were laid out the same as before. But then my father asked a question: What if the family wanted to sell the restaurant before the five years were up? That's fine, the man said. *No hay problema.*

But the man added: *"Si se mete la policía, va a haber lío. Pero no con el restaurante, ni contigo. Con tus hijos."* If the police find out, there will be problems. But not with the restaurant, he said, and not with you. With your children.

Then he listed the schools we attended, my brothers, sister and me.

My father politely declined, and the man didn't press him.

That kind of decency seems quaint in retrospect. Had my father refused the same offer today, God knows where we would be.

When I told my parents back in college that I wanted to be a reporter, my mother made the sign of the cross over my head and asked God to protect me. My father gave me a grim look.

"Está bien." It's fine, he'd said. *"Con que no te metas con esta gente"*— as long as you don't mess with those people. Drug traffickers, he meant.

"No conocen la palabra perdón," he'd said, with a wisdom learned only on the border. They don't know the meaning of forgiveness.

"Remember what I told you, right?" he asked again.

I nodded my head. In the rearview mirror, I saw my father stare back and shake his head in disgust. "Shit," he said, one of the few English words he'd learned during his six decades in the United States. Mamá looked sad. Mexico, meanwhile, was fading from view.

SEVENTEEN

I stayed on the U.S. side of the border, crossing only briefly to report in Juárez before returning to El Paso. Mexico's murder rate, which had fallen 37 percent between 1997 and Felipe Calderón's inauguration in 2006, nearly tripled in 2008. Hundreds of people had disappeared, hundreds more had been killed. At first dozens, then hundreds, and later thousands more were being displaced. People sought the relative safety of their hometowns in southern Mexico or, if they had the documents, across the United States in cities like El Paso and other parts of Texas and beyond.

The drug killings were nonstop. President Calderón had ordered the military to Ciudad Juárez that spring. Suddenly, 6,800 troops in fatigues and federal police in dark blue uniforms were patrolling the streets of the country's most important hub for *Fortune* 500 companies in Mexico. Government officials began to show up, announcing operation this or that; like the Americans, they had become fixated on the word "operation."

Miguel Monterrubio, Calderón's spokesperson, called me one spring day to tell me he'd be in Juárez with his new boss, Juan Camilo Mouriño, the interior minister. He asked me to meet him to hear about the government's crime fighting strategy. I wasn't going into Mexico much those days—mostly I just reported from the safety of El Paso—but for this I made an exception.

We met at a fancy hotel near the airport. The place was flooded with federal agents talking into their earpieces and bureaucrats announcing the details of Operación Conjunta Chihuahua, or Joint Operation Chihuahua, a combined effort of the state and federal governments.

I had grown cynical about the government's "operations," but I thought it would be good to see Miguel and pick his brain. He had gone out of his way to look into threats against me. I owed him one. Plus, I was curious whether he still thought journalists were exaggerating the violence.

We drank soft drinks while his boss met behind closed doors with the state governor and other authorities. There were so many soldiers on guard outside that Miguel quipped: *"Esto parece que se va a poner de la chingada, güey."* This looks like it's going to get fucking bad, man.

"Yeah, it looks like you're preparing for war, no?" I said, writing down his words as he diligently reminded me again we were off the record.

He didn't answer. He just changed the subject.

"So when are you coming out of hiding?" he asked, half joking, fidgeting with his cell phones as usual and looking over his back to check on any movement, any sign from his boss.

"When will Mexico be safe again?"

"Ya mero," he said. Soon enough.

"I think I'm done with Mexico for a while," I said, explaining I was waiting to hear about a fellowship that would keep me out for at least a year, until I decided what I wanted to do. "I don't see the point anymore," I said. "I'll always be an outsider in Mexico. I don't really belong."

"Güey, you're talking to me," he joked. "Don't be pessimistic like all

196

ALFREDO CORCHADO

your other colleagues, like the Americans. You're not an outsider." Sarcastically, but with kindness, he added, *"Eres un pocho, güey.* You're part of the bridge Mexico wants to build with the United States."

I wrote down his words and closed my notepad.

We agreed to meet up in Mexico City in the city's Polanco neighborhood. Just as promised he introduced me to several of his colleagues, all diplomats groomed by Mexico's foreign ministry, some of whom had graduated from the same university as Miguel. It seemed he was almost desperate for me to meet his colleagues—he'd always felt I had the wrong impression of Mexico, and he wanted to show the refined, sophisticated side. He and his diplomat colleagues were part of the once hopeful NAFTA generation, part of a cadre of thousands of college graduates inspired by the government of Carlos Salinas de Gortari to represent an up-and-coming Mexico abroad, to learn about the world and eventually transform Mexico. Salinas may have become the most disgraced former president of Mexico based on repeated allegations of corruption and because he'd left the country in economic disarray, but he hadn't been afraid of opening Mexico, making it competitive and inspiring a legion of diplomats to take up the cause. Miguel's rise was also a sign that Mexico was serious about its role as a global leader, he'd tell me. These diplomats were from my generation. Yet I knew that, had I grown up in Mexico, it was unlikely I would have ever joined their ranks. Many were connected or came from privilege, and many were from Mexico City. They were the new promise for Mexico, Miguel said. Unlike the crusty old politicians, these diplomats had seen the world. They viewed Mexico from a prism of global reality.

Among them was Cynthia Prida, who had shown up late for a reception the day he introduced me to her. But nobody really cared. In Mexico, you learn to wait, to be patient, because waiting is all you do.

When Cynthia walked in, I noticed she had a gentle face and long hair the color of almonds. The skin on her neck and shoulders seemed translucent. She wore wire-frame glasses and an elegant executive suit. She seemed like the kind of person I had met repeatedly in Mexico, the ones with the perfect makeup, impeccable dress and fake smiles and who spoke in kind but hollow phrases like *¡Qué maravilla!* or *¡Qué lindo!*—How marvelous! How beautiful!—and addressed people with syrupy diminutives like *corazón* and, of course, *cariño*—sweetheart, my dear.

"Te presento a Alfredo," Miguel said.

"Glad to meet you," Cynthia said, later referring to me as "Alfred," an impromptu nickname that rubbed me the wrong way.

"The pleasure is all mine," I responded, not really meaning it.

But as I came to know her, I discovered a complex woman who was far more sincere than I had imagined, and infinitely proud of and committed to her country. She had just returned from Europe, where she'd been working at an embassy. She was also an entrepreneur, and hoped to elevate women's role in business. When she shopped, she told me, she checked the labels to see where clothes were made, a way to measure her country's progress in the NAFTA age.

Later, when we became friends, Cynthia reminded me of what Miguel had learned while living in the United States, a lesson he'd tried to instill in me: The United States and Mexico were bound not only by trade, fast reaching $500 billion a year, but also by blood ties. In addition to some five million legal Mexican immigrants, and millions more undocumented and uncounted, there were nearly thirty million Americans who traced their roots to Mexico, or roughly 10 percent of the U.S. population. That Latino political heft could swing key U.S. states and, for better or worse, serve as a bridge between the United States and Mexico. We needed each other more than ever. Mexico had been punished for centuries, Cynthia said. Now Mexico had a chance to right its destiny, to stop being a nation of victims, to expose the corruption within. We couldn't simply walk away. I thought we should start right here, mending our own internal differences in Mexico, bridging the gap between the rich and the poor.

Yet I couldn't help but feel that I would have to walk away from Mexico. Even El Paso was starting to feel too close to the danger for comfort. I also worried whether staying with my parents was safe—not for me, but for them. The U.S. investigator continued to warn me to keep my guard up. Those twenty-four hours may have passed, he said, but the cartel was likely watching me, waiting for me to make a wrong move. My paranoia had only grown.

O n weekday mornings, one of my father's distant relatives would visit my parents' house. He and my father would sit on the back porch smoking Marlboro Reds, drinking Diet Coke from cans and reminiscing about old times. The two men had grown up in the same town in Durango and had crossed the border together, but their paths had taken different turns. My father's relative had never really taken to working the fields in California; he'd preferred the border, which he saw filled with opportunity, and danger.

"Entre más peligrosa la cosa, más dinero hay, Juanito," he would say. The dirtier the business, the more money you can make.

My father's relative had always held a combination of odd jobs, some considered dirty, some clean. He was a gifted gardener and took care of yards in El Paso. He had also, mostly in his younger years, moved money for the Juárez cartel, which was under the control of Amado Carrillo Fuentes in the 1990s.

One son seemed to have followed his father's mantra: the more dangerous the job, the greater the reward. But he'd taken it to another level. He had become a Juárez cop. He received two paychecks. One from the government, one from the cartel, in cash.

One weekend in the spring of 2008, the son showed up at our house, grim faced. He explained that things in Juárez were getting hot—too hot—and he planned to stay on the U.S. side of the border for a while. Did my parents have any work for him? My parents, loyal as always to everyone in our extended family, said they could use a gardener. Other family members hired him too. I started to wonder what had driven him out of Juárez. The Sinaloa cartel, which was fighting the Juárez cartel for territory, had recently pinned a kill list to a public monument in Juárez, next to the body of a murdered city cop. One of the names on the list was the nickname our relative went by. I finally got up the nerve to ask him about it.

"All the cops were working for the Juárez cartel," he explained. "Things are out of control. Several of my *compañeros* have been killed. Several others are here, flipping burgers, painting homes, fixing up houses."

"Are you still working for them?" I could barely get the words out.

"Nah," he said. He was a quiet guy. The conversation ended there.

But when I told my brother Mundo—not the whole story, just hinting that maybe he should keep an eye on the new gardener—he freaked. Mundo, David and Mario came down on me at a family barbecue, out of earshot of my parents. Sure, our relative was involved—U.S. authorities later nabbed him as he tried smuggling nearly $1 million for the Juárez cartel southbound from El Paso. He ended up in a U.S. federal prison. That didn't surprise them. It hurt them that I had lived a double life, kept things from them. I had done it for their own protection, to save them the worry.

"What the hell are you doing, Freddy?" Mario challenged. "You're writing all these stories. We saw the news about the journalist getting threats. That was you, wasn't it?"

"You don't tell us shit anymore," Mundo said. "You're supposed to be the big brother here. You're not protecting us. We're all exposed. Our parents are exposed. What about our kids, Fred?"

These were my little brothers, and I felt as if I had let them down, as if they didn't look up to me anymore. I got their point. I knew they weren't just worried for themselves and our parents; they were worried for me. I promised I'd stay away from the story, for now. That was the best I could do. Just don't tell *Mamá y Papá.*

R amón and I walked into a restaurant on the border in Laredo and had trouble finding a table. This was strange, because with Ramón next to me, it was almost never difficult to find a seat anywhere. Whether in Laredo or Nuevo Laredo, hosts and hostesses would pull him to the front of a waiting line. But today the headwaiter—who usually greeted us with a servile smile and all the welcoming gestures he could muster— seemed distant and ushered us unceremoniously to a table in the corner. The lunch hour din seemed quieter than usual. All eyes were directed toward a long table in the middle of the room. It had to be a celebrity, I wondered aloud.

"Nope," Ramón said. "This is no celebrity, *cabrón.* That's Toño Peña." He was referring to the man whom members of the Gulf cartel and the Zetas gang had identified as the "moneyman" on that gruesome video— the man who greased wheels on both sides of the border, the financial guru who allegedly negotiated deals between the Gulf cartel and key government officials—cops, politicians and others—so that drugs could cross smoothly. The very same man who had once helped negotiate the release of Ramón's brother.

I recognized his lunch guests—Americans officials. Strange coincidence. I pretended I didn't know anyone. Peña was dressed casually and seemed to be joking with everyone at the table.

¡Ah cabrōn!

In our story about that video, the *News* had omitted Peña's name, because we couldn't get confirmation. Yet the day after the story ran,

Ramón had called to tell me he had a message from Toño Peña, who at the time had been vacationing in Cancún.

"Bad facts can get you killed," Ramón had said, reluctantly relaying the message.

Now Peña was right there, all smiles and for all to see. Just about everyone knew him.

One of the American officials noticed me and shot me a look that said "Don't fucking think of coming over here." They paid the bill and he scrambled out.

Peña stayed behind and went around the room saying hellos and backslapping, shaking hands like a politician. He wanted to make sure everyone saw him. As he made his way closer to our table, Ramón asked if I wanted to be introduced. Sure, I said. Peña's grin grew wider when he realized who I was. He shook my hand tightly and said to call him whenever. Yeah, right, I thought. When he left, Ramón confided that there had been rumors that I was working clandestinely as an undercover agent.

"So what do you tell them?" I asked.

"That I think the U.S. government is more intelligent than that," he said, laughing. "I don't think they would rely on a reporter to be their spy. I mean, these guys have sophisticated listening devices that can track anyone from miles above earth, don't they? Why would they need you?"

"I hope for their sake they find some real spies," I said. For a few seconds I debated what offered more protection: being an American reporter or a spy? I gave up and skipped dessert and told Ramón I had to get back to my hotel. He suspected what was going on but didn't say anything. I promised to make it up to him with some tequila later that evening.

I rushed back to the hotel, took out my notepad and called one of the officials.

"You're having lunch with the Zetas' moneyman at a popular restaurant for everyone to see?" I asked. "What the fuck is going on? Am I missing something here?"

"There are things you'd rather not know," he said.

"Does this guy have U.S. immunity?" I asked.

"It's called gathering intelligence and that's all I'm gonna tell you," he said. "It's the same thing you do."

"Explain this to me like I'm ten years old, 'cause I obviously don't get it."

"Let it go," he said and, just before hanging up, added firmly, "To get to the devil sometimes you have to dance in hell."

I no longer had the courage to stay in Mexico, or even on the border. I pled with Angela to come with me on a fellowship. I had applied for a stay at Harvard—the farthest away I could think to go, geographically and mentally. Angela, meanwhile, had become increasingly committed to reporting on the bloodshed in Juárez. The city, plunged into a war among rival cartels and the government, was unraveling before us. Now she was the one who refused to leave the story.

We sat facing each other, in her stone cottage surrounded by an acre of land in El Paso. We enjoyed one of the last breezes before the dust storms took over the city and the burning dry heat desiccated the scrub into tumbleweeds that migrants sometimes tried to imitate, rolling across the border, trying to reach the promised land.

Mosquitoes buzzed, a perennial spring annoyance. Outside, trees rustled in the rough wind.

"I can't leave now," she said. "I can't just get up and abandon Juárez at a time of crisis."

Betrayal, disloyalty—these weren't in Angela's vocabulary.

But Juárez was dying. Our favorite bars and restaurants had been shuttered. Many establishments closed down rather than risk the consequences of not paying protection money. Cartels torched businesses that failed to pay, leaving them in cinders. Many business owners simply fled with their families and set up shop on U.S. soil, where they waited for calm to return. Peace remained elusive.

I heard the pain and exhaustion in Angela's voice, and I saw it in her eyes.

"I need to tell these stories, make sure people realize what's happening here," she said. "If we stop, we only add to the silence that's growing across Mexico."

"And then what? Americans will do exactly what? Stop snorting, smoking, actually give a damn?" I said. "Pressure Mexico to strengthen its courts, clean up the corruption, and maybe then democracy will actually mean something? What is democracy anyway, when people have no rule of law, when they want governments to be pragmatic? Nothing seems to be working and the United States has somehow managed to look the other way."

"We're sending $1.4 billion—remember Mérida? The story you broke," she countered. "That's a start."

"You know how much they're sending to Afghanistan? Ten, twelve times that! As long as the killings don't affect American businesses, as long as Mexico doesn't have a bomb, everything will stay the same," I said. Then, sarcastically, I added, "Tell me exactly what you plan to do, how you plan to make a difference, so I can follow your lead."

"You don't understand," she responded, exasperated.

I tried to change the tone. "I do, precious. I do. But I also need you."

Angela swatted at a mosquito. She wouldn't say another word. There was nothing more to say.

At that moment I felt we had failed each other by allowing us the freedom to be ourselves, perhaps too independently. We had stopped being a couple. Mexico had united us. Now we had fallen apart.

. . .

By the spring of 2008 the killings had gotten so bad that, like any desperate Catholic, the mayor of Juárez responded by holding personal prayer sessions during Holy Week. He prayed privately at his office, at home, inside his car, prayed over and over again that Calderón would send in more troops and federal agents. Juárez was on the verge of being overtaken by warring cartels. The more troops arrived, the more lifeless Juárez became. One morning I crossed into Juárez to report on the killing of five people in a cheap motel near the Juárez airport. At the crime scene authorities and curious bystanders were trampling everything; nothing was controlled. We haven't learned a goddamn thing, I thought. I did my interviews quickly and jumped into the cab that was waiting for me across the street. I liked that the driver wasn't much of a talker. I didn't feel like talking. I usually pepper taxi drivers with all sorts of questions. Now I just wanted to get back across the border in peace. Then the taxi driver broke the silence.

"At the rate we're going," he said, "taxi drivers should provide a death tour for visitors. What do you think?" His twinkling eyes looked at me in the rearview mirror.

I shrugged.

"We can pick up tourists right on the border and take them to see where the first woman was killed and the thousands of men and women that followed after that. This is the city of death."

I shrugged and wrote down his words.

Cars began to slow down. I rolled down the window and spotted a pickup truck in the middle of a busy intersection. As we got closer, I saw that the truck's windshield was riddled with bullet holes. The driver's-side door was open and a man's body was half hanging out. The cops were just arriving. The cabbie asked if I wanted to stop. He was so nonchalant. I felt sick to my stomach.

I said no.

We got to the bridge. I paid him, hopped out, put my three-peso toll in the slot and made my way across the Santa Fe bridge. I thought of Dante again and walked slowly at first, Juárez behind me, El Paso ahead. I put my earphones on and scrolled to Café Tacvba's "Moliendo Café," hoping to tune out the carnage I had just seen. The bodies were piling up in Juárez every day—ten, twelve, twenty a day. It was only April and hundreds had been killed so far that year. Nausea overcame me as I thought about it. I stopped in the middle of the bridge, right on the border, leaned my forehead against the cool chain-link fence and threw up.

EIGHTEEN

By the fall of that year, I was a world away from the border and all the grief that hung over it.

A crisp wind blew the leaves in slow motion outside the Walter Lippmann House, a stately white three-story New England colonial the fellows of Harvard's Nieman Foundation called home. I had been accepted to the fellowship program in May 2008 and had moved to Cambridge in August.

Angela and I talked all the time, but something wasn't right between us anymore. She called me from bed one night, the phone cradled to her ear.

"You won't recognize Juárez anymore," she said. I could hear Zorro snoring, piglike, at the foot of her bed.

"It's hard one minute to be at the scene of a mass murder wondering if the killers will come back and then the next to be back on a quiet street in El Paso," she said.

Angela was on edge, distant and tired. The wit, the humor that would make me laugh so hard was gone.

She had been at a crime scene that day, as she was most days. "I've never seen so much blood, never stood in so much blood," she said. "There was blood on my shoes today. I couldn't bear to wash it off. I tossed them in the trash."

"You did what?" I asked, incredulous. Ensconced in a tiny apartment two blocks from the redbrick buildings of the university, I was becoming American again: relaxed, callous, self-absorbed. As if coated in Teflon.

It was threatening rain on the evening of the U.S. presidential election, November 4, 2008. I left my apartment and headed for Lippmann House that night. I brought one bottle of tequila to the gathering and left another bottle at home, assuming my apartment would once again serve as the venue for the after-party. I had just walked inside the Lippmann House and saw my Nieman friends in a celebratory mood—Obama was poised to win. I walked around the room greeting friends like Chris Vognar, salivating at the sight of my tequila, and took a seat near the giant TV with live shots from Grant Park in Chicago.

My phone vibrated and I picked up. It was my pal David Suro.

"Are you watching this?" David shouted over his cell phone. He was calling me from his restaurant in Philadelphia.

"Yes, historic—incredible night," I said as Barack Obama, his wife, Michelle, and their daughters, Malia and Sasha, took center stage. "I'm watching this now. He's onstage."

David mumbled something I couldn't quite make out.

"*Qué país tan chingón, ¿no que no?*" I added. "Great country or what? You can't deny it anymore . . . Speechless? Say something, *cabrón!*"

"You don't know what just happened in Mexico City?" he shouted.

"Earthquake?" I asked, suddenly panicked. I was having trouble making out his words with all the chaotic cheering.

"An explosion!" he screamed.

I pushed a chair out of the way and pulled my computer out of my bag as my mind filled with concern for my friends and colleagues back in Mexico City—Samuel, Lonny, Javier. Angela, at least, was on the border, away from any serious fault lines. If this was an earthquake, my colleagues would be working inside my sixth-floor apartment in La Condesa, a neighborhood that shakes more fiercely during earthquakes because it sits on softer ground. Living in Mexico City, I had experienced small tremors inside my apartment. One had woken me at night. I knew how the building could sway for what seemed like forever.

This tragedy, however, had fallen from the sky.

"Mouriño's Plane Crashes Over Mexico City," read a headline. Juan Camilo Mouriño, the interior minister, who oversaw domestic security—the highest-ranking member of President Calderón's cabinet, his closest ally and probable candidate to succeed him.

Mouriño had been in San Luis Potosí, where he'd given a speech about providing safe passage for immigrants returning to Mexico that upcoming holiday season. The small Learjet he'd been traveling on was seconds away from landing at Mexico City's airport when it crashed near the busy Paseo de la Reforma during rush hour. The pictures were horrific. Pieces of the fuselage lined the street. Government IDs worn by the victims were scattered, as were human remains.

My heart sank. Whoever was on that plane was dead for sure, I thought. And my friend Miguel Monterrubio had to have been on that plane. The two men were inseparable. My heart raced as I searched for answers. I pounced on the computer and saw pictures that had been taken of Monterrubio and Mouriño together that same day, hours before, when they'd arrived from Mexico City and gotten off the plane. The picture showed a dapper Mouriño trotting hurriedly next to José Luis Santiago Vasconcelos, the man I'd once believed threatened me. Miguel was in the background, tall and skinny, his wire-rim glasses in place. Now he was almost completely bald, a change from the last time I'd seen him months before. I could see him with two phones, one to each ear—classic Miguel. I felt a sharp pain grip me from deep inside. I got up to leave the party.

Sabotage? The cartels? It had to be.

"Sorry, guys," I told my friends Bob and Nancy Giles, who were already in full celebration mode. "I need to go home and check on something."

As I retraced my path toward my apartment on Trowbridge Street, I quickened my step and punched out a text message to a contact in Washington, D.C., where I had met Miguel years before. Back when he believed in a bright future for Mexico.

Was Miguel on that plane?

I rode the elevator four flights to my apartment, unlocked the door and threw down my computer bag and the unopened bottle of tequila.

The blue glow of neighbors' TV sets—all tuned to television anchors mouthing the news of Obama's election—radiated.

The response on my cell phone came back almost immediately: *I'm afraid so.*

Outside, the celebration poured from bars and houses into the streets. President-elect Obama was in the middle of his acceptance speech. Despite the honking of cars and cheers from the street, I could hear his muffled words coming from a neighbor's TV through the thin walls. I dragged myself into my bedroom, sat on the corner of my bed, reached for a pillow and threw it on the floor. I buried my face in my hands and began sobbing.

As snow started falling in the northeast, I was headed to Mexico for a quick visit over Christmas break to take advantage of an invitation. Tony Garza, the U.S. ambassador, had invited me on his last official trip to Tamaulipas, a state bordering Texas. If any state had succumbed to organized crime, represented organized crime, it was

Tamaulipas. I found myself curious again, and, besides, I had a soft spot for Garza, who had taken immediate action and warned against threatening Americans.

The governor, Eugenio Hernández, and a group of mayors from the state were going to receive him, throw him a going-away luncheon, complete with *cabrito,* young goat, the state's signature dish. Garza and I flew together to Ciudad Victoria, named after Mexico's first president, Guadalupe Victoria, the seat of power in the state of Tamaulipas. The state and its capital were synonymous with PRI patronage. The federal government may have switched hands in 2000, but many individual states had remained firmly under PRI control, in some cases becoming small fiefdoms of power. Tamaulipas was a booming crossroads, with gateways to the United States and a long coast with busy commercial ports. Ciudad Victoria remained mostly a ranching community, and the folks who never left mixed easily with those who moved back and forth between Texas.

Along the border U.S. drones were flying, peeking over Mexico, along with U.S. helicopters manned by Mexican pilots. U.S. contractors were training Mexican soldiers and agents. Hernández provided Garza's plane. He obviously knew the ambassador well, because for kicks he provided an ice chest filled with beer, chips, nuts and a bottle of tequila. We flew from the small airport in Toluca, outside of Mexico City, in a twin-engine along with Garza's bodyguard and a personal assistant.

The plane's door opened and Garza took a moment to smile for the cameras that had accompanied the governor. Garza basked in the limelight—pats on the back, cheeks touching cheeks—especially from the women who found the handsome U.S. ambassador alluring. Beyond his natural charm, the fact that he was married to a very rich Mexican woman gave him extra cachet. He wasn't just a U.S. ambassador; he was from the border, one of them. I stood back and tried to ingratiate myself with the security guards. They often had interesting information.

"*¿Cómo están?*" I asked. "So humbled by your service. Thank you."

I rode with them to the event, where people packed the tables that had been set up in a big hall in the governor's mansion. The group gave Garza a typical Tamaulipas vest made of brown suede and white fringe. Just about everyone else was wearing a similar one. He put it on over his business shirt, laughed and then promptly took it off. I watched the men as they clinked forks and knives and devoured plates of stewed goat and liberally tossed back Chinaco, a tequila cultivated in Tamaulipas.

Seated at a table of mayors, I had a captive audience and I took advantage of it. Are the narcos setting up parallel governments in cities that suddenly appear normal again, where killings, kidnappings and extortions have allegedly stopped? Had the violence really ended, or was it just that stories of violence weren't appearing in the press because of cartel threats? I wanted to know. The mayors at our table cheerfully denied any such reports. Yes, those madmen, the Zetas, now forged an alliance with another criminal organization, the Beltrán Leyva brothers, and every now and then there were rumblings of a split with the Gulf cartel, which they were supposed to protect. But they had largely fallen in line and were beholden to their original bosses.

According to these elected officials, the state had regained whatever control it had lost. I should focus on tourism pieces, like fishing in Falcon Lake or duck hunting with .30-30 Winchester guns, so popular with those beefy Texans and their rifles. I agreed with them.

American diplomats at the luncheon smiled but said little. I followed one of the Americans into the men's room and asked more questions. He told me about SUVs with armed men circling the cities, of reporters too afraid to write anything down anymore, of locals—especially the middle and upper classes—slowly moving farther north into the United States. Some estimates showed more than two hundred thousand people had been displaced by drug violence, including several thousand from Tamaulipas. Mexico's elite once vacationed at Padre Island; they now seemed to own the beach town—people who could afford it left and many bought homes in Texas. If Tamaulipas was quiet, it was because the drug traffickers now controlled the region.

Toast followed toast. All I saw that afternoon were men worried not about the violence encroaching on them but about their accommodations with the easy money of the cartel-government alliance being increasingly threatened.

The governor's staff brought more food and drinks. Garza looked at me and asked if I had left anything on the plane, because the pilot was leaving without us. It turned out the pilot had another gig and the governor had told him not to wait around anymore. How are we going to get back to Mexico City? I thought. Garza didn't seem too worried. In Mexico, you go with the flow; something usually works out.

After two more hours of celebrating, slamming down tequilas, we were loaded into an SUV and ushered to the tiny airport, where a shiny private jet waited for us, motors roaring. The governor sat in front of me, Garza on my right. A Mexico City businessman who owned an oil rig in the city of Tampico sat next to the governor. He said little after Garza introduced me as a friend who happened to be a reporter—code for "watch your ass." There wasn't much talk, just the deafening roar of the jet engines.

First the governor's twin-engine aircraft, now the wealthy businessman's private jet. We were in a state essentially in the hands of narcos. Garza took the high road. He dealt with his counterparts not with trust but with a smile. Always listening for clues. What else could he do? he'd later asked. He looked relaxed, sipping his tequila, all part of the act of being a gracious U.S. ambassador. I knew then I could never be a diplomat. I blurted to the governor, a man suspected—like so many political leaders—of having made illicit financial gains:

"So do the Zetas control your state?"

The governor looked at me, cleared his throat and answered carefully.

"They've been a problem—thugs—but we're successfully taking them on," he said in Spanish. "The federal government has been receptive to our concerns and we're glad that the president is trying to reestablish order."

Everyone seemed nervous when I reached for a notepad to write down the governor's words. The governor looked out the window and switched gears. He pointed to the state's treasures, the rivers and waterfalls dotting the countryside.

"This state is so much bigger than the Zetas," he said. "I hope Texans know that they are safe here."

I asked him whether his wife had really been stopped by the Zetas— something I'd learned from his own bodyguards and drivers moments before. She'd been reminded on the spot, I had been told, of who the real bosses in the state were. Not her husband, the governor, and not the federal government. But the Zetas.

"That story is false," the governor said and then looked at Garza for help. Garza looked at me, his eyes darting to my notepad. I relaxed and put the notebook away. We were supposed to be off the record, but I had been besieged by curiosity. I wanted to know so much: Was Vasconcelos corrupt or a victim surrounded by crooks? More immediate, what or who had sent down that plane that had killed Vasconcelos and Miguel? I still couldn't believe Miguel was gone. I missed our bantering, and his insistence that Mexico was headed in the right direction. I needed to hear that again. I stared at my tequila glass, nearly empty.

I remembered the time Miguel, Angela and I were having dinner at a restaurant, and over mariachis he'd raised his glass to toast the Mexico he believed was imminent—not the one, he claimed, we journalists predictably portrayed with the same paintbrush. He urged me to sing along to an old song about a hopeless love worth waiting another hundred years for.

I rubbed my fingers over my eyes.

Garza gave me a sharp look and poured more tequila into my glass.

He had a saying that seemed appropriate at the time: "Remember—the best way to survive in Mexico is to be bulletproof and invisible and tequila has a way of getting you there. And remember, your ears aren't ornaments. You already know everything you're going to say, but not everything you might hear."

I slumped back in my chair and tossed back the tequila.

The moon was full. The plane began its slow descent to the Toluca airport. I saw the shadow of the volcanoes, the lights of Mexico City flickering ahead of me—those lights that go on for eternity—and thought of what must have been going through Miguel's mind those last moments as his plane fell from the sky.

Later, Garza and other senior U.S. officials reported they were convinced that the Learjet crash, which had killed Miguel, Mouriño, Vasconcelos and eleven others aboard, had been an accident caused by pilot error—nothing more, no conspiracy. A joint investigation between American and Mexican experts showed that wake turbulence, left behind by a Mexicana Boeing 767 ahead of the Learjet, had caused the pilots to lose control.

Yet Garza couldn't say much about Vasconcelos, other than that he was steamed with his staff when he realized how easily Mexican officials from the attorney general's office had entered the embassy without escorts. He was also angered by what he called his own team's naïveté when they would later express surprise that Vasconcelos's people had been sharing intelligence gathered at those meetings, at the U.S. embassy, with the cartels.

A DEA document later released accused Vasconcelos of taking bribes from a powerful cartel organization that at the time was suspected of killing those men in the video that we'd reported on, the one that had forced us to leave Mexico. Officials wouldn't say how much money Vasconcelos had received, but at least one of the two other senior Mexican law enforcement officials mentioned in the DEA report, lower in the hierarchy than Vasconcelos, was allegedly pocketing $450,000 a month.

One senior U.S. official said he "was deeply disappointed with José Luis. But I don't like talking about dead people."

Garza told me, "Look, we had heard it, and others had too. It's poker. You work with the hand you're dealt and you make the most of it. But you never trust completely and bet the ranch."

Vasconcelos also had his defenders, including Larry Holifield, who headed the DEA office in Mexico City, and who later upon retiring allegedly rented a home Vasconcelos owned in Miami. Holifield had known Vasconcelos since the 1990s, when Vasconcelos was a prosecutor: "First we honor him, and then we trash him. That's very convoluted." When I pressed him about whether his friendship with Vasconcelos was a conflict of interest, Holifield wouldn't discuss that or the allegations that he had rented his former friend's home. "I'm not going to answer any of your questions," he said. "But I thank you for calling."

Many Mexicans filed the crash away with other suspicious unsolved mysteries: the death of Luis Donaldo Colosio; the tens of thousands of other people killed so far in the drug war; the makeshift graves periodically discovered in all parts of Mexico.

Mexicans knew the government—and its "investigations" conducted by weak institutions—were not to be trusted.

The U.S. government clearly felt the same way. American officials were relying increasingly on Mexican informants. Paisana was in hot demand by American officials who still couldn't trust their official counterparts and depended more on informants like her.

I paid Paisana a visit. We met at a swanky restaurant in Texas, where we sat eating breakfast next to an American couple with a baby in a stroller. Paisana wore designer clothes, bought on her latest European trip, when she'd been working undercover to follow cocaine shipped by Colombians through the latest Mexican cartel she'd infiltrated. She wore Dolce & Gabbana sunglasses and jewelry, and had a new hairdo, courtesy of a hairdresser in Paris.

"My weakness isn't men," she boasted, "but designer clothes, chocolate and good food. That's the only upside of my job."

She was as curious as ever, fishing for information, including the identity of my sources.

"Information is the new industry," she'd say. "Tell me something I don't know."

"I know nothing," I'd respond.

"Everybody wants to be an informant these days," she said. "All this war has done is create a new generation of snitches who claim they have the next best information."

On the U.S. side, she was pretending to sell weapons to a cartel, part of a plan to help trace how and where weapons were being used and by which criminals, an operation intended to bring down the entire gun trafficking network of the cartel. The Bush administration rolled back Clinton-era restrictions on sales of high-powered weapons like AR-15s and .50 caliber machine guns. Mexico was now flooded with these powerful weapons. And the gangsters wanted more.

Paisana's ruse was to lure the cartels' gun purchasers to the U.S. side of the border—courtesy of temporary visas that she'd obtained for them as part of the U.S. sting operation. She'd obtained the visas, she'd tell the cartel men and women, through corrupt contacts inside U.S. immigration agencies. Once on the U.S. side, the buyers would hold the guns as Paisana taught them the difference between AK-47s and AR-14s and stinger missiles. The idea was to eventually arrest these low-level purchasers and gather intelligence that would help them bring cases against top kingpins who had long eluded prosecution.

"How do you do that?" I asked. "How do you lure these guys and get away with it?"

"I'm an actress," she said, and just like that she got into her role, cursing up a storm in Spanish as the young couple next to us looked bewildered. "I say, 'Hey, motherfucker, you want the fucking guns, or what the fuck do you want because I have no motherfucking time to kill. Understand me, motherfucker?'"

"And if they're caught in the U.S., don't the cartel bosses suspect you?" I asked.

"Fuck that," she said. "You act like you own the place. You are in charge! You belong, motherfucker. I tell them, 'Look, motherfucker, don't blame me if you sent out some fucking morons. I did my job and hooked them with the corrupt U.S. official. Not my fault your guy fucked up. Fuck you, motherfucker.'"

I looked sheepish, almost sorry I'd asked. She caught herself when she noticed the couple anxiously wanting to change seats. She said, "I'm so good at this shit that I forget where I am. Once I'm in acting role, watch out, motherfucker. I'm one badass bitch who takes no shit from anyone. I could easily be a soap opera star."

"And the guns that end up in Mexico?" I asked. "What then?"

"If people get killed—well, they're Mexican," she said, with a shake of her head that said, "You really think anyone gives a shit? *No te hagas pendejo como tus paisanos aquí.*" Don't play dumb, Alfredo, like your countrymen here.

The idea that the U.S. government was purposely selling weapons to the cartels sickened me. How could they possibly trace where the weapons ended up? Or who ended up dead?

I asked why she did it, why she helped the Americans. The money was hardly the reason, she said.

She still desperately wanted that green card.

NINETEEN

Death reached my family on a hot July day, just a day after I'd returned to Mexico for good. It was Tío Delfino. He had died from a heart attack that struck him as he stepped off one of those rickety white buses with the words *"Dios está contigo"* painted in lipstick red on the front fender. He was just a few feet from his home in a working-class Juárez neighborhood. Residents had grown so accustomed to bodies lying on the ground that when he stumbled, clutching his chest, some thought he was drunk or had been struck by a bullet. They watched as he gasped for help. One of the bystanders was a cousin, who realized it was Tío Delfino kicking on the ground and struggling for his last breath. He ran to him, but it was too late.

At age eighty-four, Tío Delfino was dead. I had just landed in Mexico City, after nearly a year in Boston, when I got the news. I rushed to my apartment, unloaded my bags and then repacked them. The next morning I was on a flight again, to Ciudad Juárez. I wanted to be with the man who had helped bury my umbilical cord, the man I saw as a surrogate father in Durango while my father labored in California. He had told me never to lose my Spanish and to be proud of Mexico's glorious, mystical past. History hasn't been good to us Mexicans, he'd say, but somehow we would get through it all.

Tío Delfino had wanted nothing from the United States—a country, he said, that robbed Mexico of half its territory and later exploited its people as cooks and fruit pickers before kicking them to the curb whenever xenophobia set in or the economy fell apart. That's why the United States is so powerful, he'd say—the gringos thrive off cheap labor. Hell, no—he wouldn't follow his brothers and sisters across the border. Let them labor under the hot sun and bow to the capricious wishes of the bosses in a foreign country. One moment they love you, shower you with praise; the next day they call the *migra,* the border patrol, on you.

Tío Delfino would stay in his Mexico. He'd prove everyone wrong. He had been mayor of our hometown and had taken care of my father's ranch. Later he'd settled in Ciudad Juárez. Yes, he'd tell me, life in Mexico was tough, but he still lived on Mexican soil, and that meant something. Sometimes when I went to Juárez I'd stop at the small storefront where he worked as a tailor, just as his mother had, hunched over piles of clothes. He'd always remark about my clothes. I needed a tailor, he'd say. No, Tío, I need you. Don't abandon us just because we left for the United States of America.

He had his own children by then. He raised them in Juárez, although some of them had left for the United States as soon as they were old enough.

July and August 2009 marked some of the bloodiest months yet of war in Ciudad Juárez since the revolution. It seemed that half the people were dying and the other half were clinging urgently to life. Amid a war between two rival cartels and their respective government forces, the city's morgues were packed. So many bodies awaited burial that hearses started carrying bodies to El Paso.

Without any warning, the mortician arrived at my cousin Teresa's doorstep with my *tío* in a metallic casket.

"We have your father," he informed her, and then wheeled in the light brown aluminum casket and left it in the backyard, the August sun rays burning over him. "We have no room for him at the morgue. Sorry."

My cousin Teresa—Tere to us—told me the story when I walked into her tiny living room, accompanied by my father, mother and brother Juan. For three days, Tere told me, she'd waited for family members to arrive from California, Texas and Colorado, as my *tío* lay in his casket outside, scalding in the sun. She'd borrowed two fans from neighbors to keep the area ventilated for loved ones who came to pay their last respects to her father. The fans moved hot air around the back porch, but the heat was relentless. It was the best she could do, she said apologetically. My mother embraced her.

I approached the casket, closed my eyes and slowly opened them. I hadn't seen my *tío* in years and was struck by the heavy makeup on his weathered face. His mustache neatly trimmed. His receding hairline combed just right. The tiny body—he was only four feet, eleven inches tall—dressed in a black suit and white shirt. I spotted a maggot nibbling on his neck. I didn't cry, just cursed quietly at Juárez.

Tío, was this the Mexico you believed in so much?

The question floated in the oven-baked air.

I stood there and tried crying. But I couldn't. I had become numb.

With all the family present, we waited to take my *tío* to his final resting place. It was a Tuesday. The hearse pulled up and Juan helped me carry the coffin. It didn't weigh much. We placed it gently in the back of a long station wagon. I closed the curtains so the sun wouldn't hit the coffin directly and then I realized how ridiculous that was. I got inside my old black Toyota 4-Runner and followed the hearse to the church, just a few blocks down the street. I drove, with Juan in the passenger seat and my parents in the back. We were nervous the whole ride to the church, and with good reason. Roadblocks would materialize at random in Juárez, especially in this neighborhood, as the fighting between cartels was moving to the southeastern part of the city.

Suddenly the traffic halted. I looked up and saw soldiers pointing their AK-47s and .38 caliber guns at us. The caravan screeched to a stop. Soldiers swarmed the area outside a mom-and-pop grocery store advertising cell phone cards and ice-cold Coca-Colas. The store faced the church where the funeral Mass would be held. We were just a block away. On my left I could see the bodies of three men on the ground, one strangely twisted on the sidewalk in puddles of blood. Soldiers hustled by the hearse and the train of mourners; they fanned out from trucks and took up positions, fingers always on the trigger, safeties clicking off and on. Gunmen appeared to be on the scene.

We waited for minutes, which felt like hours, all in a line, exposed to the commotion in front of us. Suddenly a man threw down his weapon. A soldier hit him across the head with the butt of his rifle. I tried snapping pictures with my cell phone, but one of the soldiers motioned for me to stop.

The soldiers finally waved us through. For a second we forgot why we were there. We all followed. There was nothing else to do.

Inside a large, ornate church with glass windows and a sea of empty pews, the fifty or so of us gathered and listened to the priest give my *tío* the last rosary. He talked about redemption and forgiveness. The ceremony felt rushed; more funerals awaited the priest that afternoon. We couldn't wait for the final blessing. We had to rush out, carrying Tío Delfino's body from the church. The hearse driver put his cell phone down and walked over to help us. As I walked to my car, I took a peek to see whether the soldiers were still across the street at the grocery store. They were. Customers ignored them as they milled about, picking up fresh tortillas and soft drinks.

This was Ciudad Juárez.

We followed the hearse to the cemetery, about three miles away. For-eign assembly plants, most of them owned by companies in the United States, dotted the land that was once cotton fields. These were the same factories that for years employed my cousins and their children, until the global recession devastated the area, or the jobs were ferried off to China. The cemetery was under expansion now, with grave diggers preparing fresh graves.

From my rearview window I suddenly saw dust rising and the snake of vehicles pulling to the right. Again I saw rifles pointed in our direc-tion, trucks coming up from behind. I pulled over, as did the hearse in front of me. The same soldiers who had earlier pointed their guns at us were forcing everyone to the side of the asphalt and onto the dirt road. They passed us. They had blank stares as if it was just another day. They were headed to another shootout near the cemetery that had left a woman and her infant dead. I watched the dust trails left by trucks with soldiers crammed together in the back, sweltering in their helmets and heavy gear.

At the cemetery, the hearse driver came over to me. At least a dozen people had been murdered that day. The morgues were rushing bodies out. More bodies awaited his service, right that minute, he said. He'd have to leave soon.

I told him to please be patient and turn his cell phone off for the next few minutes. We needed to give our proper farewell to Tío Delfino. He said he understood, but then rocked on his feet impatiently.

A few minutes later I walked up to him and told him he could leave. The grave diggers had assured me they'd stay to help us lay the coffin in the ground. The driver seemed embarrassed. I told him I understood. He tried to hand me his card. I hesitated.

We have the best service in town, he said. You never know, he added. *Nunca se sabe.*

I took his card reluctantly and thanked him.

He got in the black and gray hearse and tore out of the cemetery. Business was booming.

We stood watch as more hearses pulled in for the multiple funerals that afternoon, trails of mourners behind them. Maybe my mother had been right, I thought, when we arrived all those years ago from Durango. She had described Juárez as a garbage dump of humanity: the biggest dreamers, the most ambitious and the most vulnerable, all lured by a promise, everyone from somewhere else, a fractured mosaic of Mexico unable to build any sort of community. We were all disposable in this town.

As my *tío's* body was lowered into the ground, I whispered to my mother that I lamented not having spent more time with him, not having asked more questions, like where exactly he had buried my umbilical cord. Nina, my maternal grandmother, had died years earlier and was buried in San Luis de Cordero. Like my *tío,* she had returned to Mexico and died alone one Christmas holiday, with most of her sons, daughters and grandkids living comfortably in the United States. I wondered how Tío Delfino and Nina—the two who took care burying my umbilical cord and reminding me of its significance over the years—lived their last days. They fulfilled their promise to return, but we hadn't—the ones who now stood with our heads bowed were counting the minutes before we could leave and get away from the insanity around us.

I pressed my mother again. Was Tío Delfino the last to know? If so, I probably would never know.

"Shh," my mother said, somewhat annoyed. "That's not important now. This is not the moment."

Besides, she had other more pressing worries, she said.

"We got word that people back in Durango want to buy your father's ranch. Other than your *tío,* no one else knows who these men are. They might be drug traffickers, Chapo's men—who knows? You never know anymore."

I looked at my grieving father, my mother's hand holding his arm, and felt his pain. The loss of Tío Delfino, his older brother, was naturally painful, but the circumstances—the madness in a city once home—hurt just as much. People had confused his brother for a criminal and had done nothing to save him; no one could find a quiet, dignified moment for a proper burial. Dad was fighting off tears that he quickly wiped away. I went over to him, put my arm around him.

"'*Tá cabrón,*" he said.

I also knew my father would like nothing more at that moment than to leave Ciudad Juárez and cross back to the safe refuge of the United States.

"*Ya nos vamos, ¿no?*" he said. We should go now.

TWENTY

Seven months after my *tío*'s funeral, on a gray Sunday in midmorning, February 2, 2010, Angela, her cameraman Hugo Perez and I were on our way to Villas de Salvárcar, a working-class neighborhood where more than a dozen young people had been massacred just three days before. The area lies in what is commonly known as the "new" Ciudad Juárez: Tucked in the eastern periphery of the city, it's the part that's supposed to be more prosperous than the old.

This "new Juárez" sits at the end of Las Torres, a huge megaboulevard lined with cookie-cutter homes and squat electric towers. It was supposed to be well planned, with housing, commercial and industrial zones clustered together in an orderly fashion. In a city of workers, this layout would allow laborers to travel easily from their homes to work and to commerce. It was an improvement from older parts of the city, where people had to take several buses to get to work at old industrial parks and had almost no access to grocery stores or pharmacies near their homes. These new, integrated neighborhoods resembled company towns: They were built around a single maquila, or a single industrial park. The company had a captive pool of workers with little time for anything other

than work; employees and their children were isolated from other opportunities. Villas de Salvárcar was also home to *"minicasas,"* brightly colored row houses resembling dollhouses in both color and size. For so
many, these modest homes put the dream of home ownership within
reach. They were an improvement from the squatter villages that I had
covered as a student reporter.

There were brand-new buildings, shopping malls and a new public
hospital—all built before and after the violence ran wild, meaning the
violence didn't get much in the way of economic growth. Other than a
worldwide economic downturn, or cheaper wages in China, little did.
Now as many as fifteen thousand gang members from both sides of the
border prowled the streets of Juárez. The supply of reinforcements seemed
endless; high unemployment and limited opportunities had created a new
category of youth, and a buzzword: *ni-nis,* young people who neither studied nor worked. *Ni estudian, ni trabajan.* In a country of 112 million, there
were said to be more than eight million youths who were prime candidates
for the cartels. Some eighty thousand *ni-nis* lived in Ciudad Juárez.

Amid the growing lawlessness, everyone in Juárez was trying to cope.
Angela and her cameraman, Hugo, had their own rules. They would roll
down the windows of the company's dark blue SUV even in the cold,
even in the rain. Everyone in Juárez knew the narcos preferred to ride in
SUVs. Angela would let her blond hair blow loose out the window so
that narcos and federal police could plainly see that she was just an
American woman, not to be mistaken for a hit man. Hugo wrapped
bright yellow reflective duct tape on his camera and tripod so that it
would not be mistaken for a mounted .50 caliber weapon.

A photographer from the *News* and a freelance reporter doing a story
for National Public Radio rode with us, sitting next to Angela in the
backseat. Safety in numbers.

In the front seat, I was freezing, my hands growing numb. The wind
was so cold—not a quaint, scarves-and-hot-chocolate New England cold,

just a cold slashing wind, scattering strips of garbage, cigarette butts, old newspaper ads and food wrappings along the Francisco Torres Villarreal boulevard. Whenever I tried rolling up my window, Hugo and Angela would stop me short. At one point they threatened, jokingly, to kick me out of the SUV and force me to fetch a cab.

"Hit men make mistakes," Angela ordered firmly from the backseat. "Roll down your window."

"You gotta get rid of this goddamn truck," I fumed. "If the narcos don't kill us, this freezing wind and rain will."

"You're a long way from Harvard, the coffee shops, the big thoughts," Angela said, ribbing me. "Welcome back."

"Yeah, really," I said defensively as we zoomed across muddy streets, splashing dirty water onto sidewalks. "I see a shitload of Starbucks here too."

On that gray day, we were headed for the wake of the slain youth. Their bodies lay inside coffins in their living rooms, a common practice for Mexicans who can't afford a funeral home. Even by Juárez's ghoulish standards, the mass killings in Villas de Salvárcar were hard to stomach. The bloodbath felt like a watershed moment for Mexico: sixteen young people, mostly students, shot down by gunmen who'd burst into a birthday party. They were carrying semiautomatic assault rifles smuggled from the United States. President Calderón, traveling in Japan, had reacted prematurely and declared that the massacre had likely been the result of a turf war between rival gang members. The words would come back to bite him after it was discovered that the victims were not gathered at a bar or rehab clinic but were good kids celebrating a birthday at a private home where their parents could keep a close eye on them.

Some parents in Juárez forbade their children to leave their homes after the sun went down. They talked only with those they trusted. Large social gatherings were frowned upon, including weddings, *quinceañeras* and birthdays. The majority of these victims were teenagers, ages thirteen to nineteen; all were boys, except one teen girl. They were honor students, athletes, kids who grew up together and played sports on weekends.

On our first visit to the home, just hours after the massacre had occurred, we'd seen the bloodstains on the walls, the sneaker prints stamped in dried blood. The blood that had not yet been mopped had run down the driveway in rivulets and had caked on the tires of parked cars, including our SUV.

The rain picked up as we got closer to Villas de Salvárcar. I looked at Angela in the mirror and shook my head as if to say, "You need to get out of here, for your own sake"—just as she used to repeat to me years before urging me to leave Mexico. I started to raise the issue again, but she would have none of it. "Love you too," she said, her way of shutting me up. Angela and I were trying to pick up the pieces of our relationship.

Tall, skinny Hugo had a shaved head that I worried could easily pass for the look of one of those hit men whose faces regularly decorated the front pages of newspapers.

"Push the button and roll the goddamn windows up," I urged Hugo.

He just shrugged his shoulders, locked his jaw and left the windows down.

From my window on the passenger side I could see people going to church, heading for the grocery store, always looking over their shoulders, mindful that, at any second, the violence could explode.

At that moment all I wanted was to do my job and get out.

"How much to kill us?" I asked.

Angela chimed in from the back. "Anywhere from three hundred pesos to, I don't know, three thousand, five thousand pesos, depending on the target," she responded. Her estimates worked out to anywhere from thirty bucks to a few hundred U.S. dollars. "You? Maybe three thousand pesos, maybe less," she joked and winked. Humor on the border had become macabre. "And if they get the wrong target—well, too bad. It's not like the dead come back and say, 'Hey, you got the wrong person. Oops.'"

I didn't know what to say, so I put the issue aside and stared at the commotion, the mourning around us.

Hugo pulled the truck over around the corner from the street of Villa del Portal, where the massacre had taken place, and where most of the wakes were being held in small homes made out of cinder block. Mexican dignitaries, including the Chihuahua governor, milled about, offering condolences to parents who suspected them of being in cahoots with the very people who'd murdered their children. We waited outside on broken sidewalks for Dudley, my colleague from Houston, and separately a group of academics from the Woodrow Wilson Center, there to gauge the security situation in Ciudad Juárez. The five arrived, squeezed into a cab and slowly got out.

All eyes were suddenly on us. Residents thought we were officials from the U.S. embassy. One after another they approached us, terrified of what had happened, what would become of them, and begged for asylum. If not asylum, they wanted the FBI to investigate. If not the FBI, they wanted the United Nations to send in a team of peacekeepers to protect them. They wanted nothing to do with Juárez or Mexican authorities anymore. They wanted nothing more than to flee and save their children, to find safety as wealthier *juarenses* had already done across the border.

A young woman approached, her face filled with desperation. She stopped me and explained that her younger brother had witnessed the massacre from a crack in the closet door where he'd been hiding. Their older brother had ordered him inside when the gunmen burst into the house. That brother was now in a hospital with bullet wounds to several parts of his body.

"Please help us," she said. "We can't live here anymore."

"I'm just a journalist," I said. I felt like a fraud. She didn't believe we couldn't help. She pleaded again, this time in tears. I felt useless to ease her pain.

The rain was picking up again.

I walked into one of the homes. A wake had been laid for the son of a man named José Luis. Next to his son's coffin was another body, his cousin.

The couch was covered in plastic; on the walls, old faded photographs of family, including a smiling boy—the one now in a casket. The floor was tiled in white. The curtains looked like bedsheets. No carpeting, no overstuffed love seat, no coffee table, no flat screen. In the middle, two silver aluminum caskets, with lids on, and little glass windows to peer down into the face of the departed. Like Tío Delfino. The coffins occupied nearly the entire room.

Flower arrangements and wreaths sat on shelves and furniture, taking up what little space remained. The cheap carnations and greenery reeked of a funeral parlor, and I silently wished I could pinch my nose. The boys' grandmother, small but with sturdy bones, was covered in black. She cried loudly as she grieved over one grandchild's coffin and then the other, wailing as she pressed against the glass that kept her from touching their faces. *"¡Despierta! ¡No me dejes sola, Wicho!"* she cried, using her grandson's nickname. Wake up! Don't leave me here alone, Wicho.

José Luis, Wicho's father, was a truck driver. He had told me the day before that his son was an A student at the Autonomous University of Ciudad Juárez, one of eight universities in the city. His name was also José Luis, but people called him "Wicho." Father and son had been talking about ways to expand the family trucking business to take advantage of the trade between the United States and Mexico. Maybe young Wicho would become a customs broker someday. Together they had dreamed of making a living in Juárez, not to get rich, nothing extravagant, just to work hard and lead a quiet life with dignity. The two believed in building their own Mexican dream. Now the son lay inside a coffin, a victim of fourteen gang members who'd gotten the wrong address from a former state cop. Outside José Luis's house was a sign that read: *"Campeones de Doble A"*—Double A Baseball Champs. Double A was also the initials for Artistas Asesinos, the rival gang to La Línea.

Hearses crawled up the road.

The rain wouldn't let up. I tucked my notepad into my back pocket so that it would be shielded under my red windbreaker. Angela had taken the umbrella to help protect the camera. Dudley also ran for cover from the rain. He looked heartbroken.

José Luis emerged from his light yellow house; outside was a sign directed at President Calderón that read: "What do you want us to do? Arm our children? Justice." He led the procession, his son's coffin held aloft by pallbearers, a brother, friends, cousins. José Luis was in his late thirties but looked twenty years older. He had confided to me earlier that he felt he couldn't cry, nor did he want to: He had to stay strong for everyone else. He felt so lost that he didn't take the time to put on formal pants or a dress shirt to his own son's funeral. He wore blue jeans and a black leather jacket with the collar turned up. The rain picked up once again. José Luis caught my gaze. He and the pallbearers slid the coffin into the back of the hearse. Another hearse waited patiently for Wicho's cousin. José Luis looked back over at me again and patted his jacket pocket, as if searching for something he thought he had lost.

Suddenly he was walking toward me.

It looked like he was crying now, but it might have been the rain.

"Are you a father?" he asked. His eyes were open wide, searching mine.

Angela and I had once talked about raising a family, but when we learned we couldn't have children, we left the topic alone. Now this man—a stranger, really—was asking whether I was a father. He kept looking at me under the pouring rain.

No, I told him. But I, too, had lost someone many years ago.

From his pocket he pulled a photograph of father and son, Wicho and him, taken after a baseball game. The two held a trophy together. Double A Champs, it said.

"Here," he said. "For you. Keep it. I raised a good boy. Look at him. Don't forget him."

"I won't," I assured him and stretched my arm around his shoulders in a strained embrace.

He put his head down and turned away. I watched as he got inside his car. I felt that something was missing, something had been left unsaid.

I quickly walked over to him. He'd put his key in the ignition and turned the radio off. I blurted again how sorry I was about his loss. I gave him my business card, told him to stay in touch. We exchanged phone numbers. I asked him what he wanted readers in the United States and Mexico to understand about his son's senseless death, about the death of so many young people on that single block. He paused and looked up at me. I could now see the tears running down his cheeks, tears no longer masked by the rain.

"I want them to feel my pain," he said, adding something I couldn't understand.

"Resignation?" I asked.

He nodded, paused and then shook his head no.

"Reconciliation," he said, starting up the engine and heaving into sobs. "That's all."

I kept returning to Villas de Salvárcar after that day, drawn back by the families' decision to stay when they could have left for the United States. They chose hope against all odds. I was drawn there by the fact that I, too, wanted to believe. I always asked for José Luis, but he was never home.

One year later, I knocked on his door and his wife, Maricruz, answered. She told me her husband was on the road, his escape. That's how he dealt with the pain, she said. I announced that I had come to return the photograph that José Luis had given me. The photograph of father and son, Wicho. It didn't seem right to keep it. I had framed it.

"I thought you would like it," I said. She looked at it and smiled politely.

"I've lost my son, and no photograph of him, framed or not, will ever replace him. But thank you for the kind gesture," she said, hustling her other son to the door. They were off to baseball practice.

I spent that afternoon with Adrián Cadena, the father of another victim of the massacre, a boy named Rodrigo. He wanted me to see the new football field, part of a sports complex the families had lobbied for from the Mexican government, which had earmarked more than $390 million for security and social development throughout the city.

It was Calderón's way of making amends.

But their resentment toward the president lingered. One mother had defied the president's security detail and stood before him amid a group of dignitaries and told him he wasn't welcome in her city, not after saying that her two killed sons were gang members. The pain ached, but the neighborhood was rising up.

We walked the artificial turf. Adrián knelt, periodically, to pick up large, stray nails. Though they had contemplated leaving Juárez and even separating because the pain was too great, Adrián and his wife would never muster the courage to leave behind their son, now buried in a cemetery close to the airport, where the ground moved subtly with every takeoff and landing. The exodus grew by the day.

Instead, Adrián and his wife, Guadalupe Dávila, returned to the crime scene and faced their pain. On afternoons after he left his job as a mechanic, Adrián would go to two neighborhoods where he and his wife had started separate projects, with the help of federal money and donations, to keep kids away from gangs, drug addiction and the reach of cartels. They turned a second home that Guadalupe owned into an office to rescue kids and offer therapy to those who had lost someone. Their message was simple: We're here to invite your son or daughter to attend sports practice, learn about drug prevention and stay away from gangs. Either entrust them to us, or to El Chapo or La Línea, they said. Kids began to show up by the dozen. They were forming a community, albeit from the cruelest kind of inspiration, Adrián explained as we continued walking around the football field, a cool wind in our faces that winter afternoon.

"Before, I never gave a damn about anyone other than my family," Adrián said. "Now that family has expanded."

Then he stopped, put his hands on his hips and choked up. He took his right hand and wiped away a tear. He struggled to find his voice.

"*Vive*," Adrián assured me. "I can always feel Rodrigo's presence."

We stopped. He kneeled and noticed another nail. He picked it up, wiped a nagging tear and rose from his knees.

"Why do you do all this?" I asked. "This is so painful for you."

"We're building community with the blood of our children," he said.

In the distance, El Paso's mountains loomed like shadows.

"Every time I wonder whether we've become a nation of savages," Adrián said, "where we kill just to kill, decapitate people, hang them over bridges, end the dreams of the young and turn us old prematurely, I look to those mountains."

He nodded toward El Paso, the first and largest town built, in the 1600s, on the river in the mountain corridor that was called Paso del Norte, and the first U.S. city, in 1913, to ban marijuana. El Pasoans, like the people in most border communities, were social conservatives, associating pot smoking with crime. Prohibition had also given white Texans a tool to control the Rio Grande.

Despite the threat from Mexico, El Paso was also the safest city of its size in the United States. Mexican immigrant communities, and other new arrivals in general, represented the "culture of effort": hardworking people putting food on the table, avoiding problems and pushing to get ahead, if not for themselves, then for the next generation, their children.

The city was also swarming with the increasing presence of law enforcement: local, state and federal cops, plus Immigration and Customs Enforcement (ICE), FBI, DEA, border patrol and El Paso Intelligence, not to mention one of the country's largest military bases. Many of the new agents lived in the west side in what was becoming known as Fed Hill, partly visible from here.

"What do you see?" I asked Adrian, writing down his words.

"Our future," he said. "I see laws that work. I see people—the majority of them with roots in Mexico—living in peace."

"Would you live there?"

"It's so beautiful. People have jobs and rights. But I would feel that I would be betraying my son. We have to make sure something good comes out of this tragedy."

Adrián drove me to the international line and we rode along Tecnológico, an avenue filled with trucks carrying cargo and passenger buses heading north.

"What happens when the federal monies run out?" I asked Adrián. "When the next government takes over and the guilt is gone?"

"We've already thought of that," he responded. "Hundreds of volunteers will take over street corners to solicit donations. We'll test how far society wants to go to really change this country. I won't stop—that's for sure."

On the way, we ran into the president's convoy, the leader of Mexico hidden somewhere inside the train of SUVs hurrying to the next meeting with business leaders, protected by soldiers and federal police. Adrián barely noticed.

TWENTY-ONE

On a sweet, sunny morning following the end of the summer rainy season in 2011, I stood out on the balcony of my Mexico City apartment. White clouds rose above a skyscraper under construction on Paseo de la Reforma—a pretty backdrop in contrast to the gray clouds that had taken over the afternoon skyline for months. Four other tall buildings had risen down the road from the Torre Mayor. One was the bicentennial monument, La Estela de Luz, to celebrate the country's independence. A group of protesters had shown up at the grand opening to decry the tens of thousands killed in the drug war, calling the wafer cookie–like structure a monument to corruption and death. Another tower was rising closer to my house on Avenida Insurgentes. It seemed Mexico City was undergoing constant reconstruction.

After a brutal global recession and rising wages in China, the economy was growing slowly again and creating more jobs than ever, yet the number of Mexicans living in poverty had grown by more than four million. The ranks of the middle class had increased, academics and the president touted. But in violent regions, people hardly noticed. The wealthy continued to head to the United States.

Mexico's economy—like political power—remained highly concentrated, dominated by monopolies and oligarchies. It was not all that different from when the Spanish Crown and the Catholic Church controlled much of the nation. The country still had a powerful and corrupt teacher's union, one national oil company, two dominant television networks (though only one really mattered), one national electric company, one cement company, one dominant bread maker, one major cornmeal supplier for tortillas and—of course—one dominant telephone company. Carlos Slim, often ranked the richest man in the world, then worth about $70 billion, controlled not just the telephone industry but also chain restaurants, shopping centers, construction and so much more, and he wanted a share of television rights and tolls for new highways. Like most Mexicans, I subscribed to his cell phone service—one of the most expensive in the world—bought magazines at his department store, ate at his Sanborns restaurant chain, shopped at his malls and paid him tolls on the road.

I took the elevator down to the lobby of my building, where Samuel was waiting with my car. We hurtled down Paseo de la Reforma. Samuel was having a bad day, as he often did when he didn't have much work and was worried about money. I could tell by the way he drove—it was as if he was leaving the scene of a crime. He fiddled with the stereo, switching between songs on the newest mix CD I had given him.

I wanted to listen to "Huapango de Moncayo," a traditional Mexican song that I associate with the pain and happiness of being Mexican. The song picks up slowly; then the trumpets blare and make you feel like the angel perched on a Paseo de la Reforma roundabout—the Angel of Independence—stretching her wings to the heavens. But I didn't bother Samuel. I watched the road instead.

I cautioned him—yet again—against speeding. He just grinned, as though seventeen years in Mexico hadn't yet taught me anything. Here no one gets ticketed. We all negotiate a way out.

He winced and finally played Emmanuel's "Si Ese Tiempo Pudiera Volver" and raised the volume to drown me out or find comfort. Like most Mexicans, he used politeness as a way to skirt conflict. I'm sure he wanted to tell me to fuck off.

He asked what I knew about struggling in Mexico—me with my Condesa flat near all those new fancy restaurants—Milos, Bistro Rojo, Vucciria—and coffee shops. "Mexico is so much different than La Condesa, Alfredo," he said. "You're lucky."

I lowered the music and reminded Samuel that at age thirty he couldn't really remember a peso crisis, something other generations had weathered every six years. He took for granted all the newer vehicles on the roads, the high-rises, highways, bridges like the Puente de los Poetas under construction in the city. Competition at supermarkets meant cheaper basic foods for his family. You were too young in 1994, I said. Mexico really hit bottom then. He couldn't really remember how the PRI once ruled Mexico as the perfect dictatorship, as novelist Mario Vargas Llosa once described it, although some took issue with that term since the PRI was, if anything, a perfect mirror of ourselves. Even if the PRI came back, as many predicted and wanted—Samuel included—this wasn't the old Mexico, I said. Yes, in parts of the country, reporters were besieged—more than seventy journalists had been killed in twelve years. But freedom of expression and accountability were stronger than I could ever remember. Mexico was moving, I said—maybe not fast enough, but it was moving. Mexicans now had political choices. A supreme court, a federal electorate institute and a more independent congress. Technology was helping transform civil society. Fewer Mexicans than ever were heading to work illegally in the United States. Sure, the U.S. economy wasn't healthy enough to swallow as many as it used to, but more jobs were being created in Mexico. Hell, even a *New York Times* article had declared that Mexicans were finding the "Mexican dream" in Mexico. I wanted him to fight back, to drop the politeness and show his anger—reveal that new Mexican in us.

Samuel said: "You're joking, right?"

"You know what middle class in Mexico is?" he asked, sarcastically. "About ten dollars a day. That means Julia and I are middle class," referring to the woman who periodically cleaned my apartment and struggled daily to put food on the table. "That's insulting."

M onths later I got a bitter dose of reality.

"Alfredo, tenemos un problemita." Samuel called me early one morning as the violet-flowered jacaranda trees were in bloom. He was supposed to have picked me up thirty minutes earlier.

"You okay? My car okay?" I asked.

"Yes, car is fine," he said. "But there is a *problemita.*"

"¿Sí?" I said, perplexed. "Spit it out."

"Your car has been confiscated and I'm being detained," he said.

"¿Problemita? ¡Problemota! That's sounds like a big problem. What happened?"

"Two police officers on a motorcycle stopped me because the sticker on your car is fraudulent. The people at the verification center put a false sticker on it and the situation is bad," he said. "I need you here immediately or I will go to jail."

"What do you want me to do?"

"Bring *cinco,*" he said, code for what I naively assumed would be a five-hundred-peso bribe, then roughly forty dollars. He gave me the address of where he had been detained, a police station near the international airport.

I hopped in a cab. I had six hundred pesos in my pocket, although I had no intention of paying. I headed into the station, U.S. passport in hand, but Samuel was standing next to two police officers a few feet outside the headquarters as though they were old friends. The officers greeted me politely and told me the seriousness of the offense: Pay a fine of at least six thousand pesos or four to five years in prison.

"Officer, I agree this is a very serious matter, although I hope you believe me when I tell you we were duped," I said.

"Yes, but he can still go to prison," the officer responded, sizing up Samuel, who looked downright frightened, fully aware that in Mexico one was guilty until proven innocent.

I continued. "Well, that's up to the judge, no, Officer?"

"Look, let's not make this difficult," the officer said. "If we take him in, we'll be compensated six thousand pesos just to set foot in court, three thousand each."

"What? That's insane."

"We're compensated to do our job," he said. "If we take him in, the judge will know we weren't persuaded by anything else."

"I guess that's that, because I don't have that kind of money, Officer," I said.

"How much do you have?" he asked.

"Six hundred pesos, Officer," I said.

Both officers grinned widely and laughed simultaneously before grabbing Samuel by the arm.

"We'll see you in court," the officer said. Samuel looked horrified. "We won't know how long the process of detention is. It could be years before you see him again. Say good-bye to your friend."

Samuel looked teary-eyed.

"Can I get a moment with him, Officer?" I asked.

"Sure, but make it quick 'cause we have work to do and we've already waited long enough. We had hoped we could come to some kind of favorable arrangement for both sides, but that doesn't look possible," the officer said.

"What did you mean by *cinco*?" I asked Samuel when we were alone.

"Five thousand pesos," he said. That was more than four hundred dollars.

"This is ridiculous. Are they serious?"

"I don't really want to find out, but I'm sure they are," Samuel responded. "You gotta help me."

"What the hell happened?" I asked.

"The verification center was in cahoots with the cops," he said. "Everybody gets a cut and I get screwed."

He stood no chance. Had I been the target, I could have called the U.S. embassy for protection. Not Samuel. As in most of Latin America, Mexico has no jury system. Oral trials before a judge had begun only in a couple of states and were expected to expand by 2016 as part of the much anticipated judicial reforms. Still, some 96 percent of all criminal court proceedings were administrative, and 80 percent of those arrested never even saw a judge, as documented in the compelling film *Presunto Culpable.*

What would I tell Samuel's children if their father didn't come home that night? He's in jail because I was trying to make a point? He was facing down Mexico's corruption with zero resources—except what I could provide.

I told Samuel to calm down. I would take care of it. I changed my tone from indignant to humble.

"I repeat: I only have six hundred pesos," I said. "I'll call my attorney and see if he can lend me some more so we can find that favorable arrangement."

"Not a problem," the officer said. "Take your time."

I looked at Samuel and mumbled loud enough for all to hear, "I can't believe we live in a country where narcos who massacre people go free and someone who's duped can end up in prison for five years."

Samuel just looked at me, pleading. I took my cell phone and pretended to make a call. What I was really doing was turning my camera on and recording the moment for prosperity.

"*Sí, Paco,* I have a *problemita* here," I said, using the name of an attorney friend. "I need six thousand pesos right away. Ah, no? And that's because? Ah, I see. So I'm screwed, really fucked. *Me chingué.* Well, let me see what I can do here, see if I can find some sympathy, some flexibility. Thanks for your time."

I looked at the young officer, who seemed disappointed.

"I can do thirty-five hundred pesos," I said. "That's all."

"Five thousand," he responded. This meant there was some flexibility.

I picked up the phone and pretended to call Paco again. "I need at least forty-five hundred, or my friend goes to jail," I said. "Hm. Ah. Wow! *Maravilloso.* Yes, that would be very helpful. Paco, you're the best friend ever. *Muchas gracias.*"

"Four thousand from him and five hundred from me and I go home with a hundred for tortillas and eggs, maybe some water. Does that work?" I asked. "Otherwise a court hearing could take weeks, if not months."

Both officers readily agreed. "Deal."

"I just don't have the cash," I said. "I would need a bank to withdraw."

"Not a problem," the officer said. "The bank is a few blocks from here. We'll guide you."

"Great," I said, feigning kindness. "We'll get in the car and follow you. *Qué amable,* Officer. How kind."

We drove a few blocks, led by the two dirty cops on motorcycles, until we saw the giant Banamex sign. One of the officers nodded at the security guard outside the bank.

The guard nodded and smiled at me. I walked in, bypassed the tellers and took out my debit card. I typed in the withdrawal amount: four thousand pesos. The sound of money whooshed. I rolled the money in a wad, added the five hundred pesos and made sure my camera phone was still on. I returned to the two officers parked about a block away, next to Samuel inside my car. He looked defeated. I had the money in a neat roll and gave it to the officer.

"Here we go," I said. "You may want to count it to make sure it's all there."

"That won't be necessary," he said.

"No, of course not," I responded.

The officer took the wad of pesos and we both smiled.

"Who do I have the pleasure . . . ?"

"Officer Martínez," said one. "Officer Ortiz," said the other. I looked at the name tags on their blue uniforms and confirmed their names. Shameless.

I was opening the car door when Officer Ortiz tapped me on my shoulder. I thought the officer realized I had been taping their unfolding crime all along. Instead, the officer politely reminded me, "Be careful where you get your sticker next time," he said. "There's a lot of false places in this city. A lot of criminals."

"Thank you for being so thoughtful," I said.

We drove off. Samuel and I didn't say a word for the first few minutes as I checked the quality of the video on my camera phone. The image was shaky, but the sound, faces and names were clear. Samuel discouraged me from uploading the video to YouTube.

"Look, technology is one way to hold the government accountable," I said. "You put this on YouTube, and you denounce corruption and strengthen civil society. This is better than a *limpia*." I made a closed fist and looked for his. Both his hands remained glued to the wheel.

"I'll pay the price for that video," he said, cringing. "They have my home information. They'll find me, or my family. Forget about it, Alfredo. I'd rather leave it alone and move on. Please."

I didn't press it.

A song on that same mix CD we had been listening to for months ended and Samuel lowered the volume. His frustrations exploded. He confessed he had recently been approached by someone he knew who had offered him a job to drive cars loaded with drugs from Los Angeles to Chicago, Dallas and New York City. They would smuggle him into the United States and then he'd keep doing what he was doing now: driving.

U.S. newspapers were still losing money, and what was once an honest, steady gig—driving around foreign correspondents, helping with logistics and interviews or running bureau errands—was now an occasional job. I raised the volume to "Huapango de Moncayo," but the song now sounded shallow.

"Samuel, think this through—one mistake can cost you your life and that of your family," I said. "These assholes *no conocen la palabra perdón,*" I said, echoing my father's words. They don't know forgiveness.

"You're right," he said. "I've already thought about it and that's why I'm pissed off. I can't do it 'cause of my daughters and because I don't want to take my problems to bed. But you see how easy money can be, why so many get into the business? There's no end to poverty, or to the illegal, informal market. This is Mexico. *Everybody* is corrupt. The cops, the security guards, the verification center, their supervisors—they are all in on this. The entire system is rotten."

"Everybody is in on it?" I asked. "Were you in on it too?"

"What? No." He looked at me hard. "You do believe me, right?"

Like many Mexicans, Samuel could have left for the United States. He stayed not because he believed in a future, but because he believed in his family. The only precious thing in his life, he said, were his two daughters, who had helped cure the wounds of his own difficult childhood. He would prove to be the father he never had.

"This is a great, generous country, Alfredo. Every six years the politicians beat up the country—*le parten la madre a la patria*—and then somehow Mexico gets back on its feet again and gives us more."

It's not that Mexico is generous, I thought; it's that Mexicans have heart. Samuel was talking about himself.

"You do believe me, right?" he asked again.

If anything, Mexico had taught me to believe, even against all odds—sometimes against my own instincts—to have faith, the kind of faith my mother tried teaching me for so long, faith that chases away evil. Faith was all you could have in a country with a glorious past and a decrepit system. I was channeling my mother.

"*Te creo.*" I felt enough conviction as I said the words.

TWENTY-TWO

Angela, Hugo and I drove the 580-mile trip from Laredo to El Paso in west Texas, hugging the line with the states of Coahuila and Chihuahua. Hours upon hours of lonely desert, unless you counted the border patrol trucks cruising up and down Highway 90. Since 1990, the size of the U.S. border patrol force had increased by a factor of five. Past Del Rio, I started counting them, but I lost count of the green vans after counting more than a dozen in less than a hundred miles.

Farther into west Texas, in El Paso, shiny white-and-green border patrol trucks crawled along the fence that divided "us" from "them," part of the latest federal security buildup. As if a rusted, eighteen-foot fence stretching 650 miles—part of the $2.8 billion package that locals referred to as a "border wall"—could absolve Americans of their longing for drugs or their desire for cheap labor to keep the price of fruits, vegetables and services low. As if sheets of steel and drones could keep out the mess Americans helped create. We were bound by blood, and nothing—not even the wall—could undo that.

The dry rocky hills of spectacular Big Bend rose not far from the winding two-lane highway, the border somewhere out to our left. The winds picked up, breaking the summer heat, a sign that autumn was on the way. The vast blue skies expanded; clouds rose from the horizon.

Vast stretches of wild land and arid ranches and hills separated towns with names like Zorro and Guadalupe. It was hard to tell where Mexico ended and America began. It is one of my favorite parts of both countries.

The border, Carlos Fuentes once wrote, is a "scar." We are the wound.

I looked at Angela again. The years of absence in each other's lives hurt. I reached out for her hand, but was quickly reminded that Hugo was in the backseat. She had an aloofness that made me want to hold her tight. But Angela didn't like showing affection in front of colleagues. I always forgot this rule. I just smiled at her, and she smiled back.

I began to tell her about a recent troubling meeting with the U.S. investigator. She didn't seem surprised at all.

"I know you like him, but in the end he's just doing his job and so are you," she said. "You can't trust anyone anymore. I learned that as a child. It's time you learn that too."

"You're wrong, precious," I said, and touched her hand. "I trust you. We still have each other."

As we neared the town of Marfa, a favorite spot of Hollywood types and New Yorkers with time and cash, big skies and sheets of rain greeted us. Raindrops falling on the desert would ease a long drought in west Texas. I wasn't sure whether we were driving into a storm or chasing it away.

We stopped in Marfa and looked for Padres, formerly a funeral home, and one of the few bars open in the afternoon. The music on the jukebox, old Javier Solís songs that my mother once sang, and the spicy chili bowl were worth stopping for.

Hugo left to make some calls. Angela and I were alone now. We had been going around in circles for years, really since that afternoon she'd stormed off from Parque México in La Condesa. I felt my heart racing, hoping she'd come back. She was as beautiful as ever, her cheeks as smooth as the day I had met her at Freddy's twenty years before. Angela kept pushing me forward in spite of our imperfections. Angela represented everything I ever loved about my homeland, even though I, more than she these days, dreamed of living in Mexico.

She broke the silence by asking me what time I thought we would arrive in El Paso, whether the rain would follow us or if the storm had passed.

"Who cares?" I responded.

Angela looked at me and tightened her grip on my hand. "We really need to get our shit together." She laughed. I agreed.

Outside we could hear lightning strike. I searched for quarters in my pockets to play songs for her.

Somewhere in Mexico, away from the border—I'm not allowed to be specific—I finally met the U.S. investigator again. I wanted to finally put some issues to rest and get an answer to the question that haunted me: Who had threatened my life?

The investigator had called out of nowhere and I rushed to meet him. I still found myself looking over my shoulder, staying up late at night, wanting to make sense of the senseless. He was still chasing the feared Zetas leader, now referred to simply as Forty, or Cuarenta. He was wanted in the United States in connection with a 2006 double homicide in Texas and for conspiracy to manufacture and distribute cocaine in the United States. The Zetas had split with the Gulf cartel and had merged with the Beltrán Leyva organization. In just two years they had spread to key regions from Tamaulipas to Nuevo León, Coahuila and Zacatecas. They were now considered the second most powerful criminal organization after the Sinaloa cartel. The violence continued to spread.

"You seem obsessed by Forty," I told the U.S. investigator.

"You should be too," he responded. "We should all be."

We were drinking what seemed like an entire bottle of tequila. Yet he wouldn't talk. He seemed depressed, and so was I.

Officially, the Mexican government said forty-seven thousand people had been killed in the war on the cartels, but it had stopped counting in early 2011. Other estimates at the time had the death toll at more than eighty thousand. So many were dying, the investigator said, that no one kept count anymore. Sometimes, cartel members would pick up the fallen and bury them in clandestine graves to keep it all a secret between themselves and the corrupt officials. We were a traumatized nation, pain shared on both sides of the border.

Along the U.S. side, agents were also being recruited by the cartels, lured by money or even sexual favors. Dozens of federal agents—as many as 170 in just four years, including agents of the border patrol, DEA, FBI and ICE—had given in to temptation.

All the while, the Mexican government had kill squads working full-time to get Chapo Guzmán and Forty. The DEA and other U.S. security agencies were feeding Mexican military intelligence information on the movements of the top narcos. That information all too often made it to Mexican officials who were also sympathizers of one cartel or another. So many officials were on cartel payrolls that it increasingly wasn't a war against cartels, but a war within the government itself.

"They're too slow to react," the investigator said. "The corruption *está cabrón*. It's so deeply ingrained with government politics and economics that what we do doesn't always make sense. It doesn't matter if you have that cartel leader right now, right here, cornered. It doesn't matter."

That summer of 2012 the U.S. investigator was even more frustrated by the Mexicans' failure to kill or capture Forty, or his cohort, Heriberto Lazcano, Z-3, who was an original member of the elite army deserters; he had been caught two times by the military in Puebla and each time he'd bribed his way out. The investigator slammed down another tequila.

(Weeks later Lazcano was killed in a shootout with marines in the state
of Coahuila.)

"Mexico enjoys easy money too much," he said. "You won't see a sig-
nificant change here for another ten, twenty years. I wish Calderón had
cleaned up the house a little more before he started this, but you can't
blame Calderón. Imagine where Mexico would be today if everyone continued looking the other way, *haciendose pendejos*."

I thought about how many Mexicans might answer that question:
Yes, it would look less democratic, but it would be more peaceful. Sometimes it seemed people were so frustrated with so much violence they'd
prefer order, even smelly order, to their new freedoms. I thought about
all the banks in the United States and Europe stuffed with illicit money.
I thought about Calderón, the man who had grown up hating the PRI,
even promising at his father's grave that one day he'd remove them from
power. He used to camp outside the presidential palace or protest in the
Zócalo, pressing for change. Now he seemed poised to return power to
his old rivals—his legacy, for the moment, stained by a barbarity that
overshadowed his many other accomplishments: opening 140 public universities, miles of infrastructure projects including three thousand new
and renewed clinics, expanded health care, upgrading environmental
standards and creating 2.2 million new jobs. But all the people remembered was the bloodshed. Some said death shadowed him. Some human
rights groups vowed that Calderón would one day face criminal charges
from an international court.

The investigator's eyes were glassy and I imagined mine were too. He
told me what I had always suspected but never confirmed. Treviño
Morales—Forty—had put a price on his head. He said he slept with a
loaded shotgun at his bedside on the U.S side of the border. On the Mexican side? Well, he wouldn't say, since Mexican law prohibited U.S agents
from being armed. He suspected Forty would send hit men to his house
and take him out. He wanted to believe that no cartel would risk the

wrath of the U.S. government, but he also knew some of these guys could get so high on drugs and power that they'd forget which side of the border they were on and make a stupid move. And he'd be dead.

Then he confirmed what I'd been searching for for so long: that Forty had also been behind the death threat against me. If Forty couldn't get the investigator, he'd get me to send him a message.

"Puta madre," I said.

Cuarenta had friends and family in Dallas, and some had read stories that colleagues and I had written about the Zetas. The U.S. investigator said Forty loved Dallas, its flashy life. As late as 2005, Forty would cross the Rio Grande illegally near an inland port known as San Ignacio, just south of Nuevo Laredo, and head to Dallas to see friends and family who were now laundering millions of Forty's illicit dollars through horse racing. He had even been spotted at a strip bar. The U.S. investigator said my stories had something to do with Forty's decision to stop going to Dallas. The coverage, particularly about the peace pact, intrigued him, and he suspected the leads on the story had come from the investigator. He hated snitches and wanted to know who exactly had leaked the information to the investigator so he could cut off his balls and stuff them in his mouth. Mutilate them. The investigator had spent the past eight years trying to find Forty first. All reports from his informants—at that moment I counted four cell phones on him for snitches from each of the major cartels—showed that Forty was on the lam, or hiding beneath a giant rock.

Cuarenta now had a $5 million reward on his head placed by the U.S. government, a $2 million one by the Mexican government, and his own cartel rivals were gunning for him. He was protected by some two hundred hit men, plus corrupt cops and officials who helped form a circle of fifteen levels of security around him, difficult for anyone to penetrate, especially a government whose intelligence was often compromised. He often traveled in ambulances or low-flying planes. Treviño Morales was distrustful of everyone—except his brother Omar, Z-42—and slept inside his car, where he carried hundreds of thousands of dollars to bribe any authority who got too close. He was addicted to marijuana, antisocial and liked living in the wilderness—some called him El Chacal, the Jackal—because he was a night owl and so difficult to find in the woods.

He was no longer the gardener or the chimney sweeper. He was a madman. His other nickname, Muerte—Death—said it all. It earned him the much-denied respect. His pep talk consisted of one line: If you don't kill someone every day, you're not doing your job.

He was deeply loyal to his family, particularly his mother, who single-handedly raised him and his siblings after their father abandoned them. He was so incensed over his mother being harassed by U.S. Customs in Laredo that in October 2010 he ordered grenades tossed near the U.S. Consulate in Monterrey, the investigator said.

The Zetas under Forty had turned into a satanic cult, offering the blood and hearts of victims to the devil in return for their protection. Part of the ritual involved Forty removing a victim's heart—while the person was still alive—and taking a bite out of it. He believed it would make him invincible.

The U.S. investigator had seen so much inhumanity that whenever he came to Mexico City he would slip into the Basilica de Guadalupe to pray to the Virgin for peace and strength. He wasn't praying alone; grateful mothers along the border held sessions for him to thank him for helping find their children, dead or alive. On Sundays he'd go to confession. "Why do you rejoice at news of the killing of some big drug kingpin?" one priest asked.

"Because," he'd responded, "that kingpin was the closest thing to the devil."

He was a decent man, I thought, but at the moment I didn't know whether to be grateful for the investigator's honesty or to feel betrayed.

"So this whole time—all the tips you gave me, all the stories—I was really your mouthpiece? Your way of communicating with Forty?" I asked. "Just like the cartels that use Mexican reporters to get their message out? What the fuck?"

He looked into his glass of tequila, then raised his gaze to meet my angry eyes.

"Yeah," he said. "I used you, just like you used me. I called you with tips, but I did it 'cause I knew you gave a shit. It was more than just a story for you."

"So that's why you called to warn me?" I asked.

"I warned you not as a U.S. government official but as a friend," he said. "I didn't want anything to happen to you."

"Gee, fucking thanks!" I spit out.

The tequila was making me brave.

"Forty has too much on his mind to worry about you or me these days," he said. "I doubt he even remembers."

The last five years of running flashed through my mind and the pieces now fit together. I looked the U.S. investigator over. He seemed less cocky than when I'd first met him. He still believed in good and evil, but he also understood there were shades of evil and shades of good in each of us. He had lost at least fifteen friends, "brave sons of Mexico killed for knowing too much or trying to do the right thing."

There was police chief Omar Pimentel, whom Angela and I had kept in touch with after doing a story about why anyone would ever want the post after the last chief was killed just hours after he got the job. One day Pimentel abruptly quit and told me he did so for personal reasons. He later disappeared. He had been kidnapped and tortured, and is presumed dead. The Zetas found the phone that the U.S. investigator had given him.

"Who's this?" one of Pimentel's kidnappers asked when he dialed the number. The U.S. investigator identified himself by name.

"Fuck you, *puto,*" the gangster said and hung up.

His apparent death has never been confirmed.

The more the Mexican government confronted the cartels, the more brutal the retaliation from the criminals. There's a certain kind of wisdom in understanding that change has its own rhythm and is subject to its own time and circumstance, I thought.

"We have to keep the pressure, but we've also learned there are limitations, that we have to be flexible," he said. "Mexico has taught me—us— to be more prudent, patient. *El Diablo no duerme.*" The devil doesn't sleep. He had discovered his Mexican counterpart had sold the entire dossier to Forty.

"Aren't you tired of this?" I asked, a question I was really asking myself.

"I have gotten old in Mexico and I have realized that the timing is never right, unless Mexico believes the timing is right," he said.

"Timing for what?" I asked. "To become a country more like the United States?"

"Hey, I think everyone agrees, we all know Mexico can do better. Create more opportunities, more equality, more accountability, more justice. *¿Me entiendes?* Call that what you want. I don't care."

"So why are you still here?"

"In the United States people die either from a disease—a heart attack, cancer, shit like that—or a car accident. Here you die one minute to the next, and knowing that makes you want to live life fuller," he said. "You're reminded daily of your mortality. Plus I like the sounds of this country, the smell, the contrasts, the colors, the music, the raw feeling. Life. But I don't have to tell you that."

"Seriously, why are you here?" I pressed him again. "Why do you keep coming back?"

"Same reason you do," he said. "It's personal, no?"

TWENTY-THREE

My mother prayed for Mexico's forgiveness. We sped through the northern state of Chihuahua at dawn, bound for home in Durango. Joan Sebastian's song "Eso y Más," a tune he dedicated to his murdered son, blared from the speakers. We drove fast so we'd get there before darkness fell. It was a nine-hour drive from El Paso.

The State Department had issued travel alerts for most Mexican states, including a pointed warning against traveling on the road we were on. The meeting place between the three states of Coahuila, Chihuahua and Durango had become the dividing line between warring cartels. My mother had wanted to go by bus—alone. She was determined to visit Lupita's gravestone, she said, even if it meant breaking her promise to her children that she and my father would stay away from Mexico. She had to go, and finally relented that I could accompany her. We settled on going together, but only after I agreed to visit a *curandera* for a *limpia*. When my father saw she was serious, he reluctantly agreed to go as well.

"Are you two crazy?" my father asked, but didn't wait for an answer. He knew.

"We'll be fine," my mother assured him as he walked away. "Sometimes the perception of fear is greater than the reality."

Samuel and I took turns driving. I had invited him along for extra protection. On the highway, two separate convoys of heavily armed men in SUVs with no license plates zoomed past, headed in the opposite direction. Samuel tapped me on my arm and pointed to the vehicles. I felt ridiculous for not taking the bus, which now seemed marginally safer. If the convoy wants to mess with us, I thought, we're screwed. We'd be escorted to some isolated place—not far from where we were born—then shot and buried. Or what if they try to recruit Samuel to be a hit man and test him by having him kill us? I nervously looked to the mirror on my side to see whether the SUVs had made a U-turn and were giving chase. They were not. Instead, I saw a federal cruiser with sirens pulling us over. Samuel had hit the gas after seeing the convoys, and we were really speeding.

Samuel got out of the car and took care of the situation the only way he knew how: by bribing the cops, telling them he was simply transporting an elderly couple and their son to a cemetery. They let us proceed. He gave them five hundred pesos to share, roughly twenty bucks each.

Then a second convoy of gunmen passed and, a minute or so later, another federal police cruiser tailed us and stopped us. This time, disgusted, I got out of the car and told Samuel I would take charge. I told the cops I was taking my parents through Mexico as part of an experiment to see how safe Mexico was for immigrants wanting to come home. I'd plan to write down my experiences in a story for the *News*. I told him we were in constant communication with editors and officials at the U.S. embassy to ensure our safety. So what was the problem?

None at all, the officer said.

They were there to make sure we were fine, he indicated. Do slow down, he said. And one more thing: Try not to stop anywhere until you cross the state line.

"Who's in those convoys?" I asked. "U.S. or Mexican federal agents? . . . Zetas?"

He smirked.

I shook his hand.

I returned to the car and assured my parents we were fine. The cops were playing lookout for the cartels.

"Everything okay?" my father asked.

"Speeding," I said. "Don't worry about it."

"Slow down," my father admonished from the backseat.

We couldn't bury Tío Delfino peacefully, and now we couldn't even visit my sister's grave. *"¿Qué le pasa a México?"* my father asked. I didn't respond immediately. Things will only get better, I said, looking at Samuel. He pouted.

"Are you sure?" Samuel asked.

"Absolutely," I replied. I motioned with my foot for him to step on it. He did.

My mother hardly noticed the convoys, the commotion outside or the conversation with my father. She was too immersed in her Bible, a rosary in her hands, praying that we'd reach Lupita's grave before sunset. She read from a passage about Saint Peter's shadow, which a healer had suggested for these difficult times in Mexico. "May the light of the Holy Spirit shield us with its saintly veil. If they have eyes may they not see us; if they have tongues may they not move them." I debated whether it was my mother's relentless prayer or my crumpled blue U.S. passport that kept me alive.

At the entrance into the town of San Luis de Cordero, we saw my grandmother Rosa's crumbling home. Overgrown ocotillo trees, weeds, white trash bags, empty beer bottles tossed from the bar next door, candle wrappers tossed from the church on the other side littered the backyard, burying our umbilical cords deeper into the ground. The house was a shell of what it had been. As I tried opening a door that had been sealed with a padlock, parts of the adobe roof began to fall on my head. My mother dropped her head and muttered how sad the sight made her. Samuel stayed behind, sitting on a park bench my father had sat on when he dreamed of working in America. We drove past a plaque that honored those men and women who'd headed north on the so-called Camino Real connecting north and south. I drove toward the cemetery.

We walked aimlessly until we found my sister's grave, at the foot of our grandparents' grave site. Many other graves looked abandoned. With a pail of water, we cleaned my sister's tombstone and covered it with fresh red and white carnations and placed a singing bear that we had bought in El Paso. The bear chirped the Foundations' "Build Me Up, Buttercup," whose lyrics my parents didn't understand, though they liked the tune. My mother shed tears and my father, typically, looked away, although I could see his eyes turn watery. I put my arms around my mother, embraced her tightly and once again told her how sorry I was, just like when I was a boy. I turned away and wiped my own tears before my parents could see me. I looked over at Lupita's gravestone, the gray marble, and imagined I heard the church bells tolling.

It was Sábado de Gloria—Holy Saturday, the day before Easter— March 28, 1964, and the fair was in town. My mother had made me a promise: She'd take me to ride the Ferris wheel after church on Sunday. Mass on Saturday was interminable, but finally the church bells rang, and I bolted outside into the plaza under a brilliant sun. I was dancing, and my little sister Lupita watched me with her huge brown eyes, a wide smile, dimples and long eyelashes. She was a wobbly two-year-old, normally quiet and shy, but she clapped while I gyrated in the new shorts my grandmother had made me the night before, special for the Easter weekend.

We arrived home hungry. As my mother went to the kitchen, she asked my nine-year-old cousin, Lupe, and me to watch over Lupita while she cooked *chuales,* a traditional Easter stew made of corn with cilantro, tomato and spicy red chile. Lupita played with her dolls. I pushed a toy car along with Juan and my six-year-old cousin, Abel, and made funny engine noises.

San Luis de Cordero had no running water. My mother and neighbors fetched it from wells. Outside, my mother would fill a large tin basin so we could wash our hands, bathe or wash clothes. While my cousin and I played, Lupita decided she wanted to bathe her doll.

I heard my mother call. Lunch was ready.

"*Vénganse a comer*," she said. Come eat.

When I turned to look for Lupita, I couldn't see her. Then I spotted two white shoes dangling over the side of the basin, the doll floating on top. I screamed and ran to the tub. Lupita stared back at me, her eyes wide open, lifeless beneath the water. Just her face was immersed, her mouth turned to the side.

¡Mamá! Lupita won't move!

Suddenly my mother was lifting her baby from the basin. Sinking to her knees. Clutching Lupita. A small puddle of water growing under her knees, her apron dripping. Water soaked her blouse. My mother sobbed and screamed to the heavens. Time stopped as her cries pierced the Easter quiet. Then she stood and, holding Lupita in her arms, ran out to the street named Juárez. I ran alongside her. She searched desperately for the only doctor in town. He was nowhere. He had gone on vacation for Holy Week.

As if people don't get sick, as if children don't die, during Holy Week.

We finally reached my grandmother Rosa's house on Comercio, four blocks away. She met us at the door—she had already heard my mother screaming. Doña Rosa, as she was known, was also the town's unofficial doctor, seamstress, schoolteacher and aide to the local midwife who'd brought many of the townspeople into this world, including me. Including Lupita.

When we reached her, Lupita's brown hair was still dripping wet. My mother placed Lupita into the arms of her grandmother, saying *Save her* without uttering a word. Here, fix her. Make her come alive again. Turn back the clock. Tell me this is a nightmare and I'll wake up any second now. But all they did, my mother and Mamá Rosa, was cry over her tiny body, screaming again to the heavens for answers, begging God to intercede, appealing to the calendar of saints to do this one favor. Then she sat in a chair and didn't move for a long time.

"*¿Por qué?*" my mother bawled. "Why? Please don't take her. Please!"

I looked at them crying and drifted outside and sunk to my knees, pushing my hands in the dirt, digging for rocks, for anything. Afraid to speak.

The Ferris wheel a block away in the square began its slow churn, sending riders high above the plaza where we had just played.

Back inside, neighbors slowly joined us in the dark room, inquiring about all the screams. Once they heard the news, they bowed their heads, shed a few tears and then returned with white carnations from their small gardens blooming in early spring. Throughout the afternoon others brought roasted corn, *fideo,* cooked beans. The smell of corn on the cob permeated the room where my mother and Mamá Rosa had hastily laid Lupita on a table, her head on a pillow.

A day later, at Lupita's wake, a three-man band played "Las Golondrinas," a song for the departed. Neighbors poured in to pay their respects. I was in the middle of them, four years old, lost, screaming for Lupita to wake up. They patted me on my head. Some hugged me, whispered things into my ear that I don't remember. I didn't care what they said. My eyes were fixated on Lupita, whose rosebud face was now covered by flowers. I cried hard and loud; I believed she could somehow still hear me and would wake up. Death was not for the young, but for the old, the ones we accompanied to the cemetery from time to time when dusk fell. Death had no business with my baby sister.

A photographer came and took pictures of Lupita that Tío Delfino later hid away from my mother forever. She didn't move at the wake, her chair firmly beside Lupita, who was tucked inside a white casket and dressed in a snowy Sunday gown sewn by my grandmother overnight. Day-old tears stained my grandmother's withered face. I imagined her tears being embroidered into the white ruffled fabric. Of course, my father couldnt make it back in time for Lupita's funeral. As usual, he was in California getting the fields ready to plant cotton, sugar beets, melons, lettuce, to make sure Americans had food on the table in the seasons ahead. As a bracero, he could return only with written permission from his boss. He didn't reach the boss in time.

I stepped in for my father. I clutched my mother's hand, begging silently for forgiveness for not watching Lupita as closely as I should have.

At the funeral, my mother wasn't there—not really. She was buried in sorrow, inconsolable. She never looked up. At thirteen, she had lost her father to a fire that engulfed him while he worked in the cornfields of San Luis de Cordero; he'd never stood a chance, because there were no doctors, no clinics back then.

My mother vowed after Lupita's death that she would never sing again, that Lupita's death would be our rebirth.

Everything about that day remains so clear. The spring day, the dogs barking, the neighbors staring, the Ferris wheel, my sister's wet hair—those images still follow me. Sometimes at the strangest times or in the oddest of places, and always when I'm ready to leave Mexico, whether for a day, a week or longer, I think of Lupita. Maybe my return to Mexico, my stubbornness, my anger, my refusal to leave this country, even when all signs indicate I should go, even when I am so tired and disappointed, maybe it's really nothing more than my attempt to make amends for what I lost that day. What is my search for home if not a futile desire for resurrection, a renewal of a wounded spirit, a sentimental attempt to give meaning to not one but two lives, a reconciliation with the past?

Yes, I thought, it's personal.

TWENTY-FOUR

I looked toward the desert landscape and its ocotillo plants waving with the wind over the flat plain below the mountains. I sat next to my mother and father in our backyard overlooking the pool. My mother's gaze was firmly set, as was mine, on dry, dusty northern Mexico and the burnt orange Chihuahua mountains beyond. Her eyes were transfixed by the wood pallet shacks on the Juárez side of the Río Bravo. In 2012, we were holding a family gathering in late summer at our house. As my parents aged, Thanksgiving and Christmas reunions weren't enough anymore.

My mother walked out to the upper deck of our home and looked at the rain clouds gathering. The clouds were coming from behind the mountain, a sign, she told me, that rain would burst any minute.

"I hope it rains and rains hard," she said. "My plants, especially the roses and *bugambilias,* can use a little soaking."

The sky looked dark, ready to unleash a thunderstorm. Mundo made beef tacos and yelled to his ten-year-old son, Cristian, in English, "When the rain starts, you better get out of the pool. Get out, okay?"

One by one my family members arrived, their English more intact than their Spanish. The only time I heard Spanish was when my mother and father spoke. There were eight of us now: Juan, Mario, Frank and myself, born in Mexico; David, born just weeks after we arrived in America, and Mundo, our youngest brother; then two sisters, Monica and Linda. Most have U.S. college educations and professional jobs. My sister Monica has a master's degree in education, lived in Pittsburgh and plans to work at UTEP; my sister Linda has a law degree from Cardozo in New York City. We're all American now. Yet the other remnants of our Mexicanidad—our faith, the lurking suspicion that death or a curse, or *maldad,* is always near—remain hidden inside.

My two sisters had set three tables outside for guests. "You're not getting in the pool until you help us, *güey,*" Linda admonished me. "Make sure someone watches Fred. He's getting in the pool," added Monica.

My father sat at the end of a long table. The Chihuahua desert and its pained, broken city of Juárez loomed to the left of us. I pointed this out to my father, who seemed annoyed.

I waited by the pool for Angela, who had vowed to continue teaching me how to swim. I was determined to shed my own fears and learn, at least, how to float.

Tired of waiting, I entered the water where it wasn't too deep, where I could stand on my feet, comforted by the sight of Cristian, my nephew, who swam like a dolphin. He offered to watch over me, he told me earnestly, his eyes bigger than normal, with a soft chin and spiked hair. I closed my fist and we bumped fists twice. The waters rippled with the gentle summer winds. Rain was now moving in fast.

I felt the weight of water slowly immersing me. My body gradually grew accustomed to the coldness. Zoé, the band, took over the music system and jammed "Nada," the beat pulsating and ricocheting from the walls on the porch, my brothers' fists pumping in the air—*"Nada que pueda temer . . ."* Nothing to fear, nothing that cannot be . . . I tried moving my feet in the pool to the beat, but stopped when I noticed Cristian's worried face. He doted on me and I on him. He looked afraid now.

"Tío Fred, don't do that. Don't dance," he said. "You might drown."

"I don't understand a word you're saying," I responded in Spanish, hoping he'd answer me in my native tongue, hoping he and everyone else stopped calling me "Fred." I hated that name, a name not appropriate for a son of Mexico. But his puzzled look reminded me it was too late.

"I don't understand Spanish," he pleaded.

"*Yo no hablo inglés,*" I responded, my way of reminding him that he needed to learn Spanish, my way of forcing what was left of my culture on him. I got momentarily exasperated, then sighed, blew bubbles on the surface of the water. I gave him a gentle pat on his arms and told him it was okay. I'd be fine. I pushed him off. He really didn't understand and just floated away, his small belly over the water. He smiled with dimpled cheeks.

I left the pool and sat on the balcony and waited for the rains. I ached for rain. The clouds broke open, first gently, just as when I was in Mexico City, especially late at night inside my apartment in La Condesa, just as in San Luis de Cordero when I was only a boy. I closed my eyes and I was back in Durango, where I had all the freedom in the world, running down the street until the dirt turned to mud and rivers ran down my cheeks.

Angela finally showed up with a sheepish grin. She was late but she had nothing else planned for the rest of the day, she assured me. She just wanted to hang out and pass the time. I offered her something to eat. She said yes. Under the trickle of raindrops, I walked away to fetch her chicken tacos and a salad.

Suddenly lightning flashed and the thunder boomed louder, the skies opened wider and the rains turned ferocious, pelting everyone, forcing us to scramble for temporary shelter underneath the roof of the patio. The rain poured and it kept pouring. Zoe's "Luna" erupted—*"Silencio"*—the lyrics sweeping me away; the tide rising to the rhythm of a volcano.

It was, in my opinion, a perfect afternoon. I stared into the distance. We are the same geography, one blood, two countries dancing out of step, two souls still clashing. My feet were planted on U.S. soil. Mexico was in my sights. I did not want to be anywhere else or anyone else. At least at that moment, in my search for home, I felt I didn't have to choose anymore.

I looked toward the Rio Grande and tried finding its meandering waters. I imagined myself floating on the river, the border, underneath the rain, in the currents of a shared turmoil, without having to pick one side over the other. If only I could swim, I thought. If only.

I stepped out into the downpour. The rain pounded. I closed my eyes, turned my palms to the sky and raised my head.

In the rain, everything is washed away. Everything but our faith.

Acknowledgments

Producing a book encompassing more than fifty years of my own and my country's life incurs many debts. It was Scott Moyers's idea that I write this book and I am most grateful for the opportunity. The Penguin Press's Virginia Smith patiently and brilliantly guided me through the process, my first as an author. Thank you, The Wylie Agency.

I am forever in awe of my gifted writing coach, Lauren Courcy Villagran, who taught me the difference between being a reporter and a writer by helping me find my own voice.

This book would not be possible without the support of many people who unselfishly gave of their time and knowledge. Harvard historian John Womack read the manuscript carefully and made many important suggestions. Hope Reese taught me discipline—there's no *mañana* in book writing; June Carolyn Erlick guided me through the early stages of writing, and always asked to see more—now! Benjamin Alire Saenz brought a literary critique to enhance what he called my dry, boring reporting. Shannon K. O'Neil read the entire manuscript one weekend, made insightful suggestions and helped me make peace.

Cynthia Prida constantly challenged my ideas of what Mexico is and could be.

This book would not be possible without the generous support of the *Dallas Morning News,* in particular, Bob Mong, George Rodrigue, Tim Connolly and Alfredo Carbajal; Andrew Selee, Eric Olson and librarian Janet Spikes at the Woodrow Wilson Center's Mexico Institute in Washington D.C.; Merilee Grindle, Kathy Eckroad and Edwin Ortiz at the David Rockefeller Center for Latin American Studies, DRCLAS, at Harvard University, as well as Harvard librarian Lynn Shirey. Thank you, Dr. Diana Natalicio at my alma mater, the University of Texas at El Paso, and El Paso Community College.

I also thank Lowell House at Harvard University for providing a roof, a bed, a desk and a window with a view into autumn. Special thanks to Diana Eck and Elizabeth (Beth) Terry for the hospitality.

The *Club de los Secretos*—four aspiring writers and friends who dared each other to write a book. We did it. Thanks Karin Grundberg, Graciela Mochkofsky and Gabriel Pasquini. The idea was born in the class of Constance Hale, who enthusiastically helped shaped the concept.

The following offered not just friendship but feedback and support:

Jorge Dominguez, Dora Beszterczey, Louie Marie Gilot, Kalpana Jain, Paola Ibarra, Julie Reynolds, Chris Vognar, Alejandra Xanic, Sergio Silva-Castaneda, Anika Grubbs, Patricia Villarreal, Daniela Baptista, Billy Calzada, James Martinez, Maria Barron, Irma and Victor Salas, Pete Duarte, Cecilia Balli, Zaira and Joe Crisafulli, Veronica Martini, Lourdes Cardenas, Marysa Navarro, Lois Fiore, Monica Almeida, Andrea Pitzer, Thorne Anderson, Kael Alford, Maria Sacchetti, Laura Vargas, Camino Kavanagh, Bob and Nancy Giles, Dr. Guillermo "Jesus" Velasco, Vicki Icard and Michael Lapadot, *Miguelito.* The entire 2009 Nieman class at Harvard, the best ever, the Tepoztlan group, Freddy's Breakfast Forum, and of course, *Los Camineros.*

I also thank my cousins, aunts and uncles for helping me remember things I wish I had forgotten, and bringing to life moments that still warm the heart.

My brothers, sisters, nieces and nephews—family—who I hope will someday forgive my absence in their lives as I tried to weave our story with that of our two countries. Special thanks to my youngest sister, Linda, who helped me heal with laughter and revealed life's secret: float.

And finally, thank you, Angela, *preciosa,* for continuing to be the brightest light and biggest hope amid the darkness in our beloved country, Mexico.

Sources

This book is based on personal experience and my reporting for the *Dallas Morning News,* the *El Paso Herald-Post* and the *Wall Street Journal,* ranging from 1986 to 2012. The material is backed up by hundreds of notebooks that I have diligently saved during my career. In as many cases as possible, I have tried to confirm my notes and memories with the people who were present. When that wasn't possible, I relied on my memory.

I owe a great deal to the *Dallas Morning News* for its support and commitment to the story of Mexico. I am also indebted to scholars whose work I have consulted. At times I have borrowed from the work of some of my outstanding colleagues in Mexico, both American and Mexican, specifically Dudley Althaus, Ginger Thompson, José de Cordova, David Luhnow, Ioan Grillo, William Booth, Susana Seijas, Anne-Marie O'Connor, Keith Dannemiller, Elisabeth Malkin, Eduardo Garcia, Anita Snow, Adam Thomson, Dominic Bracco, Tracy Wilkinson, Randy Archibald, Alma Guillermo Prieto, Julian Aguilar, William Finnegan and colleagues at the Associated Press; Alfredo Quijano, Sandra Rodriguez, Victor Hugo Michel, Marcela Turati, Javier Garza Ramos, Octavio Rivera, Diego Osorno, Patricia Dávila, José Carreño Figueras, J. Jesus

Esquivel, Francisco Gomez, Jorge Carrasco Araizaga, Carmen Aristegui, Ignacio Alvarado, Jorge Zepeda Patterson, Lydia Cacho and the
staffs at *Reforma, El Universal* and *Proceso*.

I have relied on the assistance and insights of U.S. and Mexican officials, particularly John Feeley, Joseph M. Arabit, Daniel W. Fisk, Rafael
Fernandez de Castro, Arturo Sarukhán, Gustavo Mohar Alejandro
Hope, Carlos González Gutiérrez, Jacob Prado, Phil Jordan and many
others who asked to remain anonymous.

I have withheld names on request from sources citing safety concerns. The anonymous sources have been previously vetted by the *Dallas
Morning News*. With these and some other sources I shared passages
from the book for accuracy.

For background I referred to *Zapata and the Mexican Revolution* by
John Womack (Knopf, 1969) and *The Life and Times of Mexico* by Earl
Shorris (Norton, 2006). I also read *Rain of Gold* by Victor Villaseñor
(Delta, 1991) and *Carry Me Like Water* by Benjamin Alire Sáenz (Hyper-
ion, 1995).

For detail on Mexico's democratic transition, I turned to *La Transición
en México* by Sergio Aguayo Quezada (El Colegio de México, 2010) and
Opening Mexico: The Making of a Democracy by Julia Preston and Samuel
Dillon (Farrar, Straus and Giroux, 2004).

For richer historical context of the drug war in Mexico and for material I used in chapter three, I corroborated my reporting with the works
of Howard Campbell, professor of anthropology at the University of
Texas at El Paso and author of *Drug War Zone* (University of Texas Press,
2009) as well as *Cárteles Protegidos: Droga y Sangre en México* (Ediciones
Gato Azul, 2003); *El Cártel de Sinaloa* by Diego Enrique Osorno (Gri-
jalbo Mondadori, 2009); *El Narco: Inside Mexico's Criminal Insurgency* by
Ioan Grillo (Bloomsbury, 2011) and the discussion policy paper "Drug
Trafficking in Mexico: A First General Assessment" by Luís Astorga of
the Universidad Nacional Autónoma de México.

For background on the César Chávez movement in chapters nine and eleven, I relied on *The Fight in the Fields: César Chávez and the Farmworkers Movement* by Susan Ferriss and Ricardo Sandoval (Paradigm Productions, 1997), *Why David Sometimes Wins: Leadership, Organization, and Strategy in the California Farm Worker Movement* by Marshall Ganz (Oxford University Press, 2009) and *Al Norte: Agricultural Workers in the Great Lakes Region 1917–1970* by Dennis Nodin Valdés (University of Texas Press, 1991).

For information about braceros, namely in chapters six and eleven, I relied on *Braceros: El Caso de los Braceros* by Carlos A. Madrazo, and a once confidential July 1945 report, "Some Problems of the Mexican War Workers at Present Employed in the United States," *Mexican War Workers in the United States*, Division of Labor and Social Information, February 5, 1951.

For additional background on the braceros, I relied on historical data provided by the Bracero History Archive at the University of Texas at El Paso.

I was moved by the Smithsonian Institution's 2010 exhibit *Bittersweet Harvest: The Bracero Program, 1942–1964.*

I borrowed from a series of academic papers about security by the Woodrow Wilson International Center for Scholars, the Mexico Institute and the University of San Diego Trans-Border Institute. The papers covered money laundering, drug trafficking organizations in Central America, the Mérida Initiative, police reform and profiles of drug trafficking organizations. Also from the Wilson Center: "The United States and Mexico: More Than Neighbors" by Andrew Selee, Christopher Wilson and Katie Putnam, September 2010; and, for information on Vicente Fox in chapter eleven, "Mexico in Transition," edited by Andrew Selee, May 2000.

I also relied on the excellent analysis of Patrick Radden Keefe, a staff writer for *The New Yorker* and a fellow at the Century Foundation. He is author of the June 15, 2012, *New York Times* magazine piece "How a Mexican Cartel Can Make Its Billion."

Separately, I read with great interest "Between a Rock and a Hard Place: The United States, Mexico and the Agony of National Security" by Donald E. Schulz, Strategic Studies Institute, U.S. Army War College, October 1997, and *Drug War Politics: The Price of Denial* by Eva Bertram, Morris Blachman, Kenneth Sharpe and Peter Andreas (Berkeley: University of California Press, 1996).

For figures and historical data, I relied on figures provided by the Trans-Border Institute at the University of San Diego. I also relied on the daily count of people killed in Ciudad Juárez kept by Molly Molloy, a librarian at New Mexico State University.

I read with great interest the 2012 dissertation of Harvard University doctorate Viridiana Rios Contreras, "How Government Structure Encourages Criminal Violence: The Causes of Mexico's Drug War."

For background about El Paso as a drug trafficking hub and the city's history during the revolution, namely for chapters three and fifteen, I consulted Howard Campbell's *Drug War Zone* and *Ringside Seat to a Revolution: An Underground Cultural History of El Paso and Juárez, 1893–1923* by David Dorado Romo (Cinco Puntos Press, 2005).

Finally, I tried my best to translate Spanish to English without losing its original meaning. During the process, however, I realized that Spanglish has become my natural language. In most cases, however, I used the *News*'s policy of italicizing Spanish and writing the meaning in English next to it.

Index